# Contributions to Management Science

The series *Contributions to Management Science* contains research publications in all fields of business and management science. These publications are primarily monographs and multiple author works containing new research results, and also feature selected conference-based publications are also considered. The focus of the series lies in presenting the development of latest theoretical and empirical research across different viewpoints.

This book series is indexed in Scopus.

Aizhan Tursunbayeva

# Augmenting Human Resource Management with Artificial Intelligence

## Towards an Inclusive, Sustainable, and Responsible Future

Springer

Aizhan Tursunbayeva
University of Naples "Parthenope"
Naples, Italy

ISSN 1431-1941 ISSN 2197-716X (electronic)
Contributions to Management Science
ISBN 978-3-031-75265-0 ISBN 978-3-031-75266-7 (eBook)
https://doi.org/10.1007/978-3-031-75266-7



This Springer imprint is published by the registered company Springer Nature Switzerland AG
The registered company address is: Gewerbestrasse 11, 6330 Cham, Switzerland

*To Zhanel, Jasmine, and all (Future) workforce whose lives and professional journeys will be deeply intertwined with what is discussed in this book*

# Foreword

Since the 1970s, when Moore's law was empirically validated-indicating that the complexity and performance of microcircuits double every 18 months-technological innovation has seen multiple periods of rapid acceleration.

Looking at recent advances in robotics, machine learning, and artificial intelligence (AI), exponential growth is evident. The use of these technologies by businesses, institutions, and citizens has been going on for at least 10–15 years, with numerous practical applications spreading over time. However, in recent years, we have witnessed a significant leap: the advancement of machine learning systems, predictive analysis techniques, and generative AI, coupled with the development of more powerful semiconductor devices, have led to exponential growth and an ever-widening spread of these technologies.

A case in point is the rapid development of OpenAI's Generative Pre-Trained Transformer (GPT). Since its launch in November 2022, it has reached 100 million users in just two months; in comparison, it took Instagram about two and a half years, and Uber almost six years to reach the same number of users. Analyzing the communications of the companies included in the Standard & Poor's 500 indexes, in the first two quarters of 2023, the term "artificial intelligence" (or "generative artificial intelligence") was mentioned more than 5000 times, compared to around 700 in the fourth quarter of 2022.[1]

This rapid expansion has not been accompanied by equal individual, organizational, and societal progress. Significant gaps must be bridged in various areas, from knowledge of the use and functioning of these technologies to awareness of potential risks and opportunities. Moreover, medium- and long-term scenarios regarding the evolution and applications of these technologies are difficult to predict. Precisely because of these uncertainties, both the potentially irresponsible current uses and the future challenges, these issues are the subject of numerous research programs, which focus on three levels of analysis: individual, organization, and society.

[1] Cook, V. (2023). *The AI evolution: Reality justifies the hype*. Bank of America Institute. https://institute.bankofamerica.com/transformation/the-ai-evolution.html

At the individual level, the impact of new technologies manifests itself in various fields, with the main gap related to knowledge and awareness of their use and the trust placed in them. Adopting these technologies can have major implications for citizens in their daily lives and as workers. The effects are seen not only as end-users of applications but also in relation to broader issues, such as privacy, behavioral control (in social life and business), employment, new skills required by the labor market, and the transformation or disappearance of certain professions, with impacts on people's general well-being.[2] The new "fluid" forms of work, digital platform workers, and gig workers are examples of these changes, as well as the new working modalities that use platforms and Internet connections. From the workers' perspective, the increasing adoption of technologies in human resources management (HRM)-such as people analytics, chatbots, and assessment tools in recruitment and selection processes, personalized training program design, and definition of the people journey evolution-has a direct impact. These tools can be seen as positive, improving job security and employee management practice personalization, but they also offer managers greater control over workers, with possible uses in a "punitive" key. This raises the question of an ethical managerial approach maintaining the "centrality of the person." It is, therefore, crucial to understand how these technologies evolve and are used in organizational management, considering both the positive and negative impacts.[3]

The main gap concerns knowledge and awareness: according to recent research, only 61% of the European Union population will have basic digital skills by 2030, compared to a desirable target of 80%.[4] Furthermore, the quality gap concerns "digital fluency"-i.e., "the ability to ethically find, evaluate, and use digital information to solve problems"[5]-regarding awareness of risks and opportunities and the concrete and productive use of new applications.

A useful analogy can be found with the Great War Management Problem.[6] During the First World War, military technological innovations advanced exponentially (new automatic weapons, tanks, aircraft), but war tactics remained anchored to the old methods. Similarly, today, many companies do not fully exploit the opportunities of new technologies, nor do they radically change their strategies and business models. This is due to cultural resistance to change, a lack of awareness of the

---

[2] Orlikowski, W. J., & Scott, S. V. (2023). The Digital Undertow and Institutional Displacement: A Sociomaterial Approach. *Organization Theory*, *4*(2), 26317877231180896. https://doi.org/10.1177/26317877231180898

[3] Leonardi, P. M. (2020). COVID-19 and the New Technologies of Organizing: Digital Exhaust, Digital Footprints, and Artificial Intelligence in the Wake of Remote Work. *Journal of Management Studies*, *58*. https://doi.org/10.1111/joms.12648

[4] Negreiro, M. (2021). *The EU digital decade. A new set of digital targets for 2030* (No. PE 696.189). European Parliamentary Research Service.

[5] Briggs, C., & Makice, K. (2012). *Digital Fluency: Building Success in the Digital Age*. Digital Fluency.

[6] Grigorov, M. (2015). *(Un)Productivity in the Digital Age*. *18*(1), 36–45. https://www.saisjournal.eu/DOCUMENTS/VOLUMEPDFS/D9998B0D-0A01-3FFF-40FBD54CB9D6AB09.pdf

necessary investments, and risks and opportunities. Focusing on the latter, McKinsey's research[7] on generative AI identified the main areas of focus for organizations, which include cybersecurity, data accuracy, and intellectual property, while less attention is given to the impact on the workforce, corporate reputation, and equity issues.

On a societal level, the gap mainly concerns accepting new technologies and the need for appropriate regulation. For the latter purpose, early AI regulations focused on social control applications, setting limits to ensure privacy and prevent a "digital panopticon" are needed. The AI Act in the European Union is a step forward, addressing many issues related to the social acceptance of new technologies and their use in institutions, organizations, and businesses.

In an era where AI is revolutionizing industries, its application in HRM is a pivotal area that deserves in-depth exploration. The ability to leverage data and AI for people management has emerged as a critical competency in the field of human resources (HR). This shift reflects the growing recognition that data-driven decision-making and AI tools can significantly enhance HR practices' efficiency, accuracy, and strategic value. The adoption of people analytics is transforming how organizations manage talent, predict workforce trends, and personalize employee experiences.

Globally, the adoption of AI in HR is accelerating, with a 2021 study by PwC indicating that 52% of companies have already adopted AI in at least one HR function, and 86% of HR executives see AI as a key tool for the future. Nevertheless, the Boston Consulting Group (BCG) bi-annual Creating People Advantage report[8] states that only 35% of HR professionals agree that their people management function uses relevant digital technologies and that just 30% say that HR uses data and analytics to anticipate people's challenges. This is despite people and HR strategy, planning, and analytics being ranked as the #1 future people management topic.

LinkedIn data further corroborates this trend, highlighting a notable increase in HR professionals listing skills in people analytics on their profiles. These figures reflect the shifting landscape in HR, where the integration of AI and data analytics is becoming not just an option but a necessity for maintaining a competitive edge.

The implications of this trend are profound. Organizations that effectively harness the power of data and AI in their HR functions can expect to see improvements in employee engagement, retention, and overall productivity. Additionally, predicting and responding to workforce trends in real time enables organizations to be more agile and responsive in a rapidly changing business environment. As a result,

---

[7] McKinsey & Company. (2023). *The state of AI in 2023: Generative AI's breakout year*. McKinsey & Company. https://www.mckinsey.com/~/media/mckinsey/business%20functions/quantumblack/our%20insights/the%20state%20of%20ai%20in%202023%20generative%20ais%20breakout%20year/the-state-of-ai-in-2023-generative-ais-breakout-year_vf.pdf

[8] Baier, J., Beauchene, V., Bedard, J., Caye, J. M., Kolo, P., Ruan, F., Alonso, A., Ariganello, A., Helfritz, H., Morton, B., van Wees, L., & Wong, W. (2023). *Set the Right People Priorities for Challenging Times*. BCG & World Federation of People Management Associations. https://web-assets.bcg.com/c6/3e/a87495e544c4b24061806c9eab92/bcg-creating-people-advantage-2023-nov-2023.pdf

HR professionals with expertise in people analytics and AI are increasingly viewed as strategic partners in driving organizational success. However, AI and other learning tools (such as generative AI) do not just optimize the productivity of existing processes and activities but change the overall HR delivery model. However, in the face of such change, the people function should always be cautious of generative AI's many risks-especially when handling sensitive personnel information.

Tursunbayeva's book offers a comprehensive and empirically grounded analysis that fills a crucial gap in current literature by addressing AI's operational, relational, and transformational impacts on HR practices. For practitioners and scholars alike, understanding AI's role in HRM is essential for navigating the future of work, promoting ethical AI practices, and enhancing diversity and inclusion within organizations. HRM professionals can acquire the knowledge to use AI to fill a gap in their training, and HRM scholars can reflect on this research stream, which is still an open area for improvement.

This book is a helpful resource for anyone committed to responsible AI implementation in HRM, providing both theoretical insights and real-world applications that will shape the future of people management.

D'Annunzio University of Chieti–Pescara Gilda Antonelli
Pescara, Italy

University of Naples "Parthenope" Luigi Moschera
Naples, Italy

# Foreword

One might wonder why another book on Artificial intelligence (AI) when the literature on the subject is already so vast? Despite how much we already know, there is always more to learn about this rapidly evolving technology-especially one that advances faster than humans can keep up (see further discussions in Chaps. 2 and 3).

But there is another good reason for why this book is needed. Because of its focus on human resource management (HRM), the book from its very first word is positioned at the interfaces between humans and technology. While acknowledging the prospects and benefits of automation, I believe that most of value creation will be created at those interfaces, interactions between humans and technology, when both sides act with intentionality. Let me elaborate on this.

Automation refers to machines taking over tasks previously done by humans. This is becoming increasingly important in HRM, as technology plays a bigger and bigger role in how work is done in organizations regardless of their type, industry, and location. The main reason for adopting automation is to boost efficiency, often through the use of AI or machine learning, which enhances data analysis and decision-making. While Human Resource (HR) function has traditionally lagged in digital adoption, recent advancements show that the field is moving toward a more digital approach. Algorithmic management, initially developed by gig economy leaders like Uber and Deliveroo and now being implemented by traditional organizations, is highlighted in Chap. 4 as an approach that can deliver both efficiency and effectiveness. However, this potential can only be realized if the ethical challenges discussed in Chap. 7 are effectively addressed using the responsible AI principles outlined in Chap. 8.

However, there is more to this than mere substitution - technology and humans can also collaborate to perform tasks together. This approach does not just automate work but also enhances decision-making by combining human insight with data-driven analysis. By doing so, HR can move beyond merely improving efficiency to truly adding value through digital innovation. This also aligns with the idea that HR should continuously evolve and innovate its processes to stay ahead in a digital world, creating a more flexible, adaptable, and inclusive workplace. Chapter 5 offers illustrative examples of how this can be achieved throughout the employee life cycle by drawing on AI for HRM vendor case studies, including those from Strivr, Mentorloop, and Culture Amp. Most value creation happens through augmentation because it combines the strengths of both humans and technology. While automation focuses on efficiency by allowing machines to take over repetitive tasks, augmentation goes a step further by enhancing human capabilities. This partnership allows people to make better decisions, solve complex problems, and innovate in ways that machines alone cannot achieve. Chapter 6 explores how this augmentation can be realized through advanced AI insights into diversity dimensions, neuroscience-informed perspectives on employee behavior, and contributions to organizational efforts toward achieving the Sustainable Development Goals.

However, augmentation leverages technology to provide insights, data, and analytical tools, but it still relies on human skills, intuition, creativity, and emotional intelligence to interpret and apply that information effectively. This is where the barriers are that can hinder greater augmentation in HR. Many HR teams may lack the necessary skills to effectively use advanced technologies. Moreover, but related to this, HR professionals may resist adopting new technologies due to fear of job displacement, lack of familiarity, or discomfort with changing established workflows. Combining human input with AI-driven insights can be complex. Ensuring that technology complements rather than complicates human work requires careful planning and execution. Chapter 9 illustrates this through change management strategies for and with AI, as proposed by Big Four firms. In some organizations, there may be a cultural reluctance to rely on data-driven decisions, preferring traditional methods. This can slow down the adoption of augmentation.

But if we, the humans, believe that we could simply catch up in the development, we lost the race. AI learns faster than humans. In its development it has already moved on from the predictive to generative. This shift carries profound implications for industries, organizations, practices, and employees' experiences. If HRM professionals do not keep pace with rapid AI advancements, fail to upskill, and neglect to embed AI responsibly in a human-centric way throughout the employee life cycle, they risk losing their ability to remain both strategic and "human" in their roles. This failure could undermine their core purpose: managing the organization's most valuable asset-its people. The next big move for HR should be extending the scope of augmentation from the use of predictive AI for routine tasks to use of generative AI applications to solve novel problems. Consider combinations of predictive and generative AI enable two mechanisms that allow organizations to reduce their selection bias. The first mechanism is AI agents' anticipatory quantification, which is largely a substitute for humans' heuristic selection, thereby reducing bias toward local solutions. The second mechanism, interactive selection, complements humans' heuristic selection with AI's anticipatory quantification, which counterbalances humans' natural tendencies when selecting.

This synergy leads to more thoughtful and impactful outcomes, as humans can use the data provided by technology to craft strategies, build relationships, and drive innovation in ways that create greater value for organizations. The question is no longer whether HRM should use AI, but why, when, and how it should be used (see Chap. 10).

This is why this book is a must-read to any academic and professional who is aiming to succeed in this new world of working on interfaces between human and technology. Aizhan has masterfully crafted a comprehensive exploration of AI in HRM, offering readers a balanced and nuanced perspective that is both theoretically rigorous and practically applicable. This is a solid platform that stands out for its breadth and depth, covering the broad spectrum of HRM practices through the lens of AI-from operational to relational and transformational configurations.

This book is not just a timely contribution to the field of HRM; it is a visionary roadmap for the future of work. It will undoubtedly become essential reading for HR professionals, business leaders, and anyone interested in succeeding while working on the interfaces between humans and technology.

King's Business School
King's College London,
London, UK

Dana Minbaeva

# Preface

In an era of exponential technological advancements, the interplay of Human Resource Management (HRM) and artificial intelligence (AI) has emerged as a critical area of innovation and thus exploration. The potential of AI to (re)shape HRM practices is profound, yet it comes with challenges that demand careful consideration, especially in terms of ethics, inclusivity, and sustainability. This book, *Augmenting Human Resource Management with Artificial Intelligence: Towards an Inclusive, Sustainable, and Responsible Future*, aims to provide a theoretically informed and empirically grounded examination of AI's role in shaping the future of HRM.

The foundation of this book is my relevant educational background and extensive professional and research experiences. It spans my professional work experience as an HRM Business Partner with HSBC, Global Organizational Development Manager at Giunti Psychometrics, and a PhD in human resource information systems within the healthcare sector that moved to (ethics of) people analytics and now to my current focus on AI and the Future of Work. Throughout this journey, I have observed the growing diffusion of AI across HRM and the pressing need for a balanced approach that not only leverages AI's capabilities but also upholds the principles of responsible and ethical use.

The chapters within this book are thoughtfully structured to guide readers through the complex landscape of AI in HRM. The book begins by exploring Human Resource (HR) technologies, considering them through the configurational approach, which views HRM practices as a combination of operational, relational, and transformational elements. The book consistently addresses the dual perspectives on AI-both its transformative potential and the fears surrounding its disruptive impact on the future of work and management. In doing this, the book draws on my original research and works published by international colleagues.

Real-life applications of AI in HRM are also extensively covered, providing insights into algorithmic management, AI-driven relational HRM configurations, and augmented with AI HRM. The book also dedicates significant attention to the ethical implications of AI and how these could be addressed through responsible AI principles.

The content of this book is designed to equip HRM professionals, researchers, and policymakers with the knowledge and tools needed to navigate this rapidly changing landscape. One of the core themes of this book is the necessity of advancing theoretical and empirical knowledge in the field and methodologies for studying these. While AI offers unprecedented opportunities for innovation, AI hard and soft regulations must continue to evolve, along with HRM strategies. HRM research must also catch up, contributing new theories, conceptual frameworks, and methodologies. All these can guide the responsible deployment of AI.

In conclusion, this book is more than just another academic text; it aims to raise awareness, provoke thought, and inspire action. As we move forward in this AI-driven world, I hope this book inspires readers to think critically about the interplay between AI and HRM and contribute to shaping the future of work that is not only innovative but also inclusive, sustainable, and ethically sound.

Naples, Italy Aizhan Tursunbayeva

# Acknowledgments

Completing this book has been an ambitious journey set with great determination but frequently seemed unattainable. It was only possible thanks to the invaluable insights, guidance, and support of many individuals and organizations.

First and foremost, I wish to express my profound gratitude to my mentors and colleagues in HRM and artificial intelligence (AI). I am especially thankful to Professors Gilda Antonelli, Luigi Moschera, and Dana Minbaeva for graciously writing the forewords for this book, and to all those who offered their expert feedback and endorsements. Their intellectual contributions and constructive insights helped in refining the concepts and strengthening both the theoretical and empirical foundations. I am also deeply appreciative of the colleagues who collaborated with me on the research projects referenced in this book, the Springer editorial team, and the anonymous reviewer(s) who believed in my proposal and provided invaluable guidance with their supportive comments.

I am also thankful to the academic and professional communities of the European Group for Organizational Studies, the Association of Italian Organization Studies Academics, the European Academy of Management (EURAM), the British Academy of Management, the Italian Association for Information Systems, and People Analytics World. The stimulating discussions and feedback during the subthemes, symposiums, workshops, and panels at these conferences have significantly shaped the direction of this book.

I am grateful to the institutions and funding bodies whose support made the research projects reported in this book possible, including the University of Naples "Parthenope," the Italian Ministry for Universities and Research, the International Labour Organization, EURAM, and the University of Twente.

I would also like to thank my family, friends, and colleagues for their continuous support, practical help, and encouragement.

Last but not least, I thank all the future readers to whom I actually dedicate this work. May it serve as a guide and source of inspiration as we collectively navigate the evolving landscape of the Future of Work, ensuring that AI is harnessed for a brighter future that is already here.

# Expert Quotes on Book

*"Leveraging her extensive knowledge, combining rigorous academic research and experience as an HRM practitioner, Dr. Tursunbayeva masterfully dissects the challenges involved in real-life applications of AI across different HRM practices. Drawing from a wealth of current examples and her own research, Dr. Tursunbayeva puts forward a compelling case for responsible AI adoption to take forward the practice of and research in HRM. This book is a must-read for anyone seeking a holistic understanding of the paths that adopting AI will open up for the future of work."*

—Raluca Bunduchi, Personal Chair of Innovation, University of Edinburgh, UK.

*"Augmenting Human Resource Management with Artificial Intelligence: Towards an Inclusive, Sustainable, and Responsible Future is an indispensable read for HR and people analytics professionals navigating the rapidly evolving AI landscape. The book expertly combines theoretical insights with real-world applications, offering a blueprint for leveraging AI to augment HR programs, processes, and activities while addressing critical issues like diversity, responsibility, and sustainability. With its balanced approach and forward-thinking perspective, this book is an essential guide for anyone committed to making the Future of HR strategic and human-centered."*

—David Green, People Analytics leader, Managing Partner at Insight222, co-author of Excellence in People Analytics, host of the Digital HR Leaders podcast

*"Augmenting Human Resource Management with Artificial Intelligence: Towards an Inclusive, Sustainable, and Responsible Future is an essential guide that expertly navigates the intricate intersection of AI and HRM. The author provides a balanced and insightful perspective, moving beyond the hype and fear to explore AI's real implications and opportunities in HRM. This book thoroughly examines contemporary HRM practices, the evolving role of AI, and the critical ethical considerations involved. By addressing the challenges and potential of AI across organizational, group, and individual levels, this work shows the path toward a more inclusive and sustainable future in HRM. It serves as a comprehensive resource for professionals*

*and researchers. This book's combination of theoretical insights and practical applications may make it one of the cornerstones of the literature on AI in human resource management."*

—Vicenc Fernandez, Professor in Management and Business Analytics; TechTalent-Lab, Universitat Politècnica de Catalunya, BarcelonaTECH, Spain

*"This book is a unique and state-of-the-art exploration of the AI revolution in Human Resource Management (HRM). This groundbreaking work provides a comprehensive guide to how AI can transform HRM, while maintaining a strong focus on inclusivity, sustainability, and responsibility. Dr. Tursunbayeva skillfully combines cutting-edge research with practical applications, offering invaluable insights for both HR professionals and leaders looking to navigate the challenges and opportunities of AI in today's rapidly evolving workplace. This book is essential reading for anyone committed to driving innovation and positive change in the field of human resources."*

—Jose Grade, CEO, Giunti Psychometrics, Italy.

*"This book about augmenting HRM with Artificial Intelligence (AI) is an essential read for everyone seeking to understand not only the consequences but also the nuances of this rapidly evolving technology. This book stands out for its clear structure and multi-level analysis, marking the complexities that the HRM profession and scholarship face when navigating AI's emergence. Offering a balanced perspective, the book explores AI's potential application and consequences across operational, relational, and transformational HR, while also thoroughly examining the ethical implications. Drawing extensively from her own research, the author provides deep insights and actionable strategies, making this a must-read for anyone looking to integrate AI in HR effectively and ethically."*

—Maarten Renkema, Assistant Professor of HRM and Innovation, University of Twente, Netherlands.

*"Artificial Intelligence is already profoundly changing the world of work and our societies. The recent wave of technological advances in this field has opened many opportunities and risks, especially for Human Resource Management (HRM). As Dr. Tursunbayeva adeptly describes in her book, there exists a multitude of possible AI applications in HR functions, and a large variety of expectations among scholars and practitioners regarding how these applications will change the future of work and HR. Dr. Tursunbayeva provides a comprehensive overview of this debate, examining the diverse perspectives on AI's role in HR. She then analyzes how this technology can be used to address critical contemporary issues, such as desired better inclusivity, sustainability, and responsible HR practices. Her analysis highlights the potential of AI not just as a tool for efficiency but as a means to enhance the human aspects of HR, fostering a more inclusive and sustainable workplace. This book is a timely and profound reference for scholars and practitioners alike. It not only provides a thorough exploration of the current landscape of AI in HR but also offers*

*practical insights into how AI can be harnessed to create more equitable and forward-thinking HR practices. I highly recommend reading it."*

—Daniel Samaan, Senior Economist & Future of Work Specialist, International Labour Organization (ILO), Switzerland

*"There is no doubt that Artificial Intelligence (AI) will fundamentally and unrecognizably change not only job design and the way people work, but also the way people are managed at work. Although transformations based on wide application of AI have the potential to facilitate, enhance, and boost human resource management (HRM), nevertheless, its dark side should not be underestimated. This book serves as a compelling call to action for understanding inclusive, sustainable, and responsible relationship between AI and HRM. The author starts by presenting contemporary HRM, including configurations, trends, and factors of influence. Later, the attention is shifted toward AI while underscoring two core perspectives, namely hype perspective and fear perspective. Further, the author leads readers through the landscape of AI and HRM interplay, in particular focusing on the changes AI brings to HRM and revealing how AI could be applied in sustainable HRM. It is great to note that the book addresses AI Ethical Challenges in HRM, as ethical issues seem to be fundamental and not so straightforward on all levels, be it macro, meso, or individual. The book ends with the views on AI and the future of HRM work. It provides profound insights on augmenting HRM with AI, while being a timely, great, and comprehensive resource for students, teachers, IT specialists, and, most importantly, HRM professionals. I strongly encourage to read this book as it is not only a source for professional competence growth or advice on how to deal with wicked problems, but also a nice way of spending one's time and acquiring the cutting-edge knowledge in the fields of AI and HRM."*

—Živilė Stankevičiūtė, Professor at Kaunas University of Technology, Kaunas, Lithuania

# Contents

# About the Author

**Aizhan Tursunbayeva** is an Associate Professor at the University of Naples "Parthenope." Her previous roles include Assistant Professor at the University of Twente in the Netherlands, Management Consultant at KPMG Advisory in Italy, and (HRM) Manager at HSBC Bank in Canada, the United Kingdom (UK), Poland, and Kazakhstan. She is an expert in HRM and HRM technologies, people analytics, and ethics in HRM Technologies, having published extensively in this area. She has also recently become involved in research on AI and the Future of Work and HRM, where she is emerging as a recognized expert with her work shaping discourse in both academia and practice. In 2023, she was also contracted by the International Labour Organization as an expert advisor on responsible AI and the Future of work.

Aizhan has received multiple prestigious awards, including the 2023 Emerald Literati Award for Outstanding Paper for her publication, "*The ethics of people analytics: risks, opportunities and recommendations*," in *Personnel Review*. She was also recognized with the Italian Chapter of the Association for Information Systems (itAIS) Best Track award in 2023, the Best Track Chair award in 2024, the Best Reviewer award at the itAIS/Mediterranean Conference on Information Systems in 2022, and the Italian Association for Organization and HRM (ASSIOA) Best PhD Thesis award in 2018.

Aizhan is an elected member of the British Academy of Management Continental Network Board and a regular member of the Association of Italian Organization Studies Academics, the European Group for Organizational Studies, the Academy of Management, and EURAM. She is also an Associate Editor for the *European Management Journal* in the AI and Future of Work and Organizations section.

# List of Abbreviations

| | |
|---|---|
| AI | Artificial Intelligence |
| BCG | Boston Consulting Group |
| CIPD | Chartered Institute of Personnel and Development |
| CEO | Chief Executive Officer |
| ChatGPT | Chat Generative Pre-trained Transformer |
| C&B | Compensation and Benefits |
| CSR | Corporate Social Responsibility |
| CV | Curriculum Vitae |
| D&I | Diversity and Inclusion |
| EU | European Union |
| EVAAS | Education Value-Added Assessment System |
| EURAM | European Academy of Management |
| GDPR | General Data Protection Regulation |
| HR | Human Resources |
| HRM | Human Resource Management |
| HRIS | Human Resource Information Systems |
| ILO | International Labour Organization |
| ISO | International Organization for Standardization |
| OECD | Organisation for Economic Co-operation and Development |
| NLP | Natural Language Processing |
| NT | Neuroscience Tool |
| R&S | Recruitment and Selection |
| RAI | Responsible AI |
| SDG | Sustainable Development Goal |
| T&D | Training and Development |
| UK | United Kingdom |
| UN | United Nations |
| US | United States |
| VP | Vice President |
| VR | Virtual Reality |

# List of Figures

# List of Tables

# Chapter 1
# Artificial Intelligence and Human Resource Management

## 1.1 The Need for a Balanced Perspective

Technological advances over recent decades, described by the World Economic Forum as the 'Fourth Industrial Revolution' - following steam, mass production, and electronics - are advancing exponentially (Chima & Gutman, 2020) and transforming business functions. Everyone seems to agree today that such technologies, often referred to as exponential or those progressing alongside or exceeding Moore's Law, will significantly impact how people work and how they are managed in organizations. Indeed, some declare that Artificial Intelligence (AI) and intelligent robots are "coming for human jobs" (Rus & Mone, 2024). The last discussion wave about technological unemployment, or the so-called robo-apocalypse, started with the seminal work of Frey and Osborne (2013). Popular and scholarly reports are heating this (Danaher, 2019; Susskind, 2020) by discussing how technology might reduce the number of jobs (Huysman, 2020; Willcocks, 2020).

Meanwhile, opponents of this way of thinking claim that the global labor history and the latest job market statistics demonstrate a contrary trend. The agricultural economy transformed into an industrial economy, then into service, and now into an information economy, thanks to the advances in technology (Diamandis & Kotler, 2020), which they believe continues helping to create jobs and provide solutions to complex societal and organizational problems (Willcocks, 2020). To support their arguments, the proponents, for example, quote the recent United States (US) Bureau of Labor Statistics (Edwards & Smith, 2020), which in 2019 registered the lowest unemployment rate since 1990 (about 4%).

Looking at these arguments, it is not easy to grasp what has happened or is really happening in terms of the exponential technologies such as AI and the past, present, or future of work. In particular, it is unclear whether and how the exponential



A. Tursunbayeva, *Augmenting Human Resource Management with Artificial Intelligence*, Contributions to Management Science,
https://doi.org/10.1007/978-3-031-75266-7_1

technology might have impacted work or how these have evolved. Moreover, exponential technologies, such as AI, are also envisioned to disrupt how organizations manage people (Tursunbayeva, 2019).

To improve operational efficiency, customer service, and organizational image, among many others, organizations have turned to technologies to transform their employee selection, management, development, and retention. Such technologies are expected to help to launch, manage, and provide actionable insights on an entire employee life cycle, starting from recruitment and selection (R&S) and continuing through payroll and benefits administration, performance management, and career and succession planning (Meijerink et al., 2021). This led to automated Human Resource Management (HRM), People Analytics, or algorithmic management (Meijerink et al., 2021). AI in HRM is now "necessary-to-employ" and no longer only "nice-to-have" (Black & van Esch, 2020). 250 AI-related HRM tools were reported in 2021 (Khan, 2021), promising HRM to finally become a strategic organizational function (Tursunbayeva et al., 2018), as well as enable the personalization of people's experiences (Kurter, 2021), among other benefits. Thus, their user base is constantly growing (Albert, 2019). This seems to be only the beginning, as according to International Data Corporation (2024), the worldwide AI spending, including software, hardware, and services for AI-centric systems is projected to reach $632 Billion in 2028.

Appropriate management, development, and retention of employees are frequently mentioned as essential factors in responding to organizations' crucial human capital needs, facilitating their competitive advantage, and improving the quality of customer service (Tursunbayeva, 2019). Thus, it is unsurprising and somewhat encouraging that organizations stay current with new technologies and strive to enhance their effectiveness and resilience through automation and improved data utilization (Tursunbayeva et al., 2018). However, organizations perform HRM practices for employees or groups with heterogeneous demographic, individual, or cultural characteristics. Thus, these practices are recommended to consider employee diversity (Anderson et al., 2022; D'Netto et al., 2014). Diversity-focused HRM practices administered on non-prejudicial factors can increase employees' perceived procedural justice and fairness and consequently improve their commitments to the company (Richard & Johnson, 2001). More recently, such HRM practices have also been called green or, more broadly, sustainable (Guerci et al., 2023), helping organizations to achieve well-rounded Sustainable Development Goals (SDGs) set by the United Nations (UN) for 2030.

Meanwhile, AI applied in/for HRM has also been observed to expose employees, organizations, and society to new challenges, risks, and threats (Tursunbayeva et al., 2022). It has been noted that the complex and potentially high-risk nature of AI applications in HRM distinguishes it from other fields where AI has been applied (Tambe et al., 2019). For employees, the emerging risks include privacy, career options, autonomy, income, and well-being, along with heightened concerns about mirrored or amplified bias (Khan, 2021), work-by-numbers, automated decision-making, and the erosion of choice, opportunity, fairness, and ethics (Tursunbayeva et al., 2022). For organizations, these risks pertain to operational, financial, reputation, and legal aspects, especially given recent regulatory moves in several countries regarding AI use (Khan, 2021). At a societal level, they risk amplifying biases, reinforcing existing inequalities, and posing sustainability challenges-issues currently at the forefront of scientific and practitioner debates. At the World Economic Forum's annual meeting, Sam Altman, Chief Executive Officer (CEO) of OpenAI, highlighted that future AI systems will demand significantly more power, potentially overwhelming energy infrastructures (Crawford, 2024). Moreover, AI systems also require vast quantities of water for cooling, raising further environmental concerns. However, the industry's environmental costs, including energy and water use, are often underreported, with many details kept secret. Thus, there are still many questions about the long-term impacts of AI, and organizations face managerial and organizational dilemmas as they seek to embrace innovation while also avoiding harm and penalties.

Moreover, different actors have formed different expectations about AI for HRM applications, developing different visions of what the technology involves and what potential or perils it has (Swanson & Ramiller, 1997). From one side, some (e.g., HR innovators and vendors) position it as a tool for providing equal job opportunities, supporting fair employment decision-making (Johnson et al., 2020), or closing pay gaps across gender or race (Anderson et al., 2022). Thus facilitating diversity management in organizations while saving time for HR professionals and improving the accuracy of HRM practices. On the other side, AI-enabled decision-making has been suspected to be prone to (unintentional) unfairness (Hacker, 2018) against employees with some demographic characteristics, as in the case of Amazon's gender-biased recruitment algorithm, which discriminated against women and had been discontinued for this reason (Anderson et al., 2022). For this and other backfired AI for HRM cases, the European Union (EU) Commission has even labeled the use of AI for HRM as highly risky (Khan, 2021).

Nevertheless, AI applications in HRM have received relatively little scholarly attention compared to fields like education (Borenstein & Howard, 2021) or medicine (Tursunbayeva & Renkema, 2023). Existing studies have been somewhat limited in scope, focusing on legal (Borgesius, 2020), technical (Lokman & Ameedeen, 2019), or quantitative (Marda & Narayan, 2021) aspects or driven by practitioner-led investigations such as predicting the impact of AI on job numbers in various sectors (Bughin et al., 2017). Moreover, the corpus of existing literature intersecting AI and HRM could be clustered into two fragmented and somehow unbalanced perspectives. In the first group, studies are exploring primarily the application of different types of AI or analytics approaches (often using these terms interchangeably) for a wide range of specific HRM practices (Meijerink et al., 2021; Tursunbayeva et al., 2018). In the second group, articles investigate ethical or legal challenges/implications associated with such AI or analytics uses in organizations (Giermindl et al., 2022; Tursunbayeva et al., 2022). Thus, AI in HRM is an emerging innovation with uncertain consequences, requiring organizations to anticipate and mitigate risks during its development and implementation (Tursunbayeva et al., 2022), urgently calling for more balanced scholarly attention.

## 1.2 Book and Chapter Overview

This book aims to provide a balanced, theoretically informed, and empirically grounded exploration of AI in HRM. It establishes the state-of-the-art by reporting on original, already published research and real-life applications of AI across various HRM practices. Building on such state-of-the-art, the book examines these practices and their implications for HRM and the Future of Work by considering their operational, relational, and transformational focus (Ruël et al., 2004), and that they also need to be Diversity and Inclusion (D&I) (Shen et al., 2009) and sustainability (Guerci et al., 2023) focused. The book seeks to raise awareness about the diffusion of AI in HRM applications and shed light on the approaches for evaluating AI's impacts, interactions, and unanticipated complex consequences for HRM (Orlikowski & Scott, 2008) and the future of people at work. Ultimately, it aims to promote AI's ethical and responsible use in HRM (Khan, 2021).

The book chapters are carefully designed to cover various aspects of AI in HRM to lead the groundwork for more in-depth comprehension and build the need for future research. Refer to Fig. 1.1 outlining the topics discussed in this book and how they interrelate.

The journey starts with Chap. 2, which provides an overview of the evolution of HRM, primary HRM practices, and trends within them. It also discusses the main macro trends and factors shaping contemporary HRM practices-including environmental, organizational, and technological factors-and argues the importance of accommodating individual preferences in the workplace.

Chapter 3 defines AI and its multifaceted dimensions and discusses two prevailing perspectives on analyzing its consequences: the hype perspective - championing

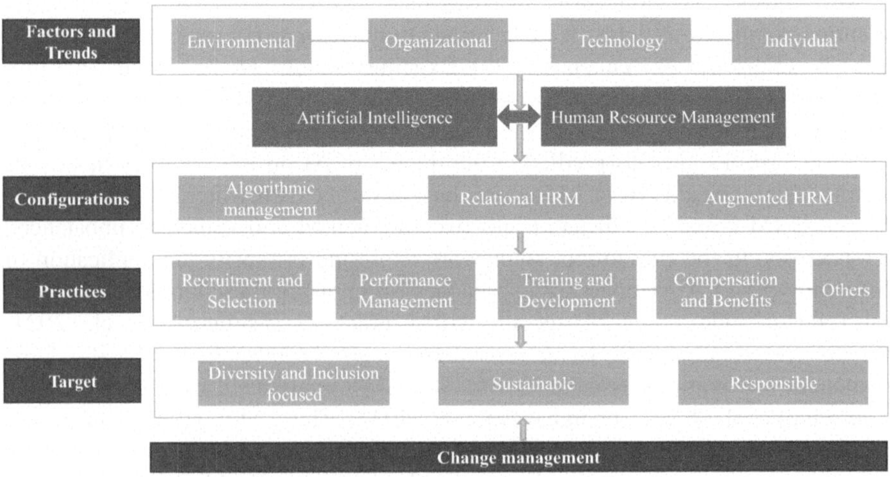


**Fig. 1.1** Topics covered in the book and their interrelationships

AI's transformative and augmentation potential-and the fear perspective, cautioning against its disruptive capabilities for reducing the number of jobs, among others. Moving forward, the chapter introduces the integration of AI into HRM and presents the configurational approach adopted in this book to disentangle AI's role in HRM.

Chapter 4 discusses a new level of HRM automation powered by AI algorithms, commonly known in the literature as algorithmic management, which now is making its way into traditional organizations. It also provides examples of algorithmic management practices within organizations, along with real-life AI-based HRM solutions that facilitate these practices.

Chapter 5 explores applications of AI in relational HRM configurations. It examines how AI can assist HRM professionals within R&S, training and development (T&D), performance management, and compensation and benefits (C&B) practices based on existing literature, AI for HRM vendor solutions, and insights from expert interviews (see Fig. 5.1 and Table 5.1). The chapter also provides illustrative examples of relevant real-life AI solutions implemented in such HRM practices.

Chapter 6 explores AI's transformative potential for HRM, emphasizing how AI techniques can augment intelligence and support organizational strategic goals. It also explores AI's implications in HRM at individual, team, and organizational levels, particularly in the context of D&I. The chapter further delves into AI's capabilities in detecting (new) diversity dimensions and attributes and advanced insights into employee behavior possible thanks to the convergent neuroscience tools. Finally, the chapter explores how AI can assist organizations in achieving the SDGs.

Chapter 7, building on the anticipated potential of AI across the three HRM configurations discussed in Chaps. 4, 5, and 6, focuses on the emerging concerns, risks, and challenges associated with implementing AI in HRM. Specifically, this chapter demystifies why AI for HRM can be considered an ethical, if not legal, minefield for both employees and organizations.

Chapter 8 builds on ongoing research and examines Responsible AI (RAI) activities at the macro level (analyzing self-developed Responsible AI guidelines), meso level (evaluating AI for HRM vendor solutions), and micro level (assessing Responsible AI competencies) that are focused on the ethical application of AI in HRM research and practice, often referred to as (RAI). It raises awareness and highlights the importance of level-by-level and cross-level analysis in understanding and implementing ethical AI practices in HRM.

Chapter 9 provides an overview of how AI can be integrated into organizations by examining it through well-known change management models, including those developed by Kurt Lewin and John Kotter. It also examines how leading change management experts, like Prosci, and the Big Four players, such as PwC, KPMG, EY, and Deloitte, leverage AI to enhance their clients' change management initiatives.

Chapter 10 examines the Future of HRM work through three specific lenses: Future of Work, Knowledge Work, and RAI. It then discusses the influence of socio-technical factors in shaping these perspectives.

Chapter 11 concludes the book, offering theoretical, practical, methodological, and policy implications and avenues for future research and practice.

## References


Albert, E. T. (2019). AI in talent acquisition: A review of AI-applications used in recruitment and selection. *Strategic HR Review, 18*(5), 215–221. https://doi.org/10.1108/SHR-04-2019-0024

Anderson, D., Bjarnadóttir, M. V., & Ross, D. G. (2022). Using people analytics to build an equitable workplace. *Harvard Business Review*. https://hbr.org/2022/01/using-people-analytics-to-build-an-equitable-workplace

Black, J. S., & van Esch, P. (2020). AI-enabled recruiting: What is it and how should a manager use it? *Business Horizons, 63*(2), 215–226. https://doi.org/10.1016/j.bushor.2019.12.001

Borenstein, J., & Howard, A. (2021). Emerging challenges in AI and the need for AI ethics education. *AI and Ethics, 1*(1), 61–65. https://doi.org/10.1007/s43681-020-00002-7

Borgesius, F. J. Z. (2020). Strengthening legal protection against discrimination by algorithms and artificial intelligence. *The International Journal of Human Rights, 24*(10), 1572–1593. https://doi.org/10.1080/13642987.2020.1743976

Bughin, J., Manyika, J., & Woetzel, J. (2017). *A future that works: Automation, employment, and productivity*. McKinsey Global Institute.

Chima, A., & Gutman, R. (2020). What it takes to lead through an era of exponential change. *Harvard Business Review*. https://hbr.org/2020/10/what-it-takes-to-lead-through-an-era-of-exponential-change

Crawford, K. (2024). Generative AI's environmental costs are soaring—and mostly secret. *Nature, 626*(8000), 693. https://doi.org/10.1038/d41586-024-00478-x

Danaher, J. (2019). *Automation and utopia. Human flourishing in a world without work*. Harvard University Press.

Diamandis, P. H., & Kotler, S. (2020). *The future is faster than you think: How converging technologies are transforming business, industries, and our lives*. https://www.amazon.com/Future-Faster-Than-You-Think/dp/1982109661.

D'Netto, B., Shen, J., Chelliah, J., & Manjit, M. (2014). Human resource diversity management practices in the Australian manufacturing sector. *The International Journal of Human Resource Management, 25*(9), 1243–1266. https://doi.org/10.1080/09585192.2013.826714

Edwards, R., & Smith, S. M. (2020). Job market remains tight in 2019, as the unemployment rate falls to its lowest level since 1969. Monthly Labor Review, U.S. Bureau of Labor Statistics. https://www.bls.gov/opub/mlr/2020/article/job-market-remains-tight-in-2019-as-the-unemployment-rate-falls-to-its-lowest-level-since-1969.htm.

Frey, C. B., & Osborne, M. (2013). *The future of employment: How susceptible are jobs to computerisation?* Oxford Martin Programme on Technology and Employment. https://www.oxfordmartin.ox.ac.uk/publications/the-future-of-employment/#:~:text=According%20to%20their%20estimates%2C%20about,an%20occupation%27s%20probability%20of%20computerisation.

Giermindl, L. M., Strich, F., Christ, O., Leicht-Deobald, U., & Redzepi, A. (2022). The dark sides of people analytics: Reviewing the perils for organisations and employees. *European Journal of Information Systems, 31*(3), 410–435. https://doi.org/10.1080/0960085X.2021.1927213

Guerci, M., Hauff, S., Panichella, N., & Radaelli, G. (2023). Sustainable HRM and class-based inequality. *Personnel Review, 52*(5), 1597–1613. https://doi.org/10.1108/PR-10-2021-0772

Hacker, P. (2018). Teaching fairness to artificial intelligence: Existing and novel strategies against algorithmic discrimination under EU law. *Common Market Law Review, 55*(4), 1143–1185.

Huysman, M. (2020). Information systems research on artificial intelligence and work: A commentary on "Robo-Apocalypse cancelled? Reframing the automation and future of work debate". *Journal of Information Technology, 35*(4), 307–309. https://doi.org/10.1177/0268396220926511

IDC. (2024). Worldwide Spending on Artificial Intelligence Forecast to Reach $632 Billion in 2028. *IDC: The Premier Global Market Intelligence Company*. https://www.idc.com/getdoc.jsp?containerId=prUS52530724

Johnson, R., Stone, D., & Lukaszewski, K. (2020). The benefits of eHRM and AI for talent acquisition. *Journal of Tourism Futures*. https://doi.org/10.1108/JTF-02-2020-0013

Khan, S. (2021). Artificial intelligence for human resources toolkit helps organizations overcome implementation challenges. World Economic Forum. https://www.weforum.org/press/2021/12/artificial-intelligence-for-human-resources-toolkit-helps-organizations-overcome-implementation-challenges/.

Kurter, H. L. (2021). 4 top HR trends and predictions for 2022. *Forbes*. https://www.forbes.com/sites/heidilynnekurter/2021/12/28/5-top-hr-trends-and-predictions-for-2022/

Lokman, A. S., & Ameedeen, M. A. (2019). Modern Chatbot systems: A technical review. In K. Arai, R. Bhatia, & S. Kapoor (A c. Di), *Proceedings of the future technologies conference (FTC) 2018* (pp. 1012–1023). Springer. https://doi.org/10.1007/978-3-030-02683-7_75.

Marda, V., & Narayan, S. (2021). On the importance of ethnographic methods in AI research. *Nature Machine Intelligence, 3*(3), 187–189. https://doi.org/10.1038/s42256-021-00323-0

Meijerink, J., Boons, M., Keegan, A., & Marler, J. (2021). Algorithmic human resource management: Synthesizing developments and cross-disciplinary insights on digital HRM. *The International Journal of Human Resource Management, 32*(12), 2545–2562. https://doi.org/10.1080/09585192.2021.1925326

Orlikowski, W. J., & Scott, S. V. (2008). Sociomateriality: Challenging the separation of technology, work and organization. *Academy of Management Annals, 2*(1), 433–474. https://doi.org/10.5465/19416520802211644

Richard, O., & Johnson, N. (2001). Understanding the impact of human resource diversity practices on firm performance. *Journal of Managerial Issues, 13*(2), 177–195.

Ruël, H., Bondarouk, T., & Looise, J. K. (2004). E-HRM: Innovation or irritation. An explorative empirical study in five large companies on web-based HRM. *Management Revue, 15*(3), 364–380.

Rus, D., & Mone, G. (2024). The robots are coming. And that's a good thing. MIT Technology Review. https://www.technologyreview.com/2024/03/05/1087646/the-robots-are-coming-and-thats-a-good-thing-2/.

Shen, J., Chanda, A., D'Netto, B., & Monga, M. (2009). Managing diversity through human resource: An international perspective and conceptual framework. *International Journal of Human Resource Management, 20*(2), 235–251. https://doi.org/10.1080/09585190802670516

Susskind, D. (2020). *A world without work: Technology, automation, and how we should respond*. Metropolitan Books.

Swanson, E. B., & Ramiller, N. C. (1997). The organizing vision in information systems innovation. *Organization Science, 8*, 458–474.

Tambe, P., Cappelli, P., & Yakubovich, V. (2019). Artificial intelligence in human resources management: Challenges and a path forward. *California Management Review, 61*(4), 15–42. https://doi.org/10.1177/0008125619867910

Tursunbayeva, A. (2019). Human resource technology disruptions and their implications for human resources management in healthcare organizations. *BMC Health Services Research, 19*(1), 268. https://doi.org/10.1186/s12913-019-4068-3

Tursunbayeva, A., Di Lauro, S., & Pagliari, C. (2018). People analytics—a scoping review of conceptual boundaries and value propositions. *International Journal of Information Management, 43*. https://doi.org/10.1016/j.ijinfomgt.2018.08.002

Tursunbayeva, A., Pagliari, C., Di Lauro, S., & Antonelli, G. (2022). The ethics of people analytics: Risks, opportunities and recommendations. *Personnel Review, 51*(3), 900–921. https://doi.org/10.1108/PR-12-2019-0680

Tursunbayeva, A., & Renkema, M. (2023). Artificial intelligence in health-care: Implications for the job design of healthcare professionals. *Asia Pacific Journal of Human Resources, 61*(4), 845–887. https://doi.org/10.1111/1744-7941.12325

Willcocks, L. (2020). Robo-Apocalypse cancelled? Reframing the automation and future of work debate. *Journal of Information Technology, 35*(4), 286–302. https://doi.org/10.1177/0268396220925830

# Chapter 2
# Contemporary Human Resource Management: Evolution, Trends, and Factors of Influence

## 2.1 Human Resource Management and Its Evolution

Organizations use three main types of resources-physical, organizational, and human-to maximize their competitive advantage and achieve desired profitability. However, considering what was labeled by McKinsey as "The War for Talent," as well as the fact that people costs normally constitute about 65–80% of the organizational total operating budget (Khatri, 2006), the importance of HR among these three was particularly acknowledged. Since HR is so important for organizations, management of HR has also been recognized as a critical priority.

There are numerous HRM definitions, which have also evolved in the last decades. One of the first references to HRM, especially its strategic importance, was made in an article published in 1923 in Harvard Business Review, stating, "When, however, we pass from tactics to the question of major strategy, industrial relations management is essentially functional rather than departmental… [It] deals with a subject matter which pervades all departments… [and] must exercise an integrating, not segregating, force on the business as a whole" (as cited in Kaufman, 2008, p. 5). Another definition refers to HRM it as to the "process of acquiring, training, appraising, and compensating employees, and of attending to their labor relations, health and safety, and fairness concerns" (Dessler, 2012). There has also been a move to substitute "human resources" and HRM with "workforce," "people," or "talent" management. However, HRM is still the most commonly used term worldwide, as illustrated by the Google Trends statistics in Fig. 2.1.

Being familiar with HRM is important for managers to hire the right people for the job, lower turnover, arrange training activities to increase the department's effectiveness, commit to fair labor practices, and engage employee experience, among others.



A. Tursunbayeva, *Augmenting Human Resource Management with Artificial Intelligence*, Contributions to Management Science,
https://doi.org/10.1007/978-3-031-75266-7_2

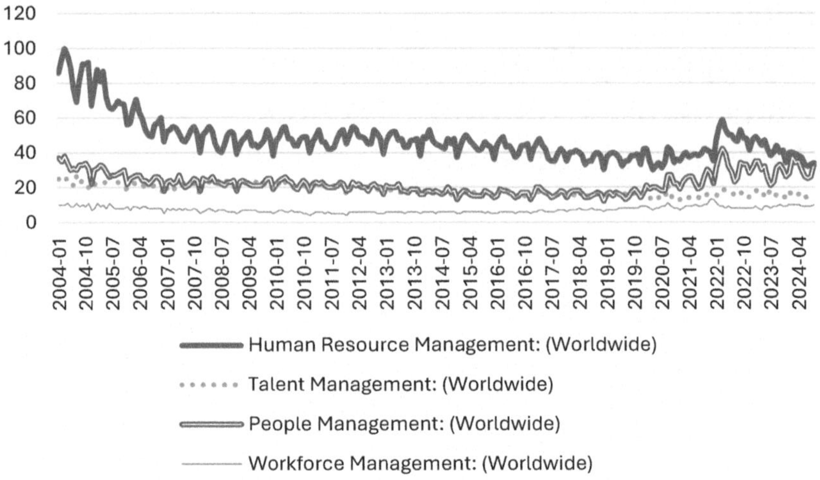


**Fig. 2.1** HRM-related terms utilization in Google Trends (Data source: Google Trends (https://trends.google.it/trends/explore?date=all&q=Human%20Resource%20Management,Talent%20Management,People%20Management,Workforce%20Management&hl=en)

Today's HRM practices are not the same as that of years past. More and more companies are looking for new ways to leverage their people as a strategic differentiator, giving them an edge over the competition. To understand modern HRM, it is vital to review its evolution, including how its functions, practices, and philosophies have adapted to align with management trends and technological advances.

A recent paper analyzing the role of HRM in the age of AI divided the evolution of HRM into four phases: administrative HRM, personnel management, strategic HRM, and business partner HRM (e.g., Fenwick et al., 2024). The earliest phase, *administrative HRM*, was prominent in the early to mid-twentieth century. During this stage, HRM focused on administrative and transactional compliance and workforce management tasks using paper-based tools (Fenwick et al., 2024; Hendrickson, 2003; Mahoney & Deckop, 1986). Such activities comprised industrial psychology practices (Fenwick et al., 2024).

*Personnel Management*, which followed and was prominent in the mid-twentieth century, marked a shift toward a more employee-oriented approach. The workforce here started being recognized as a valuable asset. This reflected the focus on the behavioral model or the impact of environmental, social, and psychological factors on employee motivation and productivity, leading to HRM practices such as T&D, employee compensation, and communication (Fenwick et al., 2024; Kaufman, 2015).

*Strategic HRM* emerged in the late twentieth century as a response to external pressures like globalization and technological advancements. This stage marked a significant shift in HR manager's role to a proactive, strategic partner essential for achieving organizational goals (Fenwick et al., 2024; Kaufman, 2008; Kim et al., 2021). The term "HRM" originated during this period, reflecting its broader scope. With the wide diffusion of computers and enterprise resource planning systems, Human Resource Information Systems (HRIS) became essential for data-driven decisions and workflow efficiency (Hendrickson, 2003). HRM practices here have started focusing on improving employer–employee relationships through better systems for performance management and career planning, leading to higher job satisfaction and productivity (Fenwick et al., 2024; Kim et al., 2021; Wright, 2008).

*Business Partner HRM* (Fenwick et al., 2024), *D&I-focused HRM*, and *Green* or *Sustainable HRM* represent the most recent developments in HRM practices. Business Partner HRM, emerging with the rise of the internet, emphasizes digital approaches (e-HRM, online HRM, digital HRM) to make data-informed decisions and add value to organizations (Wright, 2008; Malik et al., 2020). This stage views employees as key competitive advantages, focusing on enhancing the workplace through technology and people-centric approaches like D&I (Shen et al., 2009). Green HRM or Sustainable HRM highlights HR's role in contributing to the UN's SDGs through HRM practices focused on achieving D&I goals, launching sustainability-focused Corporate Social Responsibility (CSR) projects, and fostering organizational cultures that support green practices.

The primary HRM practices include R&S, T&D, performance management, and C&B (Shen et al., 2009). These are briefly introduced below, along with the latest trends in these practices. However, it is worthwhile to acknowledge that these practices are presented separately only to provide their brief overview individually. Overall, it has already been proposed that such a fragmented approach to viewing HRM and HRM practices should be overcome as part of the employee journey or their complete experiences within organizations, starting from their job application to exit from the company. "HR cannot function in a silo," says Prof. Sandy Miles, Director of Standards Development at HRCI for International Organization for Standardization (ISO)'s technical committee on HRM (ISO/TC 260). "An organization's strategy and values should be connected to talent recruitment, talent management such as remuneration, learning and development, and performance management of its employees while providing value to the organization and society as a whole. All of the strategies must work together" (ISO, 2023).

## 2.2 Recruitment and Selection

Nowadays, the war for talent remains fierce (PWC, 2023). Attracting and retaining the talent required to create a thriving post-pandemic organization was one of the top priorities for executives in 2023 (Forbes, 2023; Gartner, 2023), particularly in the context of "The Great Attrition" (De Smet et al., 2023). Thus, R&S has evolved from a critical HR process to a top strategic concern for business leaders. This practice involves attracting individuals and then selecting them for a job role. Recruiting suitable candidates is a critical activity, not just for the HRM team but increasingly also for line managers. Everyone involved in recruitment must make effective and fair recruitment decisions. The recruitment process can vary depending on an organization's size and resources. However, it often comprises the following sub-phases:

Defining the role, attracting applicants, and managing the application and selection process.

The recruitment process also involves candidates discovering more about the organization and considering whether it is where they want to work. Candidates today can share their experiences online via employer rating platforms like Glassdoor (www.glassdoor.com). Therefore, inefficient, poorly designed recruitment processes can negatively impact the employer brand and the ability to attract candidates (Chartered Institute of Personnel and Development (CIPD), 2023).

Effective R&S is about both filling an immediate vacancy and impacting the business's long-term success. It uses workforce planning data to understand the skills needed for organizational performance and bring them from the labor market of references. For instance, in a competitive talent marketplace, climate change and sustainability are becoming crucial factors in employee acquisition and retention. IBM research shows that 70% of job seekers today are attracted to employers with strong environmental practices, and nearly half would accept lower salaries to work for socially responsible organizations (Meister, 2024).

To conclude, good R&S is vital, especially when labor markets are tight. It ensures that the workforce has the relevant skills and abilities for the organization's current and future needs.

## 2.3 Performance Management

Performance management is also a critical HRM practice encompassing a range of activities to ensure employees meet organizational goals and perform at their best. It involves setting clear performance expectations, providing regular feedback, conducting appraisals, and developing plans for future performance improvement (Varma et al., 2024). Effective performance management aligns individual objectives with the organization's strategic goals, fostering a culture of continuous improvement and accountability. By systematically assessing performance, organizations can identify high performers for advancement, address areas of underperformance, and tailor development programs to enhance skills and competencies. Additionally, performance management systems that are transparent and fair contribute to employee motivation and engagement by recognizing achievements and providing constructive feedback. As such, performance management can drive organizational success and support employee development and satisfaction, making it a cornerstone of strategic HRM. For instance, the performance review outcomes can help design personalized T&D plans and inform employees of reward and remuneration plans.

As hybrid work becomes standard, the traditional face-to-face performance reviews were called to be reconsidered to address, for example, the proximity bias, where in-person workers are favored for career opportunities over remote employees. Here, leaders were also called to focus on managing through meaningful connections across locations rather than relying on physical presence as a measure of performance (Meister, 2024). Finally, leaders were called to revisit their performance appraisals as AI-powered work buddies continue to boost employee efficiency and performance (Meister, 2024).

## 2.4 Training and Development

T&D is essential in improving employees' skills, capabilities, and knowledge (Bell & Moore, 2018) to enable them to perform their jobs effectively and ensure their growth. T&D initiatives aim to unlock human potential, enhance job performance, and increase organizational effectiveness (Bell & Moore, 2018). The effectiveness of T&D depends on their alignment with the organization's strategic goals, top management's involvement, the programs' quality, and employees' willingness and ability to learn (Day et al., 2021). Therefore, organizations conduct needs assessments, create a favorable environment for learning, and evaluate the effectiveness of their T&D initiatives (Day et al., 2021).

The importance of T&D practice seems to continue increasing, as 44% of core skills are projected to evolve over the next 5 years (Meister, 2024), highlighting the need for ongoing learning and adaptation in the workforce. Key skills expected to gain prominence include cognitive abilities, technological literacy, resilience, flexibility, and a commitment to lifelong learning (Meister, 2024). Recently, employees have been concerned about AI that could replace their jobs, driving organizations to launch large-scale training on AI skills. For instance, PwC has responded by investing $1 billion in AI training for its 75,000 US employees, focusing on AI ethics, responsible use, and prompt creation (Meister, 2024). At the same time, the UK government estimated that the UK could lose up to £141 billion in GDP if it does not fix the digital skills shortage (House of Commons, 2023).

## 2.5 Compensation and Benefits

C&B or Total rewards (WorldatWork, 2024) is often referred to as the total value of an employer's financial and non-financial package to its employees in exchange for their work. This package can significantly influence job satisfaction and employee productivity (Pfeffer & Langton, 1993).

C&B packages are a great way to attract top talent and retain current employees (Andersen et al., 2012). An employer must understand employees' desires while remaining within the budget. Offering a positive company culture, opportunities for advancement, recognition, rewards, and a purpose-driven mission can also enhance talent attraction and retention.

This HRM practice is evolving as companies introduce innovative C&B programs such as wages on demand to support employees' financial well-being. For instance, LendingClub reported that 61% of American workers live paycheck to paycheck, and many lack basic financial literacy. Organizations such as Unifi, an aviation services company with over 23,000 employees, responded to such difficulty by introducing a comprehensive financial wellness program, including wages on demand, anonymous financial coaching, and customizable savings plans, with nearly 20% of frontline workers participating (Meister, 2024). Employers also have started offering innovative employee benefits. For instance, Gartner anticipates that employers will increasingly offer climate-related benefits, such as providing shelter during natural disasters (Meister, 2024).

## 2.6 Factors and Trends Shaping Human Resource Management

HRM and organizations, more broadly, are profoundly influenced by a complex set of sociotechnical dimensions comprising environmental, organizational, technological, and individual factors (DePietro et al., 1990). Understanding these factors is imperative for creating effective organizational strategies and ensuring that HRM practices are aligned with the workforce's needs and the demands of the technological landscape. For example, the WorldatWork Total Rewards Professional Association (www.worldatwork.org)-which for over 65 years has led the way in Total Rewards education across 168 countries-in their model considers economic, labor market, cultural norms, and regulatory external influences and illustrates how these can shape organizational and business strategy, and as a result organizational HRM strategy and practices. Drawing on the sociotechnical dimensions of DePietro et al. (1990), *environmental* trends such as economic and geopolitical shifts, labor market projections, *technological* advancements, relevant regulatory developments, *organizational* factors focusing on innovation, and evolving *individual* preferences are discussed below.

### *2.6.1 Environmental Factors*

#### 2.6.1.1 Economic and Geopolitical Trends

The World Economic Forum's Global Risk Report (2024) highlighted that the aftermath of COVID-19 and the ongoing Russia-Ukraine conflict have exposed societal weaknesses. Nevertheless, the global system has shown resilience, with no recession so far and a quick resolution of financial turbulence. However, uncertainty remains. The Forum's Global Risks Perception Survey 2023–2024 revealed a predominantly negative short-term outlook, with 54% of respondents expecting instability and moderate global risks, 27% anticipating more significant turbulence, and 3% foreseeing global catastrophes. Only 16% predicted stability in the next 2 years. The report, overall, suggested that economic, geopolitical, and societal vulnerabilities will persist, turning current concerns into chronic global risks. Such continuous upheaval may erode HR development and resilience investments, leaving even strong states, organizations, and individuals vulnerable to new and recurring shocks (World Economic Forum, 2024a, 2024b).

Current economic trends underscore the need for adaptive strategies in HRM to navigate a rapidly changing landscape. For instance, economic fluctuations, such as inflation and the risk of recession, can significantly influence HRM practices related to hiring, compensation, and benefits. Organizations may need to revisit their HRM budgets, restructure their workforce, or adjust compensation packages to remain competitive and sustainable during economic downturns (Cook et al., 2016). Geopolitical tensions, including political instability, conflicts, and risk of war, can further complicate HRM by affecting international operations and talent mobility. These trends demand a robust focus on risk management and compliance and developing flexible workforce strategies that respond to uncertainties. Overall, economic and geopolitical factors compel HRM professionals to be agile, strategic, and proactive in managing local and global HR challenges.

#### 2.6.1.2 Labor Market Projections

One of the significant labor market trends of concern is global unemployment. Gilbert Fossoun Houngbo, Director-General of the International Labour Organization (ILO), stated at the World Economic Forum Annual Meeting in Davos' "What to Expect From Labour Markets" session in 2023 that ILO projections indicate global unemployment could rise from 5.1% to 5.2% in 2024, adding two million job seekers. He also highlighted persistent inequalities between low- and high-income countries and noted that young people are 3.5 times more likely to be unemployed than adults. He also expressed concern over many workers struggling to pay bills (Whiting, 2024).

Another trend is that the workforce in labor markets is becoming more diverse, with more women, minorities, people with disabilities, and older workers (or employed persons aged 65 or older, as per the Pew Research Center definition). This shift and a focus on racial justice require employers to ensure equity. The World Bank found in 2020 that closing economic gender gaps could unlock $172 trillion globally. However, the World Economic Forum's Global Gender Gap Report 2023 shows that the Economic Participation and Opportunity gap is only 60% closed. Reshma Saujani, CEO of Moms First, reported in the same Davos meeting that 606 million women are not working due to unpaid care responsibilities, compared to 40 million men. She emphasized that better childcare macro-level and organizational policies can boost productivity and retention, urging leaders to treat care as an economic priority (Whiting, 2024).

The older workforce, currently around 11 million in the US, has nearly quadrupled since the mid-1980s, also requiring employers to rethink their retirement plans and the nature of jobs preferred by older workers (Fry & Braga, 2023).

Furthermore, the work people are doing is changing. Jobs today are more fluid and performed by independent contractors such as gig workers (Samaan &

Tursunbayeva, 2024). They work when they can, on what they want to work on, and when needed. Upwork (www.upwork.com) and Uber (www.uber.com) symbolize this. However, such work arrangements are also becoming standard for more traditional organizations. According to MIT Sloan Management Review, Novartis already employs 110,000 full-time staff along with 50,000 contractors and temporary workers. Similarly, Cisco has 83,000 full-time employees and over 50,000 contingent workers in various roles (Altman et al., 2023).

Moreover, after the COVID-19 pandemic, people often continue working remotely, making organizations struggle to bring them back to the offices, posing challenges to their traditional in-presence monitoring and control and, more importantly, engaging such employees. An ADP survey of 32,000 employees reveals that 64% would consider quitting if required to return to the office full-time (ADP Research Institute, 2022). Interestingly, only 7% of 500 UK CEOs reported going into the office full-time, while 25% believe returning to the office full-time is a priority (Royle, 2024). At the same time, the research by Boston Consulting Group and Scoop Technologies among 554 public companies employing 26.7 million people concluded that companies with flexible work options experienced revenue growth four times faster than those with strict office attendance policies between 2020 and 2022 (Meister, 2024).

Finally, according to the World Economic Forum's (2024b) white paper, "The Rise of Digital Jobs," global digital jobs are expected to reach 92 million by 2030 and offer higher pay. These roles could address skill shortages in high-income countries and create opportunities for young workers in low-income countries. Thus, proper management of global digital jobs can expand the talent pool for employers and provide economic growth for countries at all income levels.

### 2.6.2 *Technological Factors*

One of today's key trends is the exponential development of technology, particularly AI. The World Economic Forum (2023a, 2023b) projects that extensive AI integration could create new winners and losers globally, widening the digital gap between high- and low-income countries. Vulnerable communities in advanced and developing economies might be further marginalized, missing out on AI's benefits in productivity, finance, climate, education, and healthcare. The Global North's dominance in tech could perpetuate biases, and the Global South may struggle more with AI-related risks, such as misinformation and criminal use. Concentrated tech talent and knowledge in limited contexts are envisioned to make effective regulation difficult and enable the misuse of AI tools in countries with weak norms or regulations (World Economic Forum, 2023b).

Indeed, the development of AI has also prompted the creation of new laws and regulations due to its profound impact on various aspects of society, including ethics, privacy, accountability, and economic structures. Since 2023, AI policy and regulation have become mainstream news driven by OpenAI's Chat Generative

Pre-trained Transformer (ChatGPT) popularity that brought AI to the masses, similar to how Ford's T model brought cars to almost every American family more than a century ago. Consequently, considering the heated up discussions on AI and its implications for the future of jobs, there have been significant relevant regulatory developments in 2023 and 2024 globally.

The EU agreed on its first sweeping AI Act requiring organizations-including those developing, implementing, or using AI for HRM-to comply with new rules, including thorough system documentation and transparency about model training to minimize biases. It came into effect in August 2024 (European Commission, 2024). The law applies to all AI products and services available in the EU, classifying them according to different risk levels. Regulations for general-purpose AI models will be enacted by August 2025 (Mukherjee et al., 2023). The EU established an AI Office to oversee compliance with these rules. Companies that fail to adhere could be fined up to 7% of their annual global revenue (Mukherjee et al., 2023). The EU is also working on another bill, the AI Liability Directive, which aims to ensure that people harmed by the technology can get financial compensation (Ryan-Mosley et al., 2024).

In the US, the Senate held hearings and issued executive orders. The 2024 US presidential election will heavily influence AI regulation discussions, especially concerning generative AI's impact (Ryan-Mosley et al., 2024).

In China, AI regulation has been fragmented, with specific rules for AI applications like algorithmic recommendations, deep fakes, and generative AI. This approach envisions rapid response to emerging risks but needs a long-term perspective. This could change, as, in 2023, China's state council announced plans to develop a comprehensive AI law (Ryan-Mosley et al., 2024).

The UK has decided not to propose new laws for AI but to rely on existing regulators, such as the Health and Safety Executive and the Competition and Markets Authority, to enforce principles of safety, transparency, and accountability (Clarke, 2023). Additionally, it is offering a £2 million "sandbox" for AI developers to test regulatory compliance before launching their products (Clarke, 2023). However, more recently, the Trades Union Congress (TUC) has cautioned that the country is falling behind in regulating AI in the workplace, leaving workers at risk of exploitation and discrimination (Matheson & Jones, 2024). The TUC has suggested a legal framework requiring employers to consult trade unions when using high-risk and intrusive AI technologies. TUC Assistant General Secretary Kate Bell stated, *"UK employment law is simply failing to keep pace with the rapid speed of technological change. We are losing the race to regulate AI in the workplace"* (Matheson & Jones, 2024).

We will likely see more AI regulations introduced in other parts of the world throughout the following year(s), impacting organizations deploying and approaching AI for HRM (Ryan-Mosley et al., 2024). However, overall, at a macro level, the law is remarkably behind real-world practices, leaving many workers managed with the assistance of AI vulnerable to exploitation and discrimination (Kelly-Lyth & Thomas, 2023). In response to mounting concerns, many institutional actors, at (inter)national fronts, have developed soft-regulations or RAI guidance on AI development, deployment, and governance (see Chap. 8).

### 2.6.3 Innovative Organizations

Organizations today, to remain competitive, strive to be innovative. Indeed, it is not a coincidence that there are many world rankings of the Most Innovative Companies, such as the one by Forbes (2018). Their parameters consider companies that excel at serial innovation as they have greater opportunities to invest and position themselves for faster development than competitors. Most companies on the Forbes list, such as ServiceNow, Workday, Salesforce, Tesla, Amazon, Netflix, and Facebook (Forbes, 2018), have technology at the core of their products, services, processes, and broader business models (Columbus, 2020). Few of these companies have been around since about two decades ago. However, they continue disrupting established markets and new industries today, setting industry standards and best practices that other companies strive to follow. For instance, digital companies like Alphabet, Amazon, and Meta experienced rapid growth partly due to their innovative business models that disrupted traditional norms and regulations in the markets they entered (Birkinshaw, 2024). These companies, whose strategies focus on innovation, are claimed not only to use technologies to do things differently but also to do different things (Marr, 2020).

Organizational strategy and culture that promote innovation, collaboration, and agility are necessary for successful digital transformation (Tigre et al., 2023). Digital transformation requires changes in organizational structures, processes, and roles (Tursunbayeva et al., 2020), making it crucial to consider factors like an innovative culture, effective change management, and strategies to manage employee resistance (Lomineishvili, 2021; Agrawal et al., 2021) by building trust in AI. Thus, it is important to align AI adoption with expected outcomes and key performance indicators, considering cultural differences in trust (Choi et al., 2020). Additionally, strong organizational (digital) leadership is essential to advocate for AI adoption and foster a culture of continuous learning and experimentation (Tursunbayeva & Chalutz-Ben Gal, 2024).

### 2.6.4 Variety in the Workplace

We are living in a new world of work with a shift toward a more personalized and holistic approach to employment. There is a noticeable trend toward embracing remote and fluid work arrangements such as hybrid, 4 days-a-week, or gig work, allowing employees to achieve better work–life balance and flexibility in managing their schedules (Samaan & Tursunbayeva, 2024). This shift is driven by the aforementioned technological advancements that facilitate communication and collaboration across distances. HRM must now focus on designing flexible work policies that accommodate diverse employee needs while ensuring productivity and collaboration.

Moreover, employees increasingly prefer purpose-driven and socially responsible employers (Glavas & Kelley, 2014). They seek organizations that offer competitive salaries and benefits and are committed to positively impacting society and the environment. This emphasis on CSR influences job seekers' decisions and can significantly impact employer branding and reputation (Tkalac Verčič & Sinčić Ćorić, 2018). HRM departments are thus important in aligning CSR goals with recruitment strategies and employee engagement programs to enhance employer branding.

Employees also desire continuous learning and career development opportunities (Garofano & Salas, 2005). As industries evolve rapidly due to technological advancements and global trends, individuals seek employers who invest in their professional growth and offer pathways for skill enhancement and career advancement. Organizations with HRM practices prioritizing training programs, mentorship opportunities, and ongoing education initiatives are more likely to attract and retain top talent (Horvath et al., 2008).

Furthermore, the demand for diverse and inclusive workplaces continues to grow (Callender & Forbes Business Council, 2023). Employees value environments that celebrate diversity across all dimensions and promote a culture of inclusivity, where individuals feel respected, valued, and empowered to contribute their unique perspectives. It is in the remit of HRM to develop and implement strategies fostering inclusive environments where individuals from diverse backgrounds can feel valued, respected, and empowered to contribute their unique perspectives.

## References

Altman, E. J., Kiron, D., Jones, R., Cantrell, S., & Hatfield, S. (2023). Managing external contributors in workforce ecosystems. *MIT Sloan Management Review*. https://sloanreview.mit.edu/article/managing-external-contributors-in-workforce-ecosystems/

Agrawal, A. K., Gans, J. S., & Goldfarb, A. (2021). *AI adoption and system-wide change* (working paper no. 28811). National Bureau of Economic Research. https://doi.org/10.3386/w28811.

Andersen, L. B., Eriksson, T., Kristensen, N., & Pedersen, L. H. (2012). Attracting public service motivated employees: How to design compensation packages. *International Review of Administrative Sciences, 78*(4), 615–641. https://doi.org/10.1177/0020852312455298

Bell, B. S., & Moore, O. A. (2018). Learning, training and development in organizations: Emerging trends, recent advances and future directions. In *The SAGE handbook of industrial, work & organizational psychology: Organizational psychology* (Vol. 2, 2nd ed., pp. 215–234). Sage Reference.

Birkinshaw, J. (2024). Too little, too late? How policymakers and regulators respond to the business model innovations of digital firms. *Academy of Management Perspectives, 38*(3), 269–285. https://doi.org/10.5465/amp.2022.0233

Callender, F., & Forbes Business Council. (2023). Building an inclusive future: Diversity as key to sustainable growth. *Forbes*. https://www.forbes.com/sites/forbesbusinesscouncil/2023/10/03/building-an-inclusive-future-diversity-as-key-to-sustainable-growth/

CIPD. (2023). Recruitment: An introduction. CIPD. https://www.cipd.org/uk/knowledge/factsheets/recruitment-factsheet/.

Choi, H. H., Chang, S. D., & Kohli, M. D. (2020). Implementation and design of artificial intelligence in abdominal imaging. *Abdominal Radiology, 45*(12), 4084–4089. https://doi.org/10.1007/s00261-020-02471-0

Clarke, T. (2023). UK government to adopt "light touch" regulations around AI as concrete legislation currently tricky. *Sky News*. https://news.sky.com/story/uk-government-to-adopt-light-touch-regulations-around-ai-as-concrete-legislation-currently-tricky-12844592

Columbus, L. (2020). The most innovative companies of 2020 according to BCG. *Forbes*. https://www.forbes.com/sites/louiscolumbus/2020/06/28/the-most-innovative-companies-of-2020-according-to-bcg/

Cook, H., MacKenzie, R., & Forde, C. (2016). HRM and performance: The vulnerability of soft HRM practices during recession and retrenchment. *Human Resource Management Journal, 26*(4), 557–571. https://doi.org/10.1111/1748-8583.12122

Day, D., Bastardoz, N., Bisbey, T., Reyes, D., & Salas, E. (2021). Unlocking human potential through leadership training & development initiatives. *Behavioral Science & Policy, 7*(1), 41–54. https://doi.org/10.1177/237946152100700105

DePietro, R., Wiarda, E., & Fleischer, M. (1990). The context for change: Organization, technology and environment. In L. G. Tornatzky & M. Fleischer (Eds.), *The process of technological innovation* (pp. 151–175). Lexington Books.

De Smet, A., Dowling, B., Hancock, B., & Schaninger, B. (2023). *The great renegotiation and new talent pools* [McKinsey]. https://www.mckinsey.com/capabilities/people-and-organizational-performance/our-insights/the-great-attrition-is-making-hiring-harder-are-you-searching-the-right-talent-pools.

Dessler, G. (2012). *Human resource management*. Pearson Higher Ed.

Fenwick, A., Molnar, G., & Frangos, P. (2024). Revisiting the role of HR in the age of AI: Bringing humans and machines closer together in the workplace. *Frontiers in Artificial Intelligence, 6*. https://doi.org/10.3389/frai.2023.1272823

Forbes. (2018). The world's most innovative companies. *Forbes*. https://www.forbes.com/innovative-companies/

Forbes. (2023). Council post: 16 common concerns CEOs have in 2023 (and how to address them). *Forbes*. https://www.forbes.com/sites/forbescoachescouncil/2023/02/09/16-common-concerns-ceos-have-in-2023-and-how-to-address-them/

Fry, R., & Braga, D. (2023, December 14). *The growth of the older workforce*. Pew Research Center. https://www.pewresearch.org/social-trends/2023/12/14/the-growth-of-the-older-workforce/.

Garofano, C. M., & Salas, E. (2005). What influences continuous employee development decisions? *Human Resource Management Review, 15*(4), 281–304. https://doi.org/10.1016/j.hrmr.2005.10.002

Gartner. (2023). Top 5 trends for HR leaders in 2023. Gartner. https://www.gartner.com/en/human-resources/trends/top-priorities-for-hr-leaders-cpc.

Glavas, A., & Kelley, K. (2014). The effects of perceived corporate social responsibility on employee attitudes. *Business Ethics Quarterly, 24*(2), 165–202. https://doi.org/10.5840/beq20143206

Hendrickson, A. R. (2003). Human resource information systems: Backbone technology of contemporary human resources. *Journal of Labor Research, 24*(3), 381–394. https://doi.org/10.1007/s12122-003-1002-5

Horvath, M., Wasko, L. E., & Bradley, J. L. (2008). The effect of formal mentoring program characteristics on organizational attraction. *Human Resource Development Quarterly, 19*(4), 323–349. https://doi.org/10.1002/hrdq.1244

House of Commons. (2023). Post-pandemic economic growth: UK labour markets (No. Tenth Report of Session 2022–23). House of Commons. https://committees.parliament.uk/publications/39129/documents/192346/default/.

ISO. (2023, February 9). Three key trends shaping the new world of work. ISO. https://www.iso.org/cms/render/live/en/sites/isoorg/contents/news/2023/02/key-trends-shaping-the-work.color-C12.html.

Kaufman, B. E. (2008). The development of HRM in historical and international perspective. In P. Boxall, J. Purcell, & P. M. Wright (Eds.), *The Oxford handbook of human resource management* (1st ed., pp. 19–47). Oxford University Press. https://doi.org/10.1093/oxfordhb/9780199547029.003.0002

Kaufman, B. E. (2015). Evolution of strategic HRM as seen through two founding books: A 30th anniversary perspective on development of the field. *Human Resource Management, 54*(3), 389–407. https://doi.org/10.1002/hrm.21720

Kelly-Lyth, A., & Thomas, A. (2023). Algorithmic management: Assessing the impacts of AI at work. *European Labour Law Journal, 14*(2), 230–252. https://doi.org/10.1177/20319525231167478

Khatri, N. (2006). Building HR capability in health care organizations. *Health Care Management Review, 31*(1), 45–54. https://doi.org/10.1097/00004010-200601000-00007

Kim, S., Wang, Y., & Boon, C. (2021). Sixty years of research on technology and human resource management: Looking back and looking forward. *Human Resource Management, 60*(1), 229–247. https://doi.org/10.1002/hrm.22049

Lomineishvili, K. (2021). How entrepreneurial management and continuous learning affect the innovation and competitiveness of companies? *Economic Alternatives, 3*, 459–468. https://ideas.repec.org//a/nwe/eajour/y2021i3p459-468.html

Mahoney, T. A., & Deckop, J. R. (1986). Evolution of concept and practice in personnel administration/human resource management (PA/HRM). *Journal of Management, 12*(2), 223–241. https://doi.org/10.1177/014920638601200206

Malik, A., Srikanth, N. R., & Budhwar, P. (2020). Digitisation, artificial intelligence (AI) and HRM. In J. Crashaw, P. Budhwar, & A. Davis (Eds.), *Human resource management: Strategic and international perspectives* (3rd ed., pp. 88–111). SAGE Publications Ltd..

Marr, B. (2020). Deloitte survey finds digital maturity is critical to business success. *Forbes*. https://www.forbes.com/sites/bernardmarr/2020/05/27/digital-maturity-is-critical-to-business-success%2D%2Dnow-more-so-than-ever%2D%2Dsurvey-finds/

Matheson, L., & Jones, A. (2024, April 18). UK "losing race against time" to regulate AI in the workplace, unions warn. *The Mirror*. https://www.mirror.co.uk/money/uk-losing-race-against-time-32615500

Meister, J. (2024). The top ten HR trends that matter most in 2024. *Forbes*. https://www.forbes.com/sites/jeannemeister/2024/01/04/the-top-ten-hr-trends-that-matter-most-in-2024/

Mukherjee, S., Coulter, M., Chee, F. Y., Mukherjee, S., & Chee, F. Y. (2023, December 14). Explainer: What's next for the EU AI Act? *Reuters*. https://www.reuters.com/technology/whats-next-eu-ai-act-2023-12-14/

Pfeffer, J., & Langton, N. (1993). The effect of wage dispersion on satisfaction, productivity, and working collaboratively: Evidence from college and university faculty. *Administrative Science Quarterly, 38*(3), 382–407. https://doi.org/10.2307/2393373

PWC. (2023). 26th annual global CEO survey. *PWC*. https://www.pwc.com/gx/en/issues/c-suite-insights/ceo-survey-2023.html.

Royle, O. R. (2024). Bosses are making their staff return to the office—or quit (but they're notably absent themselves). *Fortune Europe*. https://fortune.com/europe/2024/07/29/bosses-staff-return-office-rto-quit-research-absent-workplace-iwg/

Ryan-Mosley, T., Heikkilä, M., & Yang, Z. (2024). What's next for AI regulation in 2024? *MIT Technology Review*. https://www.technologyreview.com/2024/01/05/1086203/whats-next-ai-regulation-2024/

Samaan, D., & Tursunbayeva, A. (2024). Fluid workforce management in the health sector: Navigating the changing face of workforces and their management. *International Journal of Public Sector Management*, ahead-of-print. https://doi.org/10.1108/IJPSM-10-2023-0311

Shen, J., Chanda, A., D'Netto, B., & Monga, M. (2009). Managing diversity through human resource: An international perspective and conceptual framework. *International Journal of Human Resource Management, 20*(2), 235–251. https://doi.org/10.1080/09585190802670516

Tigre, F. B., Curado, C., & Henriques, P. L. (2023). Digital leadership: A bibliometric analysis. *Journal of Leadership & Organizational Studies, 30*(1), 40–70. https://doi.org/10.1177/15480518221123132

Tkalac Verčič, A., & Sinčić Ćorić, D. (2018). The relationship between reputation, employer branding and corporate social responsibility. *Public Relations Review, 44*(4), 444–452. https://doi.org/10.1016/j.pubrev.2018.06.005

Tursunbayeva, A., Bunduchi, R., & Pagliari, C. (2020). "Planned Benefits" can be misleading in digital transformation projects: Insights from a case study of human resource information systems implementation in healthcare. *SAGE Open, 10*(2), 215824402093388. https://doi.org/10.1177/2158244020933881

Tursunbayeva, A., & Chalutz-Ben Gal, H. (2024). Adoption of artificial intelligence: A TOP framework-based checklist for digital leaders. *Business Horizons, 67*(4), 357–368. https://doi.org/10.1016/j.bushor.2024.04.006

Varma, A., Pereira, V., & Patel, P. (2024). Artificial intelligence and performance management. *Organizational Dynamics, 53*(1), 101037. https://doi.org/10.1016/j.orgdyn.2024.101037

Whiting, K. (2024). 6 work and workplace trends to watch in 2024. *World Economic Forum*. https://www.weforum.org/agenda/2024/02/work-and-workplace-trends-to-watch-2024/

WorldatWork. (2024). *Total rewards*. https://worldatwork.org/

World Economic Forum. (2023a). Global gender gap report 2023. World Economic Forum. https://www.weforum.org/publications/global-gender-gap-report-2023/.

World Economic Forum. (2023b). The 'AI divide' between the global north and the global south. World Economic Forum. https://www.weforum.org/agenda/2023/01/davos23-ai-divide-global-north-global-south/.

World Economic Forum. (2024a). Global risks report 2024. World Economic Forum. https://www.weforum.org/publications/global-risks-report-2024/.

World Economic Forum. (2024b). The rise of global digital jobs. World Economic Forum. https://www.weforum.org/publications/the-rise-of-global-digital-jobs/.

Wright, C. (2008). Reinventing human resource management: Business partners, internal consultants and the limits to professionalization. *Human Relations, 61*(8), 1063–1086. https://doi.org/10.1177/0018726708094860

# Chapter 3
# Navigating Artificial Intelligence: Implications for the World of Work and Human Resource Management

## 3.1 Artificial Intelligence

In 1999, an American inventor and futurist, Ray Kurzweil, proposed the law of accelerating returns (Danaher, 2019), according to which the rate of change tends to increase exponentially. In 2001, building on this, he also proposed an extension to Moore's law and specified that exponential technologies are disruptive technologies that bring rapid changes at a nonlinear speed. Singularity University recently precised this definition further by adding that the power of exponential technology doubles while their costs drop by half annually. Thus, exponential technologies such as AI (SingularityHub, 2021) promise a wide societal transformation by altering industries, production, consumption, and work (Bongomin et al., 2020).

The central point in AI history started in 1936 when Alan Turing, a British mathematician widely regarded as the father of theoretical computer science and AI, introduced the concept of the Turing Machine (Copeland & Proudfoot, 1999). This theoretical device laid the foundation for modern computers by showing how any computation could be performed with the proper instructions. In 1950, Turing proposed the Turing Test, originally called the imitation game, to determine if a machine can exhibit intelligent behavior indistinguishable from a human's (Kurzweil, 2024). His ideas significantly influenced early AI research, even though the term AI was coined by John McCarthy later in 1956 (Grzybowski et al., 2024).

Today, AI is a "field of computer science dedicated to creating systems performing tasks that usually require human intelligence, branching off into different techniques" (Pesapane 2018, p. 2). However, overall, there is still no consensus on the definition of AI across and within disciplinary domains due to the historical debate on what exactly "intelligence" is. AI is often employed as an umbrella term for different subsets of technologies that mimic human intelligence (i.e., computer vision,


A. Tursunbayeva, *Augmenting Human Resource Management with Artificial Intelligence*, Contributions to Management Science,
https://doi.org/10.1007/978-3-031-75266-7_3

natural language processing (NLP), machine learning, and deep learning) (Mehrotra, 2019). This book will thus follow a relatively broad yet clear definition of the technology that can be applied across the use of AI in HRM. Specifically, it will refer to AI in or for HRM as "the ability of a machine to learn from experience, adjust to new inputs, and perform human-like tasks" (Rai et al., 2019, p.III).

The progress of AI has been exponential. Back in 1995, AI could read zip codes off letters. In 1997, IBM's Deep Blue defeated the world chess champion, Gary Kasparov, by imitating the moves of human players. Twenty years later, AlphaZero, the game-playing AI created by Google sibling DeepMind, has beaten the world's best chess-playing computer program, having taught itself how to play in under 4 h (Kasparov, 2017).

Machine learning is a type of AI that has been mainly diffused and successful over the last decade, though many use these terms interchangeably. Machine learning uses algorithms to study data, learn from them, and make forecasts. The success of machine learning was associated mainly with the enormous amounts of data that became available around 2015, thanks to the diffusion of the Internet and social media and the emergence of affordable and powerful graphics processing units that can power it (Diamandis & Kotler, 2020).

However, the proper AI summer has begun with the arrival of a generative AI called ChatGPT, first released for public use in November 2022, followed by a superior version in March 2023 (ChatGPT-4). Generative AI employs machine learning models to create new content, such as audio, text, images, video, software code, and simulations, drawing on large datasets for training. ChatGPT has become famous for its ability to generate human-like responses to various questions. Its realistic and conversational interaction stems from its capability to answer follow-up questions, admit mistakes, and reject inappropriate requests. Unlike traditional AI algorithms based on machine learning, which only identify patterns in large datasets and make predictions-such as Google's autocomplete feature-ChatGPT goes further. It uses generative AI language models to create new content based on user prompts, producing various text forms like news articles, movie scripts, poetry, business plans, software codes, research manuscripts, and marketing campaigns. The quality of ChatGPT output depends on both the training data it has been exposed to and the quality of user prompts. For instance, ChatGPT-4 was trained on approximately 45 terabytes of data collected from the web until 2021 (Achiam et al., 2023), meaning its responses may lack the most recent information. To address this, supervised and reinforcement machine learning incorporates human feedback in the training process, ensuring the outputs align with users' intent and the context of their prompts (Mukobi et al., 2023).

Today, AI has encroached on every aspect of our lives, affecting how we work. ChatGPT is now used by about a third of employed Americans under 30 (McClain, 2024) (Fig. 3.1). Some employees even use ChatGPT at work secretly, as organizations are establishing guidelines and procedures on their proper use to avoid leakage of sensitive information or corporate secrets. Moreover, the workers also look for alternative AI tools, such as Perplexity, to continue benefiting from generative AI in secret (Christian, 2023). For instance, such alternatives have emerged and gained

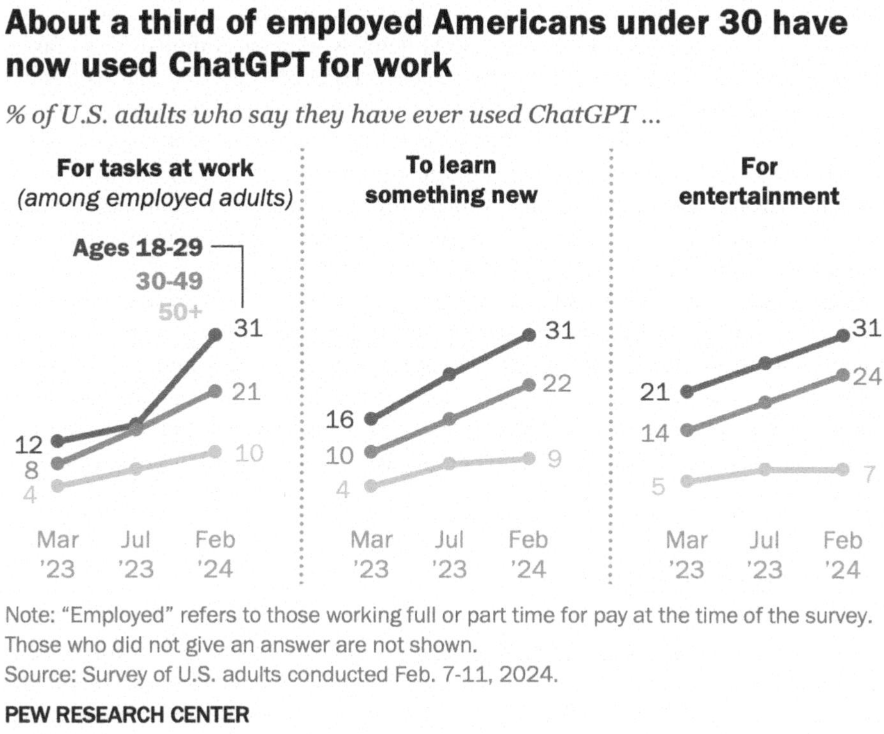


**Fig. 3.1** % of US adults who say they have ever used ChatGPT (McClain, 2024)

widespread adoption in Italy (e.g., www.pizzagpt.it) following the temporary ban on ChatGPT by the data protection authority in 2023 due to privacy concerns related to the collection of personal information (McCallum, 2023).

## 3.2 Consequences of Artificial Intelligence

The debate around AI, HRM, and the Future of Work has attracted increasing attention. Scholars, practitioners, and the general public have polarized this debate into two primary storylines: *hype* and *fear* (Willcocks, 2020).

The *hype* perspective spotlights the potential of these technologies to anticipate peoples' wants and needs and provide them with all the entertainment, food, and distractions they could ever desire (Willcocks, 2020). AI has taken care of repetitive, tedious, and knowledge-intensive tasks and has promised to assist with complex decisions often taken at work (e.g., Susskind, 2020). More specifically, AI is predicted to reshape people's work and how HRs are managed in organizations (Tursunbayeva, 2019). For example, how they are recruited (e.g., Johnson et al., 2020) or evaluated (e.g., Buck & Morrow, 2018). AI also promises to enhance worker productivity and result in higher-quality work. In 2023, various studies evaluated AI's effect on labor, indicating that AI helps workers accomplish tasks faster and improves the quality of their outputs. These studies also showed that AI has the potential to narrow the skill gap between low- and high-skilled workers (AI Index Steering Committee, Institute for Human-Centered AI, 2024). For instance, a recent paper revealed that generative AI can significantly benefit inexperienced workers. It concluded that contact center agents using a conversational AI assistant experienced a 14% increase in productivity, with the most substantial improvements observed among new or low-skilled workers (Brynjolfsson et al., 2023).

Still, others caution that using AI without proper oversight can lead to diminished performance. AI has also been accused of creating risks for displacing jobs (Talmage-Rostron, 2024), leading to increased inequalities (Acemoglu & Johnson, 2023), fewer jobs on the labor market (Susskind, 2020), and opaque decision-making, among others (Broom, 2023). This latter perspective is often referred to as the *fear* perspective. Below, these two perspectives are described in greater detail.

### 3.2.1 Hype Perspective

This storyline tells us that it will be fine, and most of us will live in a well-run technologized world where technologies will create jobs and solve multiple problems. The assumption embedded in this narrative is that technology will be a panacea that will bring many massive benefits (Willcocks, 2020). Table 3.1 provides selected quotes on AI that illustrate the hype perspective.

**Table 3.1** Famous quotes on the positive aspects of AI

| Name | Quote |
|---|---|
| Ray Kurzweil<br>Inventor, thinker, futurist; and Principal Researcher and AI Visionary at Google | *"I set the date for the Singularity - representing a profound and disruptive transformation in human capability - as 2045. The nonbiological intelligence created in that year will be one billion times more powerful than all human intelligence today"* (Karakas, 2021) |
| Peter Diamandis<br>Founder and executive chairman of the XPRIZE Foundation, and executive founder of Singularity University | *"AIs will dematerialize, demonetize and democratize all of these* [e.g., teacher, financial advisor, fashion designer] *services, dramatically improving the quality of life for 8 billion people, pushing us closer towards a world of abundance"* (Diamandis, 2015) |
| Tim Cook<br>CEO of Apple | *"What all of us have to do is to make sure we are using AI in a way that is for the benefit of humanity, not to the detriment of humanity"* (Martin, 2019) |
| Ginni Rometty<br>CEO of IBM | *"Some people call this artificial intelligence, but the reality is this technology will enhance us. So instead of artificial intelligence, I think we'll augment our intelligence"* (Martin, 2019) |

The proponents of the hype storyline invite us to look back to history, claiming that if employment has not vanished in the last several centuries because of the agricultural, industrial, and later service revolutions, thus it is unlikely to happen due to the ongoing technological revolution. Indeed, the latest job market statistics confirm this argumentation. In 2019, the US Bureau of Labor Statistics (2020) registered the lowest unemployment rate since 1990 (about 4%). Thus, more people are working these days than ever before. However, it is noted that technology might change the labor landscape (Parker & Grote, 2022). For instance, around 1800, 30–70% of the population of Western EU countries was employed in agriculture. This rate was reported to be below 5% in 2012 because of increased productivity achieved in this sector by embracing powerful machines that today can even milk or feed livestock (Danaher, 2019).

The scholarly work from the hype perspective also focuses on exploring some qualitative changes to the nature of work. Technology in this scenario is believed to be adopted first to *assist* humans by taking away the dirty or dangerous work, for example, in the agricultural sector (Danaher, 2019), and later by taking away the transactional and clerical chores (Babic et al., 2020). For example, today, bank account managers who use technologies can find some account opening fields already filled, which could help to open the bank accounts faster. Similarly, HRM managers could find the data collected from the applicants during the recruitment phase pulled directly into the employee records systems when the candidates are hired.

The proponents of the hype approach also claim that the complementary effect or *augmentation* component (Davenport & Kirby, 2015) of technology that promises an increase in productivity, rise in earnings, and growth in demand for skilled labor is often overlooked. For example, machines are often mentioned to have powers to make better, more reliable, and faster than human choices and decisions independently (Davenport & Kirby, 2015). This reframes discussions about pure efficiency-related automation outcomes to figuring out how the work could be deepened or expanded rather than diminished by greater use of machines. According to this way of thinking, machines will help us to take on tasks that are more sophisticated, more fulfilling, and better suited to our strengths (Davenport & Kirby, 2015). One example of such augmentation is enhancing human capabilities to quickly analyze large amounts of data, which is currently in high demand in organizations. This augmentation potential of technologies is already widely used by investment managers who need to analyze a large amount of constantly updating news, corporate events, or stock movements to make decisions. AI promises to make this task more manageable by almost immediately finding the most relevant news or general sentiment about events (Babic et al., 2020). For instance, Morgan Stanley has already started testing an OpenAI-powered chatbot for around 16,000 of its advisors, who are expected to benefit from the bank's enormous repository of research and data (Son, 2023).

Finally, hype proponents remind us that technologies have also created *new jobs* or *tasks* unimaginable without them, such as data scientists or information technology support officers for the former and recruiting with the help of social media (e.g.,

LinkedIn) for the latter. Indeed, a report commissioned by the World Economic Forum concluded that technologies could create 133 million new jobs while displacing 75 million of these jobs over the same period (Cann, 2018). Replacing some tasks and creating new opportunities still leave us with a net positive effect of technologies on work. However, this has opened another debate on redesigning work, rapid retraining, and upskilling humans (Tursunbayeva & Renkema, 2022). It is not any easier, as it can involve high costs and coordinated work of individuals, companies, and policymakers (Parker & Grote, 2022).

### 3.2.2 Fear Perspective

While recognizing the potential benefits of technology, many prominent figures have voiced apocalyptic concerns about AI (see Table 3.2 below for some illustrative examples).

The supporters of the fear perspective are concerned about dystopian technological unemployment or robo-apocalypse (i.e., work displacement) because of work automation (Willcocks, 2020). This technological unemployment phenomenon is projected to happen in all industries, levels of organizations (Willcocks, 2020), and geographical areas. Overall, it was claimed that the level of technological unemployment will depend on each country's work-related laws and regulations and the level of technological development of that country or individual organization (Danaher, 2019).

Existing evidence for this storyline mainly comprises studies focusing on exploring the impact of technologies on the quantities of jobs (Huysman, 2020). One of the earliest and the most influential work on technological unemployment was authored by Osborne and Frey, who, based on the analysis of 2010 O*NET database data of all US occupations, claimed that 47% of these are at high risk of being "computerized" in the next 10–20 years (Frey & Osborne, 2017). Later, the McKinsey Global Institute report suggested that 49% of the tasks currently

**Table 3.2** Famous quotes on the threats of AI

| Name | Quote |
|---|---|
| Elon Musk, Tesla, and SpaceX chief executive | *"I think we should be very careful about artificial intelligence. If I had to guess at what our biggest existential threat is, it's probably that. So we need to be very careful with artificial intelligence"* (Nguyen, 2014) |
| Stephen Hawking, Theoretical Physicist | *"The development of full artificial intelligence could spell the end of the human race"* (Cellan-Jones, 2014) |
| Shane Legg, Co-Founder and Chief AGI Scientist, Google DeepMind | *"Eventually, I think human extinction will probably occur, and technology will likely play a part in this"* (Bosker, 2014) |
| Bill Gates, Co-founder of Microsoft | *"Humans should be worried about the threat posed by artificial intelligence"* (Rawlinson, 2015) |

performed by workers have the potential to be automated (Manyika et al., 2017). Similarly, also PwC contributed to the discussion by estimating that 110 million jobs around the world are at risk of automation in the next 20 years (Hawksworth et al., 2018), while the Institute for Public Policy Research report suggested that one in three jobs in the UK are at risk of technological displacement (Elliott, 2017). Recently, International Monetary Fund's managing director Kristalina Georgieva declared, "Artificial intelligence is hitting the global labor market like a tsunami." She also added, "Artificial intelligence is likely to impact 60% of jobs in advanced economies and 40% of jobs around the world in the next two years" and that "We have very little time to get people ready for it, businesses ready for it" (Reuters, 2024).

The 2019 Office for National Statistics study found that women are disproportionately represented in jobs most at risk of automation, with 70.2% of employees in these roles being women, compared to 42.6% in jobs at low risk (White et al., 2019). This is mainly because women dominate the retail, healthcare, and administration sectors (House of Commons, 2023). A notable historical example of this trend occurred in the early twentieth century, when thousands of young women worked as telephone operators, connecting calls. However, in the late 1920s, AT&T introduced mechanical switching, which automated the process and resulted in the loss of thousands of jobs for these women (Ryssdal & Burdette, 2023). More recent research, drawing on a Goldman Sachs report that identified 15 occupations most impacted by AI, confirmed this finding, concluding that despite men outnumbering women in the workforce, 21% more women are exposed to AI automation due to the higher concentration of women in affected occupations (Frank Hawkins Kenan Institute of Private Enterprise, 2023). However, the increased use of technology in remote work has also provided new employment opportunities for women, potentially offsetting some of the risks of automation.

Although all these reports and projections are widely cited, many question their methods' reliability and results. For example, some of these reports have been criticized for being subjective and drawing conclusions primarily based on assumptions (Danaher, 2019). Undeniably, many of them do not focus on the potential of automation of future tasks and occupations, do not reveal jobs likely to be created as a result of adopting these technologies, and, last but not least, do not consider the long road of diffusion of innovation dilemma (Willcocks, 2020).

In terms of the qualitative impact of AI, the potential AI downside mentioned was its ability to alter how employees acquire, develop, share, and apply knowledge, potentially affecting both the level and value of their expertise (Renkema & Tursunbayeva, 2024). The reliance on AI, particularly in knowledge work, might limit informal and incidental learning opportunities, thereby hindering knowledge development (Evers & Van der Heijden, 2017). When workers entirely depend on AI for decision-making, they lose the chance to learn from and understand the performance of these technologies (Faraj et al., 2018). Additionally, integrating AI in knowledge work, such as in academia, could facilitate fraud and academic misconduct, which may be difficult to detect, at least initially. For example, generative AI, like ChatGPT, has raised concerns among scholars about its impact on research and

**Table 3.3** Implications of AI from hype and fear perspectives

| Implication of AI | Quantitative | Qualitative |
|---|---|---|
| *Hype* | Creating new tasks and jobs | Assisting humans<br>Augmenting humans |
| *Fear* | Replacing humans through automation | Hampering human knowledge |

teaching (e.g., Dwivedi et al., 2023), leading colleges to urgently address threats to academic integrity (Cotton et al., 2023).

Drawing on these generic perspectives from both the fear and hype storylines, it is possible to conclude that AI will have both qualitative and quantitative implications, including replacing humans or hampering their knowledge for fear perspective and assistance, augmentation, and the creation of new jobs or tasks for the hype perspective (see Table 3.3).

## 3.3 Applications of Artificial Intelligence in Human Resource Management

Mustafa Suleyman, the co-founder of DeepMind and CEO of Microsoft AI, has proposed a wave-based analysis of applications of exponential technologies (Suleyman & Bhaskar, 2023). Josh Bersin, a prominent HR technology analyst, has suggested a similar approach to analyze the application of technologies in HRM. He referred to HRM Technologies as comprising the waves of the Systems of Record, Systems of Talent, Systems of Engagement, and Systems of Work (Bersin, 2021). This approach aligns with the evolution of the HRM function, as described in the previous chapter, which includes waves of administrative or operational HRM, personnel management, and strategic management.

According to Josh Bersin, the Systems of Records (between the 1970–1980s) were used by Human Resource Management, payroll, and finance functions and focused on transactional automation and record keeping. The first need to adopt such technologies in HRM related to the establishment of the US Equal Employment Opportunity Commission in 1964 and subsequent legislations that forced companies to improve their personnel data management procedures. Interestingly, the impact of technology on jobs was already a topic of discussion. For instance, in January 1965, Newsweek estimated that automation eliminated 25,000 US jobs weekly (Kim et al., 2021). Thus, this was also when HRM managers started playing a crucial role in retraining workers in response to the risk of job displacements caused by automation.

The second wave (between 1977 and 1996) was characterized by the arrival of personal computers and their affordability, which permitted the development of HRIS. Bersin referred to such a system as the Systems of Talent, dedicated to HRM and Line Managers for different HRM practices (Bersin, 2021).

The third period commenced with the unprecedented wave of large-scale investment in consumer Internet services that led to a rapid growth of the US technology industry, as exemplified by the founding of Yahoo (1995) and Google (1998). Since this period, many HRM activities, such as recruitment and training, have started incorporating Internet technologies. Such user-friendly and mostly cloud-based integrated HR technologies were classified by Bersin (2021) as Systems of Engagement (2010s through today), and access to them was also given to employees. This period has also witnessed the rise of new work and management systems, including agile software development, lean manufacturing, management, holacracy, and self-managing teams (Mollick, 2024).

Finally, Bersin's Systems of Work (2021 and beyond) are now integrated into communication and collaboration platforms such as Teams or Slack, focusing on the whole employee journey. They can also be used by fluid employees, such as gig workers (Samaan & Tursunbayeva, 2024).

According to a recent report, organizations typically spend about $274 per employee on HR technologies (Harris, 2020). The global market for these technologies is valued at approximately $158 billion (Bersin, 2021). HR technologies are widely utilized within HR departments and by candidates, employees, managers, and organizational leaders for their daily tasks and interactions (Bersin, 2021).

These technologies supporting HRM's administration, management, and development practices can be referred to in myriad terms. A systematic literature review on HRIS (Tursunbayeva et al., 2015) identified around 50 relevant terms and concepts (see Fig. 3.2), such as electronic HR or E-HR (e.g., described as a "created real-time, information, based, self-service, interactive work environment" (Lengnick & Moritz, 2003), or as an electronic HRM or e-HRM system defined as "a way of implementing HR strategies, policies, and practices in organizations through conscious and directed support of and with the full use of web-technology-based channels" (Ruël et al., 2004).

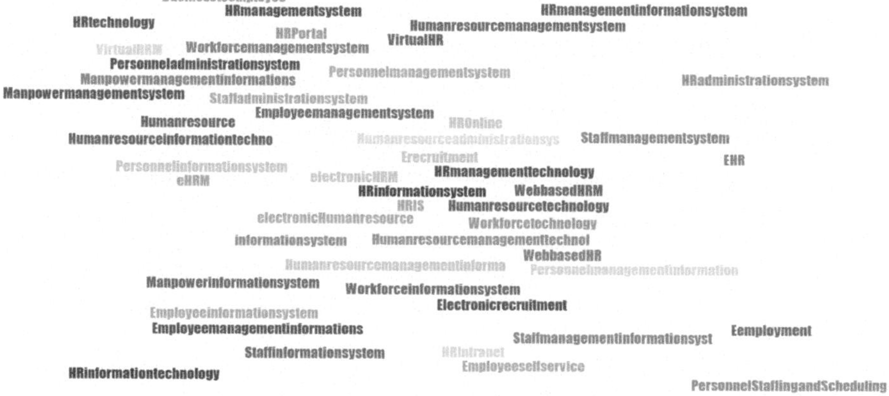


Fig. 3.2 HR Technology-related keywords (Adopted from Tursunbayeva et al., 2015)

These terms often refer to standalone information systems for HR, whereas, in complex organizations, HRM functions may be embedded within broader Enterprise Resource Planning systems. More recently, HR technologies have started to be referred to also as People Analytics (Tursunbayeva et al., 2018, p. 231)-defined as "an area of HRM practice, research and innovation concerned with the use of information technologies, descriptive and predictive data analytics and visualization tools for generating actionable insights about workforce dynamics, human capital, and individual and team performance that can be used strategically to optimize organizational effectiveness, efficiency, and outcomes, and improve employee experience" or aggregated under an umbrella "digital HRM" term (Strohmeier, 2020). The most recent development was a proposal for a new "Algorithmic HRM" term "to synthesize insights on issues of common concern, including the growing use of digital data to support HR decision-making, the deployment of software algorithms that process digital data at work, and the partial or full automation of HR decision-making, all of which are profoundly shaping how labor is management and HR practices are performed" (Meijerink et al., 2021, p. 2546).

Leveraging technologies has brought numerous benefits and opportunities for HRM practices execution, delivery, and quality (Tursunbayeva et al., 2023). These include strategic orientation, operational efficiency, improving HRM service delivery, empowering managers and employees to perform some HRM activities, and improving organizational image or strengthening employer branding (Parry & Tyson, 2011). Such benefits can be achieved by various stakeholders, ranging from candidates to top managers (Tursunbayeva, 2018; Tursunbayeva et al., 2019). Illustrative examples of these benefits, drawn from real customer stories on HR technology vendor websites, are provided in Table 3.4 below.

One of the most influential approaches for analyzing digital technology use and their implications in HRM has been configurational, providing a framework for explaining various contextual conditions (Strohmeier & Kabst, 2014), such as organizational differences, and linking them to significant organizational outcomes (Martini et al., 2020; Meyer et al., 1993; Short et al., 2008). Its underlying assumption is that organizations initiate HR technology projects with specific goals in mind, and the configurational approach here helps identify and achieve these goals (Martini et al., 2020). The configurational approach categorizes HR technologies (Martini et al., 2020; Parry & Tyson, 2011; Ruël et al., 2004; Strohmeier & Kabst, 2014) into operational, relational, and transformational types.

This approach, already established in generic HRM literature (Lepak & Snell, 1998), was proposed to be valuable also for studying emerging digital technologies like big data, analytics, and AI in HRM, as it helps navigate their complexity and interactions through a structured framework (Poba-Nzaou et al., 2020). Previous literature emphasized the need for further research on HR technology configurations, mainly focusing on new technologies such as AI due to their significant impact on modern HRM. Thus, this book follows a configurational approach to address the evolving challenges associated with the increasing complexity of AI-based HR technologies.

**Table 3.4** Benefits of HR technologies as reported by their users

| Benefit | Example |
|---|---|
| Strategic orientation | *"Based on the analysis conducted for the Gulf region, Almarai was able to link employee participation in PARADIGM to impactful results, including:*<br>– *47% reduction in Lost Sales for Gulf (2021* vs *2022)*<br>– *2% increase in Order Accuracy for Gulf (2021* vs *2022)*<br>*Depot supervisors have also grown more comfortable on the platform, requiring only occasional scenario-based question support and getting more attuned to what PARADIGM can do"* William Samuel, Head of Learning & Development, Sales Division at Almarai about Axonify (n.d.) |
| Operational efficiency | *"The real-time nature of the platform is like nothing I've ever seen before. It's incredibly fast to make changes, to get results, and to derive insights. We get a very unbiased objective view of what people are saying, what people are feeling, what they want, and what they need"* Amy Toppen, Vice President (VP) of HR at Soulcycle about Culture Amp (n.d.) |
| Service delivery | *"Greenhouse improves both candidate and hiring team experience - and the numbers back this up. From 2022 to 2023, candidate experience satisfaction at CrowdStreet grew from 69% to 86% and the offer acceptance rate climbed from 91% to 96%, while neither time-to-hire nor time-to-fill increased despite the loss of a dedicated Talent Acquisition team"* Shaquaya Perdue, Talent Experience Partner at CrowdStreet about Greenhouse (n.d.) |
| Empowerment | *"Fond's rewards and recognition platform helped Delta Dental empower managers and employees to value and appreciate each other at work.*<br>– *93% increase in employee recognition*<br>– *72% of managers say employees feel more appreciated*<br>– *93% of managers say recognition is easier to give"* |
| Organizational image | *"By leveraging Energage tools and Top Workplaces awards, Fairway has strengthened its employer brand, gather valuable employee feedback, gain insights from benchmarking data, and earn recognition for its people-first workplace culture"* Julie Fry Chief Human Resources Officer at Fairway Independent Mortgage about Energage (n.d.) |

The capacity of the HRM function to integrate AI within existing organizational business intelligence systems to aid problem-solving and decision-making, drawing on a configurational approach, can have positive HRM-specific *operational, relational,* and *transformational* implications (Prikshat et al., 2021). In the following three chapters, these three implications of AI application for HRM are described, taking into account the generic consequences of AI outlined in this chapter (see Table 3.3), such as automating traditional HRM practices, assisting HRM professionals with relational activities, and augmenting HRM transformational activities.

## References

Acemoglu, D., & Johnson, S. (2023). Choosing AI's impact on the future of work (SSIR). *Stanford Social Innovation Review*. https://doi.org/10.48558/N8MF-TW30

Achiam, O. J., Adler, S., Agarwal, S., Ahmad, L., Akkaya, I., Aleman, F. L., Almeida, D., Altenschmidt, J., Altman, S., Anadkat, S., Avila, R., Babuschkin, I., Balaji, S., Balcom, V.,

Baltescu, P., Bao, H., Bavarian, M., Belgum, J., Bello, I., ... Zoph, B. (2023). GPT-4 technical report. https://www.semanticscholar.org/paper/GPT-4-Technical-Report-Achiam-Adler/163b4d6a79a5b19af88b8585456363340d9efd04.

AI Index Steering Committee, Institute for Human-Centered AI. (2024). *The AI Index 2024 annual report*. Stanford University. https://aiindex.stanford.edu/report/

Axonify. (n.d.). How Almarai connects the dots between employee training and business results. *Axonify*. Retrieved August 22, 2024, from https://axonify.com/en-uk/customer-stories/almarai/

Babic, B., Chen, D. L., Evgeniou, T., & Fayard, A. L. (2020). A better way to onboard AI. *Harvard Business Review*.

Bersin, J. (2021). *HR technology 2021: The definitive guide: Everything you want to know about buying, implementing, and investing in HR Technology.*

Bongomin, O., Gilibrays Ocen, G., Oyondi Nganyi, E., Musinguzi, A., & Omara, T. (2020). Exponential disruptive technologies and the required skills of industry 4.0. *Journal of Engineering*, 4280156. https://doi.org/10.1155/2020/4280156

Bosker, B. (2014, January 29). *Google's new A.I. ethics board might save humanity from extinction*. HuffPost. https://www.huffpost.com/entry/google-ai_n_4683343.

Broom, D. (2023). AI: These are the biggest risks to businesses and how to manage them. World Economic Forum. https://www.weforum.org/agenda/2023/07/ai-biggest-risks-how-to-manage-them/.

Brynjolfsson, E., Li, D., & Raymond, L. R. (2023). Generative AI at work. National Bureau of Economic Research. https://www.nber.org/papers/w31161.

Buck, B., & Morrow, J. (2018). AI, performance management and engagement: Keeping your best their best. *Strategic HR Review, 17*(5), 261–262. https://doi.org/10.1108/SHR-10-2018-145

Cann, O. (2018). Machines will do more tasks than humans by 2025 but robot revolution will still create 58 million net new jobs in next five years. World Economic Forum. https://www.weforum.org/press/2018/09/machines-will-do-more-tasks-than-humans-by-2025-but-robot-revolution-will-still-create-58-million-net-new-jobs-in-next-five-years/.

Cellan-Jones, R. (2014, December 2). Stephen Hawking warns artificial intelligence could end mankind. BBC News. https://www.bbc.com/news/technology-30290540.

Christian, A. (2023). The employees secretly using AI at work. BBC. https://www.bbc.com/worklife/article/20231017-the-employees-secretly-using-ai-at-work.

Copeland, J., & Proudfoot, D. (1999, April 1). Alan Turing's forgotten ideas in computer science. Scientific American. https://www.scientificamerican.com/article/alan-turings-forgotten-ideas-in-com/.

Cotton, D. R. E., Cotton, P. A., & Shipway, J. R. (2023). Chatting and cheating: Ensuring academic integrity in the era of ChatGPT. *Innovations in Education and Teaching International*, 228–239.

Culture Amp. (n.d.). An employee experience that people love. Culture Amp. Retrieved August 22, 2024, from https://www.cultureamp.com/home.

Danaher, J. (2019). *Automation and Utopia. Human flourishing in a world without work*. Harvard University Press.

Davenport, T. H., & Kirby, J. (2015). Beyond automation. Strategies for remaining gainfully employed in an era of very smart machines. Harvard Business Review.

Diamandis, P. H. (2015). AI bring it on. https://www.diamandis.com/blog/ai-bring-it-on.

Diamandis, P. H., & Kotler, S. (2020). *The future is faster than you think: How converging technologies are transforming business, industries, and our lives*. Simon & Schuster.

Dwivedi, Y. K., Kshetri, N., Hughes, L., Slade, E. L., Jeyaraj, A., Kar, A. K., Baabdullah, A. M., Koohang, A., Raghavan, V., Ahuja, M., Albanna, H., Albashrawi, M. A., Al-Busaidi, A. S., Balakrishnan, J., Barlette, Y., Basu, S., Bose, I., Brooks, L., Buhalis, D., et al. (2023). Opinion paper: "So what if ChatGPT wrote it?" Multidisciplinary perspectives on opportunities, challenges and implications of generative conversational AI for research, practice and policy. *International Journal of Information Management, 71*, 102642. https://doi.org/10.1016/j.ijinfomgt.2023.102642

Elliott, L. (2017). Robots to replace 1 in 3 UK jobs over next 20 years, warns IPPR. *The Guardian*. https://www.theguardian.com/technology/2017/apr/15/uk-government-urged-help-low-skilled-workers-replaced-robots

Energage. (n.d.). Building and branding top workplaces. *Energage*. Retrieved August 22, 2024, from https://www.energage.com/

Evers, A. T., & van der Heijden, B. I. J. M. (2017). Competence and professional expertise. In M. Mulder (Ed.), *Competence-based vocational and professional education: Bridging the worlds of work and education* (pp. 83–101). Springer. https://doi.org/10.1007/978-3-319-41713-4_4

Faraj, S., Pachidi, S., & Sayegh, K. (2018). *Working and organizing in the age of the learning algorithm*. University of Cambridge. https://doi.org/10.17863/CAM.23960

Fond. (n.d.). Employee rewards and recognition made easy. Fond. Retrieved August 22, 2024, from https://www.fond.co/

Frank Hawkins Kenan Institute of Private Enterprise. (2023). Will generative AI disproportionately affect the jobs of women? Frank Hawkins Kenan Institute of Private Enterprise. https://kenaninstitute.unc.edu/kenan-insight/will-generative-ai-disproportionately-affect-the-jobs-of-women/.

Frey, C. B., & Osborne, M. A. (2017). The future of employment: How susceptible are jobs to computerisation? *Technological Forecasting and Social Change, 114*, 254–280. https://doi.org/10.1016/j.techfore.2016.08.019

Greenhouse. (n.d.). Candidate satisfaction grows by 17% at CrowdStreet. *Greenhouse*. Retrieved August 22, 2024, from https://www.greenhouse.com/customer-stories/candidate-satisfaction-grows-by-17-at-crowdstreet.

Grzybowski, A., Pawlikowska-Łagód, K., & Lambert, W. C. (2024). A history of artificial intelligence. *Clinics in Dermatology, 42*(3), 221–229. https://doi.org/10.1016/j.clindermatol.2023.12.016

Harris, S. (2020). Sierra-Cedar 2019–2020. HR Systems Survey Findings. Sierra-Cedar. https://cdn.ymaws.com/www.clevelandshrm.com/resource/collection/09E0F41E-BD60-41C0-A2FD-AAD4D5A44B59/The_Future_of_HR_Technology_Virtual_Learning-_February_2020_.pdf.

Hawksworth, J., Berriman, R., & Cameron, E. (2018). Will robots really steal our jobs? An international analysis of the long term potential of automation. PWC.

House of Commons. (2023). *Post-pandemic economic growth: UK labour markets* (No. Tenth Report of Session 2022–23). House of Commons. https://committees.parliament.uk/publications/39129/documents/192346/default/.

Huysman, M. (2020). Information systems research on artificial intelligence and work: A commentary on "Robo-Apocalypse cancelled? Reframing the automation and future of work debate". *Journal of Information Technology, 35*(4), 307–309. https://doi.org/10.1177/0268396220926511

Johnson, R., Stone, D., & Lukaszewski, K. (2020). The benefits of eHRM and AI for talent acquisition. *Journal of Tourism Futures*. https://doi.org/10.1108/JTF-02-2020-0013

Karakas, F. (2021, January 26). Why You Should Read "The Singularity is Near: When Humans Transcend Biology". *Medium*. https://medium.com/predict/why-you-should-read-the-singularity-is-near-when-humans-transcend-biology-f8066b5921ed

Kasparov, G. (2017). AlphaZero AI beats champion chess program after teaching itself in four hours. www.kasparov.com. https://www.kasparov.com/blog-post/alphazero-ai-beats-champion-chess-program-after-teaching-itself-in-four-hours/.

Kim, S., Wang, Y., & Boon, C. (2021). Sixty years of research on technology and human resource management: Looking back and looking forward. *Human Resource Management, 60*(1), 229–247. https://doi.org/10.1002/hrm.22049

Kurzweil, R. (2024). *The singularity is nearer: When we merge with AI*. Viking.

Lengnick-Hall, M. L., & Moritz, S. (2003). The impact of e-HR on the human resource management function. *Journal of Labor Research, 24*(3), 365–379. https://doi.org/10.1007/s12122-003-1001-6

Lepak, D. P., & Snell, S. A. (1998). Virtual HR: Strategic human resource management in the 21st century. *Human Resource Management Review, 6*(3), 215–234.

Manyika, J., Chui, M., Miremadi, M., Bughin, J., George, K., Willmott, P., & Dewhurst, M. (2017). *A future that works: Automation, employment, and productivity*. McKinsey Global Institute.
Martin, N. (2019). 13 best quotes about the future of artificial intelligence. *Forbes*.
Martini, M., Cavenago, D., & Marafioti, E. (2020). Exploring types, drivers and outcomes of social e-HRM. *Employee Relations: The International Journal, 43*(3), 788–806. https://doi.org/10.1108/ER-10-2019-0404
McCallum, S. (2023, March 31). ChatGPT banned in Italy over privacy concerns. *BBC*.
McClain, C. (2024). *Americans' use of ChatGPT is ticking up, but few trust its election information*. Pew Research Center. https://www.pewresearch.org/short-reads/2024/03/26/americans-use-of-chatgpt-is-ticking-up-but-few-trust-its-election-information/
Mehrotra, D. (2019). *Basics of artificial intelligence & machine learning*. Notion Press.
Meijerink, J., Boons, M., Keegan, A., & Marler, J. (2021). Algorithmic human resource management: Synthesizing developments and cross-disciplinary insights on digital HRM. *The International Journal of Human Resource Management, 32*(12), 2545–2562. https://doi.org/10.1080/09585192.2021.1925326
Meyer, A. D., Tsui, A. S., & Hinings, C. R. (1993). Configurational approaches to organizational analysis. *The Academy of Management Journal, 36*(6), 1175–1195. https://doi.org/10.2307/256809
Mollick, E. (2024). Co-intelligence: Living and working with AI. Portfolio. https://www.amazon.com/Co-Intelligence-Living-Working-Ethan-Mollick/dp/059371671X.
Mukobi, G., Chatain, P., Fong, S., Windesheim, R., Kutyniok, G., Bhatia, K., & Alberti, S. (2023). *SuperHF: Supervised iterative learning from human feedback* (No. arXiv:2310.16763). arXiv. https://doi.org/10.48550/arXiv.2310.16763.
Nguyen, D. V. (2014, October 27). Elon Musk calls artificial intelligence "our biggest existential threat." Silicon Republic. https://www.siliconrepublic.com/machines/elon-musk-calls-artificial-intelligence-our-biggest-existential-threat.
Parker, S. K., & Grote, G. (2022). Automation, algorithms, and beyond: Why work design matters more than ever in a digital world. *Applied Psychology, 71*(4), 1171–1204. https://doi.org/10.1111/apps.12241
Parry, E., & Tyson, S. (2011). Desired goals and actual outcomes of e-HRM. *Human Resource Management Journal, 21*(3), 335–354. https://doi.org/10.1111/j.1748-8583.2010.00149.x
Pesapane, F. (2018). Artificial intelligence in medical imaging: Threat or opportunity? Radiologists again at the forefront of innovation in medicine. *European Radiology Experimental, 2*(1). https://doi.org/10.1186/s41747-018-0061-6
Poba-Nzaou, P., Galani, M., & Tchibozo, A. (2020). Transforming human resources management in the age of Industry 4.0: A matter of survival for HR professionals. *Strategic HR Review, 19*(6), 273–278. https://doi.org/10.1108/SHR-06-2020-0055
Prikshat, V., Malik, A., & Budhwar, P. (2021). AI-augmented HRM: Antecedents, assimilation and multilevel consequences. *Human Resource Management Review, 100860*. https://doi.org/10.1016/j.hrmr.2021.100860
Rai, A., Constantinides, P., & Sarker, S. (2019). Next generation digital platforms: Toward human-AI hybrids. *Management Information Systems Quarterly*.
Rawlinson, K. (2015, January 29). Microsoft's Bill Gates insists AI is a threat. *BBC News*.
Renkema, M., & Tursunbayeva, A. (2024). The future of work of academics in the age of Artificial Intelligence: State-of-the-art and a research roadmap. *Futures, 163*, 103453. https://doi.org/10.1016/j.futures.2024.103453
Reuters. (2024). Artificial intelligence hitting labour forces like a "tsunami"—IMF chief. *Reuters*. https://www.reuters.com/technology/artificial-intelligence-hitting-labour-forces-like-tsunami-imf-chief-2024-05-13/
Ruël, H., Bondarouk, T., & Looise, J. K. (2004). E-HRM: Innovation or irritation. An explorative empirical study in five large companies on web-based HRM. *Management Revue, 15*(3), 364–380. https://www.jstor.org/stable/41783479.
Ryssdal, K., & Burdette, L. (2023). *AI lessons from the telephone operators of the 1920s* [Marketplace]. https://www.marketplace.org/2023/08/17/automation-ai-switchboard-telephone-operators/.

Samaan, D., & Tursunbayeva, A. (2024). Fluid workforce management in the health sector: navigating the changing face of workforces and their management. *International Journal of Public Sector Management, 37*(4), 593–609. https://doi.org/10.1108/IJPSM-10-2023-0311

Short, J. C., Payne, G. T., & Ketchen, D. J. (2008). Research on organizational configurations: Past accomplishments and future challenges. *Journal of Management, 34*(6), 1053–1079. https://doi.org/10.1177/0149206308324324

SingularityHub. (2021). *About SingularityHub* [SingularityHub].

Son, H. (2023, March 14). Morgan Stanley is testing an OpenAI-powered chatbot for its 16,000 financial advisors. CNBC. https://www.cnbc.com/2023/03/14/morgan-stanley-testing-openai-powered-chatbot-for-its-financial-advisors.html.

Strohmeier, S. (2020). Digital human resource management: A conceptual clarification. *German Journal of Human Resource Management: Zeitschrift Für Personalforschung, 34*(3), 345–365. https://doi.org/10.1177/2397002220921131

Strohmeier, S., & Kabst, R. (2014). Configurations of e-HRM-an empirical exploration. *Employee Relations, 36*(4), 333–353.

Suleyman, M., & Bhaskar, M. (2023). *The coming wave: Technology, power, and the twenty-first Century's greatest dilemma*. Crown.

Susskind, D. (2020). *A world without work: Technology, automation, and how we should respond*. Metropolitan Books.

Talmage-Rostron, M. (2024). *How will artificial intelligence affect jobs 2024-2030*. Nexford University. https://www.nexford.edu/insights/how-will-ai-affect-jobs

Tursunbayeva, A. (2018). *Human resource management information systems in healthcare. Processes of development, implementation and benefits realization in complex organizations*. FrancoAngeli. https://www.francoangeli.it/Ricerca/scheda_Libro.aspx?codiceISBN=9788891768759.

Tursunbayeva, A. (2019). Human resource technology disruptions and their implications for human resources management in healthcare organizations. *BMC Health Services Research, 19*(1), 268. https://doi.org/10.1186/s12913-019-4068-3

Tursunbayeva, A., & Renkema, M. (2022). Artificial intelligence in health-care: Implications for the job design of healthcare professionals. *Asia Pacific Journal of Human Resources*. https://doi.org/10.1111/1744-7941.12325

Tursunbayeva, A., Pagliari, C., Bunduchi, R., & Franco, M. (2015). Human resource information systems in health care: Protocol for a systematic review. *JMIR Research Protocols, 4*. https://doi.org/10.2196/resprot.4922

Tursunbayeva, A., Di Lauro, S., & Pagliari, C. (2018). People analytics—A scoping review of conceptual boundaries and value propositions. *International Journal of Information Management, 43*, 224–247. https://doi.org/10.1016/j.ijinfomgt.2018.08.002

Tursunbayeva, A., Bunduchi, R., Franco, M., & Pagliari, C. (2019). What kind of benefits different stakeholders can expect and obtain from HRIS implementations: An Italian case study. In A. Lazazzara, R. C. D. Nacamulli, C. Rossignoli, & S. Za (Eds.), *Organizing for Digital Innovation* (pp. 39–48). Springer International Publishing.

Tursunbayeva, A., Berni, A., & Moschera, A. (2023). Artificial intelligence in human resource management: Objectives and implications. In F. P. Appio, D. La Torre, F. Lazzeri, H. Masri, & F. Schiavone (Eds.), *Impact of Artificial Intelligence in Business and Society*. Routledge.

U.S. Bureau of Labor Statistics. (2020). *Charting the labor market: Data from the current population survey (CPS)*. U.S. Bureau of Labor Statistics. https://www.bls.gov/web/empsit/cps_charts.pdf

White, S., Lacey, A., & Ardanaz-Badia, A. (2019). The probability of automation in England. Office for National Statistics. https://www.ons.gov.uk/employmentandlabourmarket/peopleinwork/employmentandemployeetypes/articles/theprobabilityofautomationinengland/2011and2017.

Willcocks, L. (2020). Robo-Apocalypse cancelled? Reframing the automation and future of work debate. *Journal of Information Technology, 35*(4), 286–302. https://doi.org/10.1177/0268396220925830

# Chapter 4
# Leaving (Operational) Human Resource Management to Artificial Intelligence

## 4.1 From "Traditional" Automation to Algorithmic Management

HRM largely depends on document-driven processes. Thus, many HRM departments are drowning in administration and paperwork required for time-consuming and manual processing across operational HRM tasks. There was a time when there was no alternative. Now, automation comes to the rescue. HR technology experts predict, "It won't be long before everything that can be automated within HR will be" (Shani, n.d.).

So far, HR technologies helped to automate repetitive and time-consuming tasks, including employee onboarding administration, payroll, timekeeping, and benefits administration. Substantial evidence indicates that this offered such operational advantages as the potential to decrease HRM personnel, expedite processes, cut costs, and free up staff from administrative duties (Ruël et al., 2004; as cited in Parry & Tyson, 2011). As a result, the expectation was that HRM professionals would focus on more strategic tasks that are more valuable to the company. For example, on culture building, people's practices, being a workplace champion, and a communications expert. It was also claimed to improve efficiency and security while reducing the potential for human error.

Algorithms have long been used for such automation, but their role has evolved significantly in recent years. An algorithm is a "computational formula that autonomously makes decisions based on statistical models or decision rules without explicit human intervention, [such as] a sequence of instructions telling a computer what to do within a set of precisely defined steps and rules designed to accomplish a task" (Duggan et al., 2020, p. 6). Modern AI-driven algorithms possess enhanced capabilities due to their autonomous learning and ability to handle large datasets (Kellogg et al., 2020; Schafheitle et al., 2020). Unlike traditional pre-programmed



A. Tursunbayeva, *Augmenting Human Resource Management with Artificial Intelligence*, Contributions to Management Science,
https://doi.org/10.1007/978-3-031-75266-7_4

algorithms, AI algorithms can be powered by machine learning technologies, which start with minimal programming and learn from extensive, unstructured data sets (Leicht-Deobald et al., 2019). For example, a machine learning algorithm predicting employee performance would be trained on millions of records, improving through trial and error. Thus, AI algorithms stand out from previous systems by learning autonomously, continuously improving, and sometimes outperforming humans in decision-making and managing complex data (Kemper & Kolkman, 2019).

Algorithms are increasingly applied to the roles traditionally held by managers or HRM managers (Gal et al., 2020; Kellogg et al., 2020). The term "algorithmic management" was introduced by Lee et al. (2015) within the ridesharing industry and has since been explored in various sectors (McDaid et al., 2023). Parent-Rocheleau and Parker (2021) identified six managerial and HRM functions impacted by algorithmic management: monitoring, goal-setting, performance management, scheduling, compensation, and job termination. Meijerink and Bondarouk (2023) also noted algorithmic-enabled HRM activities, categorizing them into descriptive, predictive, and prescriptive functions, each with distinct applications in performance evaluation, forecasting, and decision-making (Leicht-Deobald et al., 2019).

Descriptive algorithms can analyze worker-generated data by processing and integrating information from various sources to produce simple statistics like mean scores and variable associations (Meijerink & Bondarouk, 2023; Di Lauro et al., 2024). These algorithms can help managers monitor critical metrics such as worker performance, absenteeism, and personality traits. Predictive algorithms can forecast the likelihood of specific events or outcomes, employing advanced regression, machine learning, or data mining techniques (Meijerink & Bondarouk, 2023; Di Lauro et al., 2024). These algorithms aid decision-makers in recruitment by predicting a candidate's future potential or workforce planning by predicting employee turnover. While predictions may not be perfect, they can provide valuable guidance for HRM managers in decision-making. Prescriptive algorithms build on predictive algorithms by using simulations and scenario-based techniques to recommend actions based on potential scenarios (Meijerink & Bondarouk, 2023). They can support HRM decision-making by suggesting a course of action or can fully automate decision-making.

Overall, AI algorithms specifically for HRM emphasize efficiency and overall performance outcomes (Vrontis et al., 2022) and are usually typical to organizations that primarily employ technologies for operational configuration or to increase their HRM department's effectiveness (Parry & Tyson, 2011). Algorithmic management has also been linked to earlier management methods like scientific management, which Frederick Taylor introduced in the early 1900s. For instance, Kathleen Griesbach et al. (2019) note that while algorithmic control is new, it shares many features with older labor control mechanisms. However, others argued that algorithmic management is a distinct approach specific to platform economies (Stark & Pais, 2020). Indeed, algorithmic management was once mainly associated with specific industries and settings where work can be easily broken down into discrete, quantifiable tasks, such as in the gig economy. Thus, the term has become closely linked with app-based work or companies like Uber and Deliveroo, which rely heavily on independent contractors rather than conventional full-time employees. These contractors enjoy the freedom to select their own working hours and locations. However, unlike traditional organizations that primarily hire full-time or part-time employees, these contractors lack regular employees' benefits, such as paid sick leave, vacations, and pension contributions (Samaan & Tursunbayeva, 2024). There were attempts, though, to recognize such independent contractors as regular workers, as the one fought for 7 years by the Independent Workers' Union of Great Britain. However, in 2023, the UK's Supreme Court ruled that Deliveroo riders cannot be recognized as workers or be represented by trade unions for collective bargaining because someone else can complete their deliveries, and they have the freedom to reject work or work for competitors (Criddle, 2023). This decision is significant for the gig economy as it may influence how other gig economy companies structure their employment relationships.

Algorithmic management in companies like Uber or Deliveroo differs from the traditional HRM practices typically handled by line managers (see Table 4.1 below). At Uber, for instance, conventional HRM practices are largely replaced by an algorithmic system that executes these tasks with minimal human intervention (Wiener et al., 2023). Thus, their R&S process for drivers is streamlined, focusing primarily on background checks, vehicle requirements, and essential regulatory compliance without involving interviews (Zippia team, 2022). Performance management at Uber is a star rating system where passengers rate drivers after each trip, and drivers with consistently low ratings risk deactivation from the platform (PerformYard, n.d.). Uber offers mainly basic training and orientation for drivers centered around using the app, customer service, and safety protocols specific to each region or country (Uber, n.d.). Regarding C&B, Uber drivers are paid per ride, with earnings

**Table 4.1** Algorithmic management practices at Uber

| HRM practice | Algorithmic management at Uber |
|---|---|
| R&S | *"You can apply online, and no interview is required. You will need to have a valid driver's license, registration card, and proof of insurance. The company will then perform a background check and vehicle inspection. If all of this checks out, you'll be hired as a driver"* (Zippia team, 2022) |
| T&D | *"The driver safety course [for All driver partners] is designed to equip you with the most up-to-date knowledge to keep yourself and others safe on the road.*<br>*We're working with a third-party provider to make the driver-partner safety education modules available. There are different learning modules that only take 30 min to complete"* (Uber, n.d.) |
| Performance management, promotions, and dismissals | *"Goals:New drivers are provided with clear goals and expectations, including specific rules and ways their accounts can be deactivated*<br>*Feedback:After each ride, a continuous feedback process occurs, where frequent ratings from different passengers help monitor performance and balance out biases*<br>*Reviews: Performance appraisal is ongoing. Drivers with ratings below 4.6 are dismissed, while consistently high-rated drivers receive VIP status with additional benefits"* (PerformYard, n.d.) |

fluctuating based on the number of trips, distance, time, and demand (i.e., surge pricing). Here, Uber also uses a GPS dashboard to monitor driving behavior and employs systems for sorting and matching, which can penalize drivers for slow trip acceptance. The company also uses video gamification and non-cash rewards to motivate drivers. At the same time, communication is managed through help menus and question and answers chatbots, highlighting broader issues related to workers' authority and legal status (McDaid et al., 2023).

Such algorithmic management was found to influence workers' experiences. A special issue in the Journal of Industrial Relations on the organization and experience of work in the gig economy (Kaine & Josserand, 2019) revealed that while gig workers may enjoy the variety in their work, they often face negative emotions like devaluation (Sheehan & Pittman, 2019), anxiety, and fear due to job insecurity and unpredictable income (Petriglieri et al., 2019). These emotions are associated with poor platform communication (Carmody & Fortuin, 2019) and career uncertainty (Schwartz, 2018). However, some studies suggest that social connections, mainly through online communities, can help mitigate these negative experiences (Kaine & Josserand, 2019). Gig workers are thus recommended to actively build relationships with other workers, clients, and supporters to cope with the emotional challenges of gig work, as they lack stable social connections (Ashford et al., 2018).

More recently, we evidence that algorithmic management approaches are spreading from gig platforms and logistics warehouses into other sectors and occupations (O'Connor, 2022), re-adjusting and re-evaluating traditional HRM professionals' practices and roles in the organizational context. The employment arrangements in standard organizations used to be long-term oriented, open-ended, and emotionally bonded (Rahman et al., 2017). The increased use of gig workers and blended teams of standard and gig workers disrupts and transforms standard HRM practices due to gig work's transactional, short-term nature. A recent report by the Dutch Organization for Applied Scientific Research and the Rathenau Institute suggested that every worker today faces some form of digital or algorithmic management (NL Times, 2024). Also, the UK's House of Commons (2023) report mentions that AI is sometimes utilized to determine performance objectives. Meanwhile, the Telegraph reported that HR Revenue & Customs is using AI to recruit staff, with some customer service agents being hired without interacting with a human until their first day on the job (Hinchliffe, 2024). Their recruitment process includes candidates submitting a Curriculum Vitae (CV) and a 1000-word statement, then participating in a video interview with an automated system, where they need to answer six questions. An AI platform is used then to analyze these videos and evaluate candidates based on civil service standards (Hinchliffe, 2024). Finally, founded in Beijing in 2017-Bianlifeng-a chain of convenience stores in China, uses a rating system to assess employee performance, potentially reducing their pay if scores are insufficient (Gong, 2024). To do this, the company employs robots and cameras.

Most scholarly efforts on this topic so far have focused on the experiences of gig workers and how individuals adapt to this new way of working, thus overlooking how organizations manage and integrate algorithmic management into workforce ecosystems. However, as it disrupts and transforms established organizational HRM practices and creates unique challenges, it is crucial to examine algorithmic management's impact on HRM strategies, processes, and the changing role of HRM professionals in organizations in more detail. This was set as a goal for a recent research exploring whether or how HRM professionals apply standard HRM practices for gig workers in traditional organizations (Bellesia et al., 2024). The preliminary findings of this research through the analysis of more than 500 YouTube videos of HRM professionals revealed that the most discussed and thus potentially the most critical 10 HRM practices for gig workers in traditional organizations are T&D (14%), organizational culture (11%), motivation (10%), leadership (9%), job design (7%), C&B (7%), health and safety (6%), R&S (6%), and D&I (5%). This result is somewhat unexpected, as, for example, the common assumption in the literature portrays gig workers as solely responsible for their T&D (Cropanzano et al., 2023). Meanwhile, the least discussed 10 HRM practices are career progression (5%), talent management (4%), performance management (4%), employee relations (2%), CSR (1%), employer branding (1%), employee support (1%), decision-making (0.2%), and planning (0.04).

The expansion of algorithmic management beyond platform and app-based work can be linked to technological advancements, their convergence, and the decreasing cost of technology. For example, Uber was only possible thanks to the smartphones equipped with GPS, which rely on satellites made possible by rockets (Suleyman & Bhaskar, 2023).

Today, there is also a significant increase in AI tools that can enable algorithmic management in standard organizations provided by both big and small HR technology vendors (O'Connor, 2022). Thus, in 2021, the World Economic Forum reported that there are already 250 HR tools that use AI for all aspects of HRM (Khan, 2021). In the same year, Coworker.org, a worker organizing platform, compiled a database of over 550 workplace monitoring or "Bossware" products offered by "little tech" companies, reporting that around 30% were developed between 2020 and 2021 (O'Connor, 2022). Another longitudinal research on AI for HRM revealed that, at present, there are more than 220 verified AI for HRM vendors offering solutions for a wide range of HRM practices (Tursunbayeva & Bunduchi, 2024). Many such tools promise to help organizations improve productivity gains, cost reduction, safety improvements, and other operational efficiencies like accuracy, speed, and resource employment (Malik et al., 2023). Others focus on employee benefits such as health and safety or data security, particularly in remote work settings (O'Connor, 2022). Some of such applications position their products as offering specifically algorithmic solutions. For example, HR technology vendor Vervoe offers a solution embedding a machine learning algorithm to analyze human behavior; Appcast proposes data-driven, source-neutral job ad distribution; while Percolata (O'Connor, 2016) promises to power staffing optimization (see Table 4.2 for their brief description).

**Table 4.2** Exemplary algorithmic management vendor solutions

| Vendor | Solution/tool | Description | Website |
|---|---|---|---|
| Vervoe | AI-powered job simulation platform | *"Vervoe's AI We use a set of* ***algorithmic*** *models that measure the quality and interaction of a candidate's responses against millions of other similar responses and actions"* (Vervoe, n.d.) | www.vervoe.com |
| Percolata | Staffing optimization | *"OUR VISION Our vision is to help retailers with a fully managed service to optimize staffing and marketing. We also apply our predictive analytics technology to power* ***algorithmic*** *trading at Pika.group" (Our Vision, n.d.)* (Percolata, n.d.) | www.percolata.com |
| Appcast | Data-driven, source-neutral job ad distribution | *"Our vast trove of market data informs our* ***algorithmic*** *bidding engine, and our software starts to smartly advertise your jobs that need applications on general, niche, and diversity job sites... as well as search, social, and consumer sites across the web"* (Appcast, n.d.) | www.appcast.io |

## References


Appcast. (n.d.). Appcast Xcelerate. https://www.appcast.io/appcast-xcelerate/.

Ashford, S. J., Caza, B. B., & Reid, E. M. (2018). From surviving to thriving in the gig economy: A research agenda for individuals in the new world of work. *Research in Organizational Behavior, 38*, 23–41. https://doi.org/10.1016/j.riob.2018.11.001

Bellesia, F., Mattarelli, E., Ghaedipour, F., Cameron, L., Thomason, B., Idowu, A., Bertolotti, F., Keplinger, K., Tursunbayeva, A., Singh, V., & Di Lauro, S. (2024). Beyond and behind platforms and algorithms: Exploring the lived experiences of gig workers. *Academy of Management Proceedings, 2024*(1), 14769. https://doi.org/10.5465/AMPROC.2024.14769symposium

Carmody, P., & Fortuin, A. (2019). "Ride-sharing", virtual capital and impacts on labor in Cape Town, South Africa. *African Geographical Review, 38*(3), 196–208. https://doi.org/10.1080/19376812.2019.1607149

Criddle, C. (2023). UK Supreme Court rules Deliveroo riders are not workers in an employment relationship. *Financial Times*.

Cropanzano, R., Keplinger, K., Lambert, B. K., Caza, B., & Ashford, S. J. (2023). The organizational psychology of gig work: An integrative conceptual review. *The Journal of Applied Psychology, 108*(3), 492–519. https://doi.org/10.1037/apl0001029

Di Lauro, S., Tursunbayeva, A., Antonelli, G., & Moschera, L. (2024). Disrupting human resource management with people analytics: A study of applications, value, enablers and barriers in Italy. *Personnel Review*., ahead-of-print. https://doi.org/10.1108/PR-11-2023-0927

Duggan, J., Sherman, U., Carbery, R., & McDonnell, A. (2020). Algorithmic management and app-work in the gig economy: A research agenda for employment relations and HRM. *Human Resource Management Journal, 30*(1), 114–132. https://doi.org/10.1111/1748-8583.12258

Gal, U., Jensen, T. B., & Stein, M.-K. (2020). Breaking the vicious cycle of algorithmic management: A virtue ethics approach to people analytics. *Information and Organization, 30*(2), 100301. https://doi.org/10.1016/j.infoandorg.2020.100301

Gong, M. (2024). Robot-tended Chinese convenience chain Bianlifeng finds limitations of automation. *The Star*.

Griesbach, K., Reich, A., Elliott-Negri, L., & Milkman, R. (2019). Algorithmic control in platform food delivery work. *Socius: Sociological Research for a Dynamic World, 5*, 237802311987004. https://doi.org/10.1177/2378023119870041

Hinchliffe, R. (2024, May 19). Customer service staff hired at HMRC—without speaking to a human. *The Telegraph.* https://www.telegraph.co.uk/money/jobs/customer-service-staff-hired-hmrc-without-speaking-to-human/

House of Commons. (2023). *Post-pandemic economic growth: UK labour markets* (No. Tenth Report of Session 2022–23). House of Commons. https://committees.parliament.uk/publications/39129/documents/192346/default/.

Kaine, S., & Josserand, E. (2019). The organisation and experience of work in the gig economy. *Journal of Industrial Relations, 61*(4), 479–501. https://doi.org/10.1177/0022185619865480

Kellogg, K., Valentine, M., & Christin, A. (2020). Algorithms at work: The new contested terrain of control. *Academy of Management Annals, 14*(1), 366–410.

Kemper, J., & Kolkman, D. (2019). Transparent to whom? No algorithmic accountability without a critical audience. *Information, Communication & Society, 22*(14), 2081–2096. https://doi.org/10.1080/1369118X.2018.1477967

Khan, S. (2021). *Artificial Intelligence for Human Resources Toolkit Helps Organizations Overcome Implementation Challenges*. World Economic Forum. https://www.weforum.org/press/2021/12/artificial-intelligence-for-human-resources-toolkit-helps-organizations-overcome-implementation-challenges/.

Lee, M. K., Kusbit, D., Metsky, E., & Dabbish, L. (2015). Working with machines: The impact of algorithmic and data-driven management on human workers. *Proceedings of the 33rd annual ACM conference on human factors in computing systems*, (pp. 1603–1612). https://doi.org/10.1145/2702123.2702548.

Leicht-Deobald, U., Busch, T., Schank, C., Weibel, A., Schafheitle, S., Wildhaber, I., & Kasper, G. (2019). The challenges of algorithm-based HR decision-making for personal integrity. *Journal of Business Ethics, 160*(2), 377–392. https://doi.org/10.1007/s10551-019-04204-w

Malik, A., Budhwar, P., & Kazmi, B. A. (2023). Artificial intelligence (AI)-assisted HRM: Towards an extended strategic framework. *Human Resource Management Review, 33*(1), 100940. https://doi.org/10.1016/j.hrmr.2022.100940

McDaid, E., Andon, P., & Free, C. (2023). Algorithmic management and the politics of demand: Control and resistance at Uber. *Accounting, Organizations and Society, 109*, 101465. https://doi.org/10.1016/j.aos.2023.101465

Meijerink, J., & Bondarouk, T. (2023). The duality of algorithmic management: Toward a research agenda on HRM algorithms, autonomy and value creation. *Human Resource Management Review, 33*(1), 100876. https://doi.org/10.1016/j.hrmr.2021.100876

O'Connor, S. (2016). When your boss is an algorithm. *Financial Times*.

O'Connor, S. (2022, February 22). Never mind Big Tech—'little tech' can be dangerous at work too. *Financial Times*. https://www.ft.com/content/147bce5d-511c-4862-b820-2d85b736a5f6

Parent-Rocheleau, X., & Parker, S. K. (2021). Algorithms as work designers: How algorithmic management influences the design of jobs. *Human Resource Management Review*, 100838. https://doi.org/10.1016/j.hrmr.2021.100838

Parry, E., & Tyson, S. (2011). Desired goals and actual outcomes of e-HRM. *Human Resource Management Journal, 21*(3), 335–354. https://doi.org/10.1111/j.1748-8583.2010.00149.x

Percolata. (n.d.). Our vision. Percolata. https://www.percolata.com/.

PerformYard. (n.d.). How does Uber do performance management? Retrieved August 16, 2024, from https://www.performyard.com/articles/how-does-uber-do-performance-management.

Petriglieri, G., Ashford, S. J., & Wrzesniewski, A. (2019). Agony and ecstasy in the gig economy: Cultivating holding environments for precarious and personalized work identities. *Administrative Science Quarterly, 64*(1), 124–170. https://doi.org/10.1177/0001839218759646

Rahman, U. U., Rehman, C. A., Imran, M. K., & Aslam, U. (2017). Does team orientation matter? Linking work engagement and relational psychological contract with performance. *Journal of Management Development, 36*(9), 1102–1113. https://doi.org/10.1108/JMD-10-2016-0204

Ruël, H., Bondarouk, T., & Looise, J. K. (2004). E-HRM: Innovation or irritation. An explorative empirical study in five large companies on web-based HRM. *Management Revue, 15*(3), 364–380. https://www.jstor.org/stable/41783479

Samaan, D., & Tursunbayeva, A. (2024). Fluid workforce management in the health sector: Navigating the changing face of workforces and their management. *International Journal of Public Sector Management.*, ahead-of-print. https://doi.org/10.1108/IJPSM-10-2023-0311

Schafheitle, S. D., Weibel, A., Ebert, I. L., Kasper, G., Schank, C., & Leicht-Deobald, U. (2020). No stone left unturned? Towards a framework for the impact of datafication technologies on organizational control. *Academy of Management Discoveries*. https://doi.org/10.5465/amd.2019.0002

Schwartz, D. (2018). Embedded in the crowd: Creative freelancers, crowdsourced work, and occupational community. *Work and Occupations, 45*(3), 247–282. https://doi.org/10.1177/0730888418762263

Shani, J. (n.d.). What is HR automation? A guide with practical examples [www.aihr.com]. *Academy to Innovate HR*. https://www.aihr.com/blog/hr-automation/.

Sheehan, K. B., & Pittman, M. (2019). Straight from the source? Media framing of creative crowd labor and resultant ethical concerns. *Journal of Business Ethics, 154*(2), 575–585. https://doi.org/10.1007/s10551-017-3484-8

Stark, D., & Pais, I. (2020). Algorithmic management in the platform economy. *Sociologica, 14*(3), 47–72. https://doi.org/10.6092/issn.1971-8853/12221

Suleyman, M., & Bhaskar, M. (2023). *The coming wave: Technology, power, and the twenty-first Century's greatest dilemma*. Crown.

Tursunbayeva, A., & Bunduchi, R. (2024). *Legitimizing Artificial Intelligence (AI) for Human Resource Management (HRM) tools through Responsible AI: Insights from a longitudinal Analysis of AI for HRM vendors*. 6th Edition of European Academy of Management Research Grants Scheme. https://euram.academy/euram?service=grants.

Uber. (n.d.). *Driver safety education*. https://help.uber.com/en/driving-and-delivering/article/driver-safety-education?nodeId=e6fc610b-8582-4a8f-b3a1-6b9b03a054cb.

Vervoe. (n.d.). Vervoe's AI. https://vervoe.com/ai-assessments/.

Vrontis, D., Christofi, M., Pereira, V., Tarba, S., Makrides, A., & Trichina, E. (2022). Artificial intelligence, robotics, advanced technologies and human resource management: A systematic review. *The International Journal of Human Resource Management, 33*(6), 1237–1266. https://doi.org/10.1080/09585192.2020.1871398

Wiener, M., Cram, W. A., & Benlian, A. (2023). Algorithmic control and gig workers: A legitimacy perspective of Uber drivers. *European Journal of Information Systems, 32*(3), 485–507. https://doi.org/10.1080/0960085X.2021.1977729

Zippia Team. (2022). *What is the hiring process at Uber?* https://www.zippia.com/answers/what-is-the-hiring-process-at-uber/.

# Chapter 5
# Artificial Intelligence Applications to Assist with Relational Human Resource Management

## 5.1 Artificial Intelligence Assistance

Organizations use relational HR technologies to manage and enhance employee relationships by empowering them at work. These technologies improve interactions with line managers, employees, and candidates and enhance HRM service delivery through digital communication and collaboration tools (Strohmeier & Kabst, 2014). Historically, relational HR technologies have enabled remote access to HRM information, helping employees and managers connect with different departments and external organizations, thus facilitating independent HRM task execution (Parry & Tyson, 2011). Today, AI applied to HRM has been envisioned to have even more substantial implications for HR empowerment and enhance trust in the HRM department (Prikshat et al., 2021). For the former, the implementation of AI in HRM is claimed to improve the relationship between HRM and line managers and result in empowering individual employees, line managers, and senior managers to perform HRM tasks themselves, thus reducing response time and improving service levels (Parry & Tyson, 2011; Prikshat et al., 2021). For the latter, AI implementation in HRM is thought to help employees better understand the activities and criteria behind HRM policies, thereby increasing their trust in the HRM department and reinforcing its credibility (Bissola & Imperatori, 2019). The assumption is that advanced AI technologies can transform HRM from merely "descriptive and diagnostic" to "prescriptive and predictive" (DiClaudio, 2019). This shift can potentially improve coordination among employees and build stronger social connections within the organization.

Below, a review is provided on how AI can be adopted across different relational HRM practices, considering that such practices are D&I-focused (Shen et al., 2009). This is done by drawing on original research results of the analysis of existing literature, AI for HRM vendor solutions, and expert interviews, as illustrated in Fig. 5.1, Table 5.1, and described in Appendix to this chapter.



A. Tursunbayeva, *Augmenting Human Resource Management with Artificial Intelligence*, Contributions to Management Science,
https://doi.org/10.1007/978-3-031-75266-7_5

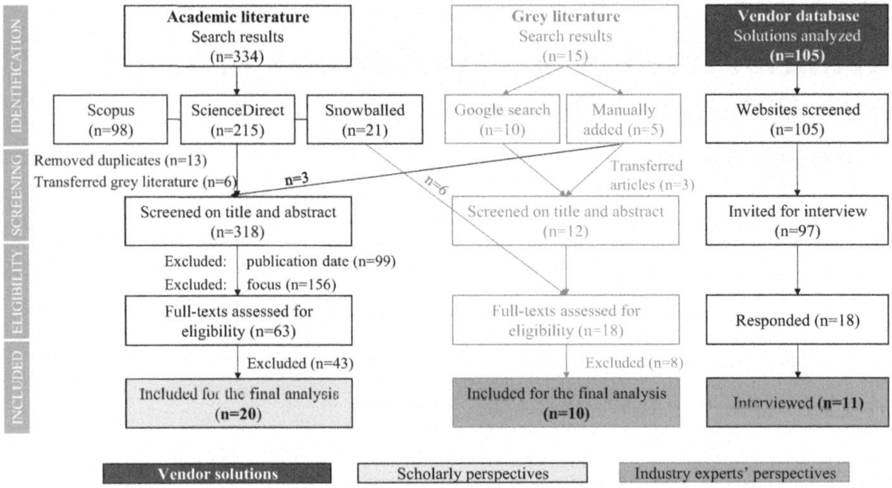


**Fig. 5.1** Data sources analyzed in the research

### *5.1.1 Artificial Intelligence in Recruitment and Selection*

The way companies hire talent has changed due to the growth of digitalization of both job and candidate information, the emergence of professional networking platforms, and the rise of AI, among other factors (Black & van Esch, 2020; Kim et al., 2021; Murphey, 2020). In 2014, it was reported that 33% of organizations had adopted AI for identifying, recruiting, and selecting job applicants (Gonzalez et al., 2019). Six years later, 55% of US organizations claimed to use AI and predictive analysis in their talent acquisition process (Mercer, 2020). According to Fumagalli et al. (2022), AI is increasingly used in decision-making within labor markets.

Albert (2019) identified 11 areas where AI algorithms could be applied across the hiring process. At that time, those larger, tech-focused, and innovative firms that adopted AI in hiring primarily relied on the same three applications: chatbots/CRM apps, admin-related task automation, and screening software. Since then, a lot has changed. For instance, the AmazingHiring (www.amazinghiring.com) sourcing platform provides a list of the most relevant candidates for the role that needs to be filled. To do so, this AI-sourcing technology searches candidates across over 50 networks, creates a candidate profile with information from multiple sources, and contacts candidates directly with personalized and automated outreach campaigns. The job site ZipRecruiter (www.ziprecruiter.ie) uses a matching algorithm to help job seekers discover jobs for which they are qualified. Job seekers are given feedback about how strong a match they are for every job. According to Ian Siegel, ZipRecruiter CEO and co-founder, their matching platform "gives job seekers information about what companies are looking for and how to make their applications more successful" (HR Tech Guy, 2021). Likewise, candidate assessment solutions provide recruiters with additional information to help them make more informed

**Table 5.1** Analyzed sources

| N | Description | HRM practice | Diversity attributes (see Chap. 6) |
|---|---|---|---|
| *Experts' perspectives* | | | |
| E1 | de Gruijl, J. (n.d.). Addressing AI Bias: Diversity-by-Design. AIHR Analytics. https://www.analyticsinhr.com/blog/ai-bias-diversity-by-design/ | R&S | Surface |
| E2 | Knight, W. (2019, December 19). AI Is Biased. Here's How Scientists Are Trying to Fix It. Wired. https://www.wired.com/story/ai-biased-how-scientists-trying-fix/ | R&S | Surface<br>Deep |
| E3 | Dastin, J. (2018, October 11). Amazon scraps secret AI recruiting tool that showed bias against women. https://www.reuters.com/article/us-amazon-com-jobs-automation-insight-idUSKCN1MK08G | R&S | Surface |
| E4 | z_ai. (2020, July 14). Bias in Artificial Intelligence: Inequality, racism and discrimination in the Era of Big Data. Towards Data Science. https://towardsdatascience.com/bias-in-artificial-intelligence-a3239ce316c9 | R&S | Surface |
| E5 | Cain Miller, C. (2015, June 25). Can an Algorithm Hire Better Than a Human? The New York Times. https://www.nytimes.com/2015/06/26/upshot/can-an-algorithm-hire-better-than-a-human.html | R&S | Surface |
| E6 | Garr, S.S., and Jackson, C. (2019). Diversity & Inclusion technology: The rise of a transformative market. Mercer | Numerous | Surface<br>Deep |
| E7 | Campbell, A. F. (2018, May 31). Facebook, Amazon, and hundreds of companies post targeted job ads that screen out older workers. Vox. https://www.vox.com/policy-and-politics/2018/5/31/17408884/facebook-amazon-job-ads-age-discrimination-lawsuit | R&S | Surface |
| E8 | Stinson, J. (2014, August 25). Hiring Bias Against the Unemployed: Should There Be a Law? PEW. https://www.pewtrusts.org/en/research-and-analysis/blogs/stateline/2014/08/25/hiring-bias-against-the-unemployed-should-there-be-a-law | R&S | Surface |
| E9 | Silberg, J., and Manyika, J. (2019). Notes from the AI frontier: Tackling bias in AI (and in humans). McKinsey Global Institute | R&S | Surface |
| E10 | Zhang et al. (2019). The role of AI in mitigating bias to enhance diversity and inclusion. IBM Smarter Workforce Institute | R&S | Surface |
| E11 | Vendor 1 | T&D | Surface<br>Deep |
| E12 | Vendor 2 | Employee Engagement | Surface<br>Deep |
| E13 | Vendor 3 | R&S | Surface<br>Deep |

(continued)

**Table 5.1** (continued)

| N | Description | HRM practice | Diversity attributes (see Chap. 6) |
|---|---|---|---|
| E14 | Vendor 4 | R&S | Surface |
| E15 | Vendor 5 | R&S | Surface<br>Deep |
| E16 | Vendor 6 | T&D<br>HR Analytics<br>C&B | Surface<br>Deep |
| E17 | Vendor 7 | Employee Engagement<br>HR Analytics<br>C&B | Surface<br>Deep |
| E18 | Vendor 8 | Employee Engagement<br>HR Analytics | Surface<br>Deep |
| E19 | Vendor 9 | R&S | Surface<br>Deep |
| E20 | Vendor 10.1 | Numerous | Surface |
| E21 | Vendor 10.2 | Numerous | Surface |
| *Scholarly perspectives* | | | |
| S1 | Deva, S. (2020). Addressing the gender bias in artificial intelligence and automation. OpenGlobalRights. https://www.openglobalrights.org/addressing-gender-bias-in-artificial-intelligence-and-automation/ | R&S<br>C&B | Surface |
| S2 | Miller et al. (2018). AI x I = AI2: The OD imperative to add inclusion to the algorithms of artificial intelligence. OD PRACTITIONER, 50(1) | R&S | Surface |
| S3 | Todolí-Signes, A. (2019). Algorithms, artificial intelligence and automated decisions concerning workers and the risks of discrimination: The necessary collective governance of data protection. Transfer: European Review of Labour and Research, 25(4), 465–481. https://doi.org/10.1177/1024258919876416 | Performance management | Surface<br>Deep |
| S4 | Coates, D. L., and Martin, A. (2019). An instrument to evaluate the maturity of bias governance capability in artificial intelligence projects. IBM Journal of Research and Development, 63(4/5), 7:1–7:15. https://doi.org/10.1147/JRD.2019.2915062 | R&S | Surface<br>Deep |
| S5 | Allen, R., and Masters, D. (2020). Artificial Intelligence: The right to protection from discrimination caused by algorithms, machine learning and automated decision-making. ERA Forum, 20(4), 585–598. https://doi.org/10.1007/s12027-019-00582-w | R&S<br>Employee engagement | Surface<br>Deep |
| S6 | Datta et al. (2015). Automated Experiments on Ad Privacy Settings: A Tale of Opacity, Choice, and Discrimination. ArXiv | R&S | Surface |

(continued)

**Table 5.1** (continued)

| N | Description | HRM practice | Diversity attributes (see Chap. 6) |
|---|---|---|---|
| S7 | Griffy-Brown, C., and Chun, M. (2020). Avoiding Bias and Identifying Risks when Deploying Artificial Intelligence. Graziadio Business Review, 23(1) | R&S | Surface |
| S8 | Ntoutsi et al. (2020). Bias in data-driven artificial intelligence systems—An introductory survey. WIREs Data Mining and Knowledge Discovery, 10(3), e1356. https://doi.org/10.1002/widm.1356 | R&S | Surface |
| S9 | Amrein-Beardsley, A. (2017). Breaking News: A Big Victory in Court in Houston. VAMboozled! http://vamboozled.com/breaking-news-victory-in-court-in-houston/ | Performance management | Surface |
| S10 | Ali et al. (2019). Discrimination through Optimization: How Facebook's Ad Delivery Can Lead to Biased Outcomes. Proc. ACM Hum.-Comput. Interact., 3(CSCW). https://doi.org/10.1145/3359301 | R&S | Surface |
| S11 | Nguyen, L.S., and Gatica-Perez, D. (2016). Hirability in the Wild: Analysis of Online Conversational Video Resumes. IEEE Transactions on Multimedia, 18(7), 1422–1437. https://doi.org/10.1109/TMM.2016.2557058 | R&S | Surface |
| S12 | Ajunwa et al. (2016). Hiring by Algorithm: Predicting and Preventing Disparate Impact | R&S<br>C&B | Surface<br>Deep |
| S13 | Prince, A.E.R., and Schwarcz, D. (2020). Proxy Discrimination in the Age of Artificial Intelligence and Big Data. IOWA LAW REVIEW, 105, 1257–1318 | R&S<br>C&B | Surface<br>Deep |
| S14 | Edwards, J.S., and Rodriguez, E. (2019). Remedies against bias in analytics systems. Journal of Business Analytics, 2(1), 74–87. https://doi.org/10.1080/2573234X.2019.1633890 | R&S<br>Performance management | Surface |
| S15 | Borgesius, F.J.Z. (2020). Strengthening legal protection against discrimination by algorithms and artificial intelligence. The International Journal of Human Rights, 24(10), 1572–1593. https://doi.org/10.1080/13642987.2020.1743976 | R&S | Surface |
| S16 | Hacker, P. (2018). Teaching Fairness to Artificial Intelligence: Existing and Novel Strategies Against Algorithmic Discrimination Under EU Law. Common Market Law Review, 55, 1143–1186 | R&S<br>Performance management | Surface |
| S17 | Daugherty et al. (2018). Using Artificial Intelligence to Promote Diversity. MIT Sloan Management Review. | R&S | Surface |
| S18 | Žliobaitė, I., and Custers, B. (2016). Using sensitive personal data may be necessary for avoiding discrimination in data-driven decision models. Artificial Intelligence and Law, 24(2), 183–201. https://doi.org/10.1007/s10506-016-9182-5 | R&S<br>C&B | Surface<br>Deep |
| S19 | Manyika et al. (2019). What Do We Do About the Biases in AI? Harvard Business Review | R&S | Surface |

(continued)

**Table 5.1** (continued)

| N | Description | HRM practice | Diversity attributes (see Chap. 6) |
|---|---|---|---|
| S20 | Derous, E., and Ryan, A. M. (2019). When your resume is (not) turning you down: Modelling ethnic bias in resume screening. Human Resource Management Journal, 29(2), 113–130. https://doi.org/10.1111/1748-8583.12217 | R&S | Surface<br>Deep |

decisions. Pymetrics (www.pymetrics.ai), considered by Forbes (2023) one of America's best start-up employers in 2022, is a soft skills platform that uses data-driven behavioral insights and audited AI to help companies build diverse teams of top performers. This company uses gamified behavioral assessments to evaluate a candidate's potential according to customized algorithms based on each company's definition of top talent. However, hiring with AI does not just happen behind the scenes. Social AI robots offer the opportunity to conduct job interviews by delivering a human-like experience. This is the case of Tengai Unbiased (www.tengai.io), a conversational AI programmed to conduct objective job interviews that can establish a "human" connection with candidates during the job interview, which is crucial to the immersive candidate experience (Tengai, 2022).

AI in hiring has evolved from "nice-to-have" to "necessary-to-employ" (Black & van Esch, 2020). Why? AI-enabled recruiting tools promise to help save time, remove human bias, and generate the best candidate matches (LinkedIn, 2018). Indeed, AI-powered tools can speed up the recruitment process by doing the groundwork in job postings, candidate sourcing, applicant screening, and candidate interviews (Jones, 2022; Van Hooijdonk, 2021). Doing so promises traditional recruiters to focus on higher-value relational tasks (i.e., at the bottom of the applicant funnel), a productivity and motivational boon (Cathey & Prabhakar, 2021). Furthermore, algorithmic R&S seems less subject to cognitive or unconscious biases that can be present when hiring (Black & van Esch, 2020; Jones, 2022). Many companies pitch their AI-based recruiting tools as enablers of faster decision-making, which help recruiters and hiring managers respond to candidates faster and earlier. Improved time-to-fill and time-to-hire metrics bring actual cost savings to organizations since "an empty seat is always an expensive proposition, and delays in responding to applicants is a sure way to lose them" (Jones, 2022). Even candidates are pitched to benefit from algorithms. The promises of candidates' benefits include improved communication between candidates and organizations and availability of support whenever they need it (Barua, 2021). However, recently, Big Four companies and City law firms in the UK banned candidates from using ChatGPT or other AI tools to complete applications or online assessments to prevent potential cheating (Mawardi, 2024), as well as to reduce the surge in the number of applications generated and submitted with AI (Criddle & Strauss, 2024).

The research of existing literature, AI solutions, and expert interviews revealed (see Fig. 5.1 and Table 5.1) that AI specifically for R&S can have wide-ranging functionality and promise to assist HRM professionals in various ways. For example, such solutions can help monitor diversity numbers or targets, thus increasing organizational intelligence and performance ("*If 50% of the applicants are women, then the shortlist should also have a 50% or be in the range of a woman applicant. So unless, you know, there is a huge discrepancy between the number of applicants of a protected group versus their numbers in the shortlist, you know, we're achieving our target of ensuring that there are no subgroup differences*" [E15: see Table 5.1]). They also promise to assist with suggesting inclusive wordings for job descriptions, offering personalized, targeted job ads, searching, identifying, and filtering candidates with diverse attributes (including passive ones), which, as also envisioned by scholars, can help organizations increase the diversity of their workforce ("*What if, instead of selecting only the job candidates who fit our existing organization profile, AI selected an array of candidates who provide the perspectives we currently lack?*" [S2: see Table 5.1]). However, scholars also cautioned that such personalization would not come without some drawbacks ("*Vendors such as Facebook need to build extensive user interest profiles and track ad performance to understand how different users interact with different ads, and that future ads are used to steer future ads. This again relies on historical data*" [S10: see Table 5.1]).

Experts also mentioned matching AI capabilities to predict the best fit between individuals, their values, capabilities, skills, behaviors, job preferences, teams, or organizational cultures. Other AI solutions for hiring claim to identify whether some unconscious human bias may be present in the process (e.g., by collecting data on recruiters' unconscious bias moments) and to mitigate this bias by standardizing the process or "nudging" recruiters to remind them of bias-reducing behaviors. The biases in the R&S process are even promised to be prevented with AI by creating or delivering anonymized or "blind" to some visible or surface-level predefined candidates' characteristics/attributes such as gender, name, race/ethnicity, or educational background ("*We are trying to divide candidates based on things that are not solely their education or work performance or something like this. The technology is blind to the bias, so to a bias where I do not know if we staff people like this, but if there is a recruitment manager who sees two people that are different and he or she chooses one based on their own discrimination of the other, this does not exist at all because the tool is nicely blind to differences between people except the ones that are actually relevant to the team and the role. So I think in that way, it is blind to race or gender or ethnicity*" [E19: See Table 5.1]).

Several experts also associated the changes AI solutions bring to the "traditional" R&S process with how the recruitment process altered in the US orchestras after they "blinded" candidates' auditions ("*We are trying to find the critical skill set in a resume and a job description and trying to have a match and then presenting all the qualified people. Independent of their diversity status*" [E3: See Table 5.1]). The US orchestras implemented "blinded" auditions, where candidates performed behind a screen, to address and reduce selection bias. By focusing solely on the sound and quality of the performance, orchestras created a fairer and more meritocratic selection process, thereby fostering greater D&I within their ranks. Studies showed that such blinded auditions significantly increased the likelihood of women being selected for orchestral positions. Specifically, the proportion of female musicians in the US top five orchestras rose from 6% in 1970 to 21% in 1993 (Goldin & Rouse, 2000).

Similarly, introducing AI-enabled blinded R&S, as per some scholars [S4; S5: see Table 5.1], promises to reduce or eliminate human bias and increase candidates' perceptions of equal opportunities provided by organizations and their fairness ("*What if our systems were taught to ignore data about race, gender, sexual orientation, and other characteristics that are not relevant to the decisions at hand? AI can do all of this*" [S17: see Table 5.1].

Proponents of AI argue that algorithms may be as reliable as, or even more accurate and predictive than, human decision-makers because, for example, their decisions could be traced [E9: see Table 5.1]. It was also mentioned that AI does not have some bias typical to humans, such as hindsight bias-believing past predictions and forecasts were closer to what really happened than they actually were-[S14: see Table 5.1]. Though others suggested that humans and AI can have some biases in common caused by the (in)completeness or order of information received and that AI can introduce additional biases not typical to human processes (e.g., AI cannot contextualize data like humans) [S14: see Table 5.1]. Moreover, AI was mentioned to magnify the effects of preexisting human, organizational, and societal biases [S2: see Table 5.1], as these systems are created, trained, and refined by humans, and they only seem rational, neutral, or unbiased [S15: see Table 5.1]. Scholars also warned to watch out for the "masking" phenomenon [S18: see Table 5.1], suggesting that when particular characteristics are correlated, it may be possible to use trivial characteristics as indicators of sensitive characteristics. For instance, when people living in a particular zip code area represent some ethnical groups, recruiters may use the zip code to indicate a race/ethnicity and thus use the trivial information as a selection criterion [S18: see Table 5.1].

### *5.1.2 Artificial Intelligence in Training and Development*

Approximately a decade ago, the significance of evaluating each employee's unique development needs and creating customized T&D plans was highlighted (D'Netto et al., 2014). AI is now fulfilling this vision by identifying the workforce that needs to learn in a specific situation and offering them a personalized curriculum (Kaushal et al., 2021). This individualized approach is a significant shift from the previous standardized gap analysis.

AI solutions for T&D can cover a wide range of topics. These include personalized career pathing and development, knowledge assessments, and fully immersive, micro, or anonymous employee training on handling difficult situations at work. For instance, Landit (www.landit.com) offers personalized coaching and career pathing, which has been well-received by their customers. A testimonial from Wendy Mayer, VP of Business Transformation at Pfizer, highlights the impact: "Landit has helped us bring our colleague development into the 21st century, providing personalized tools and resources traditionally reserved for a select few to a broader colleague population."

Some T&D activities today are provided in virtual, extended, or mixed reality. For instance, in specific industries, such as aviation and oil and gas, virtual reality (VR) is ordinary for training when workers need to operate in hazardous environments (Conboye, 2023). In other organizations, such training is used to let employees experience inappropriate behaviors like exclusion or sexual harassment in an interactive form. For instance, Strivr (www.strivr.com) offers AI-backed immersive learning experiences delivered through its platform, which it reports can bring tangible results.

**Verizon Protects and Empowers Retail Associates with Immersive Learning**

Adopted from Strivr (n.d.)

In response to increasing retail theft and armed robberies across its 1600 retail locations, Verizon sought to protect better and prepare its frontline associates. Considering traditional safety training methods inadequate for equipping employees with hands-on experience, Verizon partnered with Strivr to implement an immersive VR training program for 22,000 retail associates. This program used video simulations based on actual robbery footage, allowing employees to practice recognizing and responding to armed robbery scenarios.

The 20-minute training, which consisted of three modules, significantly boosted employees' confidence and preparedness. 97% of participants reported feeling more ready-to-handle dangerous situations, while the leadership team observed high engagement levels during the training.

T&D practices should prioritize diversity (Shen et al., 2009) to ensure, for instance, that coaching and mentoring can help mitigate the potential challenges of ethnic diversity within group dynamics (Kochan et al., 2003). This approach also aims to prevent the "glass ceiling" effect - attitudinal or organizational biases that create artificial barriers, limiting qualified individuals' advancement within the organization (Powell & Butterfield, 1994). Such T&D can improve employee morale and job satisfaction and assist in retaining qualified employees. Some AI-based applications (Garr & Jackson, 2019) are designed to enhance D&I in T&D by identifying low diversity representations among specific employee categories, such as high performers. These applications can also utilize passive organizational network analysis integrated into succession planning, including the 9-box analysis. Mentor searching and matching solutions create opportunities to establish relationship networks and find career mentors in communities and within companies. See in the textbox below a Ziff Davis case study on how the Mentorloop AI-based tool (www.mentorloop) assisted them in creating regular interactions between mentors and mentees for exchanging ideas, challenging existing perspectives, and co-creating solutions.

**Case Study: Creating 1000+ Connections Between a Family of Brands, Through Mentoring**

Adopted from Pierre (n.d.)

Before engaging with Mentorloop, Ziff Davis, a digital media and internet company, faced challenges in providing networking and development opportunities for employees across its various brands. They discovered the demand for mentorship, leading to the creation of a mentorship program. This program has become one of the most active at Ziff Davis, fostering nearly 700 relationships last year and creating almost 400 new ones this year.

The program's impact includes broadening professional networks, offering fresh perspectives, and facilitating career growth, with some employees receiving promotions due to their mentoring relationships. Additionally, employee-led group leaders are rewarded with VIP mentor matches with C-suite-level leaders, enhancing their skills and career prospects.

Looking ahead, the DEI Team and Mentorship Ambassadors leading the program continue to refine it, introducing initiatives like the "Mentoring All-Star of the Month" series to boost engagement. The team also plans to gamify the experience with Mentorship Program Bingo and work with Mentorloop to create new resources for program support.

### *5.1.3 Artificial Intelligence in Performance Management*

Effective performance management requires appraisal practices to be objective, job-relevant, fair, and equitable to all employees (Schuler et al., 1993). Thus, it must be culturally neutral, focus on performance, not personality or demographic characteristics, and free of stereotyping (Fulkerson & Schuler, 1992). However, many such organizational processes are still gender-biased (D'Netto et al., 2014).

Performance management AI solutions promise to reduce or avoid unconscious bias by finding and flagging gender biases in performance scores. AI-based performance management tools also promise to structure performance feedback and address "language" issues in performance reviews. For instance, Textio (www.textio.com) offers real-time coaching to write bias-free performance review feedback. See also the text below for a case study from Taboola on adopting an AI-based performance management tool (Culture Amp, n.d.).

**Case Study: Taboola Built a Culture of High Performance**

Adopted from (Culture Amp, n.d.)

Taboola, a leading discovery platform with 1400 employees and over 1.4 billion monthly users, faced challenges managing employee career growth as the company rapidly expanded. With employee churn increasing, Taboola implemented Culture Amp's platform to run employee engagement surveys and to revisit their performance and engagement processes, which focused on real-time feedback, regular check-ins, quarterly goal-setting, and biannual feedback discussions focused on both past achievements and future development.

The new approach led to a noticeable improvement in employee satisfaction, with significant increases in perceptions of learning, development, and career opportunities. Taboola also uses surveys to monitor the effectiveness of performance management changes and has extended Culture Amp's tools to onboard and (soon) exit processes, allowing them to track the entire employee life cycle. Taboola believes this transparency and data-driven approach have been crucial in driving continuous improvement and maintaining employee engagement.

Research findings on AI for D&I-focused HRM (see Fig. 5.1 and Table 5.1) suggested that algorithms do not make decisions but produce outcomes. In this regard, a human always makes the decisions: either the person programming the algorithm or applying the algorithm's outcome [S3: see Table 5.1]. It has been suggested here to observe the extent of overall human involvement in AI-assisted processes ("*whether the decision was fully automated or enacted by HR officer receiving an "alert*" [S3: see Table 5.1]). It has also been noted that AI has empowered HRM professionals to collect and process large amounts of (external) information for performance management. This was previously impossible due to the natural human capacity to process such information. Such information can include social media data as political opinion or digital reputation *("dismissal of an employee because his digital reputation is less than 4.6 out of 5"* [S3: see Table 5.1].

### *5.1.4 Artificial Intelligence in Compensation and Benefit*

AI's application in C&B is a relatively unexplored area in the literature (Kaushal et al., 2021). AI vendor solutions descriptions for this practice and experts promise to provide pay equity analysis capable of uncovering potential (gender) pay gaps in organizations and recommend actions to improve (gender) equity. These are also expected to reduce bias and permit comparisons against industry benchmarks, thereby improving organizational intelligence. For instance, Tom Studdert, Senior VP of Customer Experience at Payscale, used by 8600 current customers with more than 54 million employees, stated that "*There are many parts of the compensation management process that require time-consuming and tedious work, but through leveraging the latest technologies, including AI, and providing our customers with educational resources that set them apart in their field, we hope to support compensation and HR professionals drive outcomes - and free up their time to focus on high-impact work...Even more critically, getting these processes right allows compensation and HR professionals to focus on equitable outcomes, which leads to our ultimate goal of helping organizations achieve fair pay for all"* (Payscale, 2024a).

There are also AI-based solutions that promise to deliver job matches based on multiple factors, such as job titles, survey matches, or industry. These seem to be very well-received by the users. *"The* [Payscale] *Peer Auto-Match functionality is awesome! This is something we've been eagerly waiting for, and found the new feature to be 99% user-friendly," said Shirley Rawson, Senior Compensation Analyst at VF Corporation. "It effortlessly auto-matches jobs for us based on multiple factors and has definitely been a time saver for our team. The tool is especially helpful for those of us who love working in compensation but find the job matching process tedious"* (Payscale, 2024a).

However, Payscale's own latest (2024b) Compensation Best Practices Report revealed that 50% of more than 3000 respondents surveyed reported that they are still gathering information about AI and its use in C&B management, 31% already have guardrails for using AI for pay decisions, 12% prohibit their employees from using AI for compensation-related tasks, while only 7% encourage reliance on AI in this HRM practice.

Research findings on AI for D&I-focused HRM (see Fig. 5.1 and Table 5.1) proposed to be cautious with the rational use of averages in models and the desire for individualized treatment of employees in C&B. This is because, despite legislative efforts, discrimination in employment compensation continues to be an active issue (Anderson et al., 2022) *("In City of Los Angeles, Department of Water and Power v. Manhart, the Supreme Court reviewed a pension system where female employees paid larger contributions than men for the same monthly benefit due to higher life expectancies. The majority ultimately determined that this scheme violated Title VII of the 1964 Civil Rights Act, because it assumed individuals would conform to broader trends associated with their sex. Such discrimination, the court suggested, is troubling from a civil rights perspective because it fails to treat individuals as individuals, as opposed to merely members of the groups to which they belong"* [S13: see Table 5.1]). This is despite generic HRM research already highlighting that organizations without diversity-focused C&B policies are likelier to promote or rate highly subordinates with similar cultural backgrounds and experiences (D'Netto et al., 2014).

## 5.2 Appendix

This and the following chapters draw on original research informed by the approach adopted by Palas and Bunduchi (2021) in combining the perspective of different sets of actors (see Fig. 5.1 and Table 5.1). Specifically this research draws on:

- academic literature capturing scholarly perspectives;

- a database of existing AI applications for HRM providing state-of-the-art on the already available solutions (Garr & Jackson, 2019);
- grey literature and interviews of AI for vendors capturing practitioner experts' perspective.

Coding involved a combination of deductive coding and inductive coding (Miles & Huberman, 1994) relying on the data to elicit interpretations, rather than only deductive coding, involving solely the application of a predefined list of codes to the data. This list of codes, coming from Diversity management literature, included:

- HRM practices that can be supported by AI and incorporate D&I: R&S; T&D; Performance appraisal; and C&B (D'Netto et al., 2014; Khan, 2021).
- The categories of the diversity dimensions including surface-level job-oriented (organizational and team tenure; educational, functional, and occupational background) and relations-oriented (sex, age, race/ethnicity, nationality, and religion) attributes; as well as deep-level job-oriented (knowledge, skills, experience, and abilities) and relations-oriented (values, personality, social status, and attitude) attributes (Yadav & Lenka, 2020).
- The outcomes from diversity management for individuals (turnover and behavior intention, recruitment, absenteeism, psychological attachment, promotion, job satisfaction, work tension, organizational citizenship behavior, self-perception, perceived discrimination, performance, and individual creativity); teams (cooperative response, idea generation, commitment, decision-making, communication, problem-solving, satisfaction, team turnover, group cohesiveness, conflict and cooperativeness, strategic consensus, team effectiveness, group development, group performance, and team creativity), and organizations (commitment, performance, competitiveness, innovation, and fairness) (Yadav & Lenka, 2020).

Some codes' ambiguity was resolved by examining their wider context. The categories that did not fit these frameworks' categories were open-coded.

Out of the returns generated with the search strategy (see Fig. 5.1), the findings draw on the analysis of 105 AI solutions; 20 publications that present scholarly perspectives; and 10 grey publications and 11 interviews that represent the views of expert practitioners (see Table 5.1). The number of relevant article/s listed in Table 5.1 is placed in the text in square brackets-[]-with "S" for scholarly articles and "E" for grey literature publications and expert interviews. Exemplary quotes that support the findings are provided within the text.

## References

Albert, E. T. (2019). AI in talent acquisition: A review of AI-applications used in recruitment and selection. *Strategic HR Review, 18*(5), 215–221. https://doi.org/10.1108/SHR-04-2019-0024

Anderson, D., Bjarnadóttir, M. V., & Ross, D. G. (2022, January 27). Using people analytics to build an equitable workplace. *Harvard Business Review*. https://hbr.org/2022/01/using-people-analytics-to-build-an-equitable-workplace

Barua, M. (2021). AI recruitment: How candidates feel about faceless hiring. *UNLEASH*.

Bissola, R., & Imperatori, B. (2019). *HRM 4.0 for human-centered organizations*. Emerald Group Publishing Limited.

Black, J. S., & van Esch, P. (2020). AI-enabled recruiting: What is it and how should a manager use it? *Business Horizons, 63*(2), 215–226. https://doi.org/10.1016/j.bushor.2019.12.001

Cathey, G., & Prabhakar, A. (2021). Ethical AI: A new strategic imperative for recruiting and staffing. *MIT SMR Connection*. https://s3.amazonaws.com/marketing.mitsmr.com/custom/CSTCSRandstadNative0921/TCS-Randstad_ExecCon_FINAL_8-16-21.pdf.

Conboye, J. (2023). The high costs and slow take-up of virtual reality for employee training. *Financial Times*. https://www.ft.com/content/1f71b21b-93b3-4057-91cf-0ac813187e29.

Criddle, C., & Strauss, D. (2024). Jobhunters flood recruiters with AI-generated CVs. *Financial Times*.

Culture Amp. (n.d.). How Taboola built a culture of high performance. *Culture Amp*. Retrieved August 17, 2024, from https://www.cultureamp.com/case-studies/taboola.

DiClaudio, M. (2019). People analytics and the rise of HR: How data, analytics and emerging technology can transform human resources (HR) into a profit center. *Strategic HR Review, 18*(2), 42–46. https://doi.org/10.1108/SHR-11-2018-0096

D'Netto, B., Shen, J., Chelliah, J., & Manjit, M. (2014). Human resource diversity management practices in the Australian manufacturing sector. *The International Journal of Human Resource Management, 25*(9), 1243–1266. https://doi.org/10.1080/09585192.2013.826714

Forbes. (2023). Council post: 16 common concerns CEOs have in 2023 (and how to address them). *Forbes*. https://www.forbes.com/sites/forbescoachescouncil/2023/02/09/16-common-concerns-ceos-have-in-2023-and-how-to-address-them/.

Fulkerson, J. R., & Schuler, R. S. (1992). Managing worldwide diversity at Pepsi-Cola international. In S. E. Schuler (Ed.), *Diversity in the workplace: Human resources initiatives* (pp. 248–276). Guilford Press. https://psycnet.apa.org/record/1992-97954-010

Fumagalli, E., Rezaei, S., & Salomons, A. (2022). OK computer: Worker perceptions of algorithmic recruitment. *Research Policy, 51*(2), 104420. https://doi.org/10.1016/j.respol.2021.104420

Goldin, C., & Rouse, C. (2000). Orchestrating impartiality: The impact of "Blind" auditions on female musicians. *American Economic Review, 90*(4), 715–741. https://doi.org/10.1257/aer.90.4.715

Garr, S. S., & Jackson, C. (2019). Diversity & Inclusion technology: The rise of a transformative market. *Mercer*.

Gonzalez, M., Capman, J., Oswald, F., Theys, E., & Tomczak, D. (2019). "Where's the I-O?" Artificial intelligence and machine learning in talent management systems. *Personnel Assessment and Decisions, 5*(3), 10.25035/pad.2019.03.005.

HR Tech Guy. (2021). ZipRecruiter boosts matching tech for job seekers. *HR Tech Guy*.

Jones, K. (2022). How AI is transforming the talent acquisition process. *TechTarget*.

Kaushal, N., Kaurav, R. P. S., Sivathanu, B., & Kaushik, N. (2021). Artificial intelligence and HRM: Identifying future research Agenda using systematic literature review and bibliometric analysis. *Management Review Quarterly*. https://doi.org/10.1007/s11301-021-00249-2

Khan, S. (2021). Artificial intelligence for human resources toolkit helps organizations overcome implementation challenges. *World Economic Forum*.

Kim, S., Wang, Y., & Boon, C. (2021). Sixty years of research on technology and human resource management: Looking back and looking forward. *Human Resource Management, 60*(1), 229–247. https://doi.org/10.1002/hrm.22049

Kochan, T., Bezrukova, K., Ely, R., Jackson, S., Joshi, A., Jehn, K., Leonard, J., Levine, D., & Thomas, D. (2003). The effects of diversity on business performance: Report of the diversity research network. *Human Resource Management, 42*(1), 3–21. https://doi.org/10.1002/hrm.10061

LinkedIn. (2018). LinkedIn 2018 report highlights top global trends in recruiting. *LinkedIn*. https://news.linkedin.com/2018/1/global-recruiting-trends-2018

Mawardi, A. (2024, March 2). Big four accountants ban grads from using AI to write job applications. *The Telegraph*. https://www.telegraph.co.uk/business/2024/03/02/big-four-accountant-ban-grad-using-ai-write-job-application/

Mercer. (2020). Win with empathy. *Mercer*. https://www.mercer.com/content/dam/mercer/attachments/global/gl-2020-mercer-gtt-2020-infographic-global.pdf

Miles, M. B., & Huberman, A. M. (1994). *Qualitative data analysis: An expanded sourcebook* (2nd ed.) xiv, 338.

Murphey, D. (2020). How recruitment has changed over the past decade. *MHR*.

Palas, M. J. U., & Bunduchi, R. (2021). Exploring interpretations of blockchain's value in healthcare: A multi-stakeholder approach. *Information Technology & People, 34*(2), 453–495. https://doi.org/10.1108/ITP-01-2019-0008

Parry, E., & Tyson, S. (2011). Desired goals and actual outcomes of e-HRM. *Human Resource Management Journal, 21*(3), 335–354. https://doi.org/10.1111/j.1748-8583.2010.00149.x

Payscale. (2024a). Payscale enhances AI capabilities in product suite, Improving Workflows for Compensation Professionals. *Payscale*. https://www.payscale.com/press-releases/payscale-enhances-ai-capabilities-in-product-suite-improving-workflows-for-compensation-professionals/.

Payscale. (2024b). 2024 *Compensation best practices report. Payscale*. https://www.payscale.com/research-and-insights/cbpr/.

Pierre, P. (n.d.). Case study: Ziff Davis | Mentorloop mentoring platform. Mentorloop mentoring software. Retrieved August 17, 2024, from https://mentorloop.com/customers/case-study-ziff-davis/.

Powell, G. N., & Butterfield, D. A. (1994). Investigating the "Glass Ceiling" phenomenon: An empirical study of actual promotions to top management. *The Academy of Management Journal, 37*(1), 68–86. https://doi.org/10.2307/256770

Prikshat, V., Malik, A., & Budhwar, P. (2021). AI-augmented HRM: Antecedents, assimilation and multilevel consequences. *Human Resource Management Review*, 100860. https://doi.org/10.1016/j.hrmr.2021.100860

Shen, J., Chanda, A., D'Netto, B., & Monga, M. (2009). Managing diversity through human resource: An international perspective and conceptual framework. *International Journal of Human Resource Management, 20*(2), 235–251. https://doi.org/10.1080/09585190802670516

Schuler, R. S., Dowling, P. J., & De Cieri, H. (1993). An integrative framework of strategic international human resource management. *Journal of Management, 19*(2), 419–459. https://doi.org/10.1016/0149-2063(93)90059-V

Strivr. (n.d.). Verizon protects & empowers retail associates with immersive learning. https://www.strivr.com/customers/verizon.

Strohmeier, S., & Kabst, R. (2014). Configurations of e-HRM-an empirical exploration. *Employee Relations, 36*(4), 333–353.

Tengai. (2022). An AI robot interview enhances the candidate experience. *Tengai*. https://tengai.io/resources/tengai-robot/.

Van Hooijdonk, R. (2021). Is the use of algorithms in recruitment a good idea? Richard van Hooijdonk Blog. https://blog.richardvanhooijdonk.com/en/hired-by-an-algorithm-is-the-use-of-ai-in-recruitment-a-good-idea/.

Yadav, S., & Lenka, U. (2020). Diversity management: A systematic review. *Equality, Diversity and Inclusion: An International Journal, 39*(8), 901–929. https://doi.org/10.1108/EDI-07-2019-0197

# Chapter 6
# Augmenting Human Resource Management with Artificial Intelligence: From Diversity and Inclusion, and Sustainability to Neuroscience Insights

## 6.1 Augmentation of Human Resource Management

Previous chapters focused on the partial or complete algorithmic management enabled by AI for HRM and assisted HRM relational practices. This chapter discusses the third-transformational-configuration of AI for HRM. In this configuration, augmentation is achieved by leveraging technologies and techniques that enhance intelligence within HRM functions, thus improving the strategic orientation of HRM. This can contribute to organizations' strategic objectives or outcomes (Parry & Tyson, 2011), such as fostering organizational culture or supporting the achievement of SDGs. Augmenting HRM with AI, however, does not necessarily mean having the latest AI technologies to deliver HRM practices. It is mostly about utilizing AI's untapped potential in HRM to enhance human–machine symbiosis and achieve higher HRM domain-specific outcomes by/for individuals, teams, and organizations.

Thus, the first section of this chapter focuses on the transformational outcomes achievable through AI applications in HRM. Addressing the call for multilevel thinking in HRM research (Renkema et al., 2017), these implications have been analyzed at the individual level (candidates or employees), team level, and organizational level (HRM departments or the organization as a whole). Considering that HRM practices overall should be D&I-focused (Shen et al., 2009) and can be multidimensional at each level, these implications are discussed according to the framework of D&I outcomes in organizations (Yadav & Lenka, 2020).



A. Tursunbayeva, *Augmenting Human Resource Management with Artificial Intelligence*, Contributions to Management Science,
https://doi.org/10.1007/978-3-031-75266-7_6

This is followed by a discussion of the augmentation of HRM practices through new insights into different characteristics or attributes of diversity. Understanding the diversity dimensions that AI can detect is necessary for developing AI systems that are equitable and free from biases; it can allow AI developers and users to identify and mitigate potential discrimination in AI-driven decision-making processes. Additionally, recognizing the scope of AI's detection capabilities can help set ethical standards and regulations to ensure that AI technologies are used responsibly and do not inadvertently reinforce existing social inequalities.

Then, the chapter briefly overviews how relevant or convergent with AI neuroscience tools (NT) can reveal advanced and unconventional insights previously unavailable to be collected with traditional data collection approaches or technologies. By leveraging NTs, HR professionals can gain nuanced perspectives on cognitive and emotional states (Poeppel et al., 2020), decision-making processes (Hannah et al., 2013), and stress responses of employees (Rogers, 2021). These insights can be instrumental in augmenting recruitment strategies, optimizing performance management, personalizing employee development programs, and enhancing overall organizational well-being (Petrou & Rammata, 2021).

Finally, the chapter reviews AI-enabled HRM practices that can contribute to SDGs. Sustainability has become a critical issue in the twenty-first century, driven by climate change, overpopulation, and social inequalities. Thus, it is becoming the strategic goal of many organizations. In response, sustainable HRM has emerged as an important concept, aiming to integrate financial, social, and ecological objectives. Relevant approaches like green and socially responsible HRM also seek to embed sustainability into organizational practices. The UN's SDGs offer a framework for organizations to tackle global challenges. AI applied to HRM can contribute to SDGs by analyzing workforce data or assessing the impact of sustainability initiatives.

## 6.2 Artificial Intelligence Implications at Organizational, Team, and Individual Levels in the Context of Diversity and Inclusion

The diversity of workforce characteristics is often associated with effective organizational (and societal) functioning, competitiveness (Harvey, 1999), and team performance (Horwitz & Horwitz, 2007). For instance, Fortune 500 publicly traded companies with a higher number of women senior managers were reported to generate higher returns compared to their peers (Catalyst, 2004), and the countries that responded best to coronavirus all have women leaders in common (Wittenberg-Cox, 2020). Overall, organizational diversity-related actions focus on enriching organizational demography, making everyone valued, and reaching their full potential. As the meaning of the former notion differs from the latter, they were split into two parts-diversity and inclusion. The diversity here shifted in meaning to aiming to have or having a high degree of minorities in every position and inclusion to representing both "a person's ability to contribute fully and effectively to an organization" (Roberson, 2006), as well as "an environment in which employees feel valued and recognized, where they have a voice, and where they feel engaged" (Thomas et al., 2010, p. 300). The former definition could be interpreted as focusing on individual performance, while the latter focuses on their organizational experience.

Many leaders have realized that increasing demographic variation cannot augment organizational effectiveness and thus started exploring the meanings of being fully diverse and inclusive organizations. Meanwhile, some scholars have also started investigating how indicators of inclusion parallel or differ from indicators of diversity, confirming a division of these concepts and approaches to their management. Despite these, overall, the terms are still often used interchangeably (Sherbin & Rashid, 2017), implying little understanding about whether something has changed in organizations or their outcomes since the emergence of inclusion or organizations only rebrand D&I initiatives to reduce criticism against the same initiatives (Linnehan & Konrad, 1999). Considering these distinctions, both definitions have been followed in the research reported in this chapter.

Despite some existing debates about the implications of D&I for organizations (Bendl et al., 2015), D&I-focused organizational culture has become a specific strategic priority for organizations. Some scholars have connected it to the implications of D&I for talent management (Romanelli & Ferrara, 2024), employee engagement (Jerónimo et al., 2021), team innovation (Abiew et al., 2021), and overall organizational performance (Kundu & Mor, 2017). Diverse teams were shown to bring varied perspectives and problem-solving approaches, fostering creativity and driving innovation. Inclusive environments ensure that all employees feel valued and can contribute fully, leading to higher job satisfaction (Hur, 2020) and retention rates (Hanappi-Egger, 2012). Furthermore, a strong D&I culture enhances an organization's reputation (Confetto et al., 2023), attracting top talent from a broad talent pool (Jonsen et al., 2021) and improving customer relationships by better reflecting diverse markets. Research indicates that organizations with robust D&I practices tend to outperform their peers in profitability and market value (Ely & Thomas, 2020). Thus, cultivating a culture of D&I is not only a moral imperative but can become a critical driver of competitive advantage and long-term success (Jonsen et al., 2021). Generic literature on D&I states that achieving positive D&I outcomes involves many approaches and consequences at the individual, group, and organizational levels (Bendl et al., 2015; Yadav & Lenka, 2020). These are outlined in Table 6.1.

This is also true for D&I in the era of AI. Specifically, the research findings (see Appendix to Chap. 5 for methodology) demonstrate that the value of AI for D&I is expected to be mainly at the organizational level. This is understandable because organizations are the actual "buyers" and primary users of D&I-focused AI tools. Indeed, a similar trend has also been observed in the analysis of other HRM innovations, such as People Analytics, where the benefits from technology were also considered primarily for organizations (Tursunbayeva et al., 2018).

**Table 6.1** Consequences of diversity management (adopted from Yadav & Lenka, 2020)

| Individual | Group | Organization |
|---|---|---|
| Turnover intention | Cooperative response | Commitment |
| Recruitment | Idea generation | Organizational performance |
| Behavior intention | Commitment | Organizational competitiveness |
| Absenteeism | Decision-making | Organizational innovation |
| Psychological attachment | Communication | Organizational fairness |
| Promotion | Problem-solving | |
| Job satisfaction | Satisfaction | |
| Work tension | Team turnover | |
| Organizational citizenship behavior | Group cohesiveness | |
| Self-perception | Conflict and cooperativeness | |
| Perceived discrimination | Strategic consensus | |
| Performance | Team effectiveness | |
| Individual creativity | Group development | |
| | Group performance | |

### 6.2.1 Organizational Level

Generic research on D&I suggested that effective D&I at this level includes workforce diversification practices, practices that make the organizational culture more equitable and inclusive, and practices that demonstrate the organization's commitment to D&I (Bendl et al., 2015).

The primary organizational-level outcome that emerged from the research on D&I-focused AI for HRM is that such applications need to help organizations go beyond the only diversity-focused HRM practices already widely diffused today and make them also more inclusive. "[Diversity] *is an important thing, but just having a diverse workforce will not help to address the problem that companies have in terms of how inclusive they are*" [E16: see Table 5.1]. Here, AI is claimed by some experts to be "*the bridge between diversity and inclusion*" [V7.2: see Table 5.1] by, for example, increasing the awareness of people on their biases (e.g., "*we have done something that's really, truly groundbreaking in this industry…. And that is, we can help users check for unconscious bias in the messages they write to other employees*" [E17: see Table 5.1]).

Descriptions of AI solutions and experts' insights suggested that AI can collect and analyze internal organizational communications, such as those on Slack, and multi-language employee feedback, experiences, and engagement. They can also facilitate anonymous surveying, reporting on misconduct, harassment, or discrimination, and voting on organizational initiatives. These functionalities can contribute to organizational intelligence, innovation, and customized/personalized communication or engagement actions. Often, such solutions were mentioned in relation to COVID-19 and remote work that the pandemic has triggered (*"The future of workplace and workforce will be hybrid. Now, when you overlay a hybrid workforce and use the lens of D&I or gender or ethnicity or people of color, you can start to see patterns of how, say, for example, men and women network differently at the workplace in a hybrid working environment because both the genders have different styles of operating and networking with peers, colleagues, stakeholders, up the hierarchy"* [E16: see Table 5.1]).

The research also identified additional organizational-level outcomes, including an expanded pool of diverse and skilled candidates and organizational fairness, innovation, and intelligence in people management. These improvements are achieved through blind and skills-focused assessments or facilitated by AI analytics functionality. The "Big data analytical capability" (Arunachalam et al., 2018) in HRM is often called People Analytics (Tursunbayeva et al., 2018; Di Lauro et al., 2024). It is expected to increase organizational intelligence and contribute to better organizational performance, development, and generally a positive organizational change (*"We are providing a better opportunity for inclusivity and equity...so that someone can have a sense of belonging versus....I have been excluded even though my qualifications surpass all [others]. So that is the positive outcome for the individual. For the team, we know, based on research, that when you have a variety of diverse groups working together, you are going to be more innovative, you are going to be more creative. And that result in more revenue because with that innovation, you are thinking way outside the box to really drive your industry forward or your products forward"* [E14: see Table 5.1]).

### 6.2.2 *Team Level*

Generic D&I research has found that certain team-level practices are effective in realizing the benefits of D&I. These practices include fostering a shared purpose, creating an inclusive and welcoming environment, structuring interactions, promoting social integration, and offering optional contact. These approaches help cultivate a sense of belonging, group acceptance, and psychological safety among individuals (Bendl et al., 2015).

Research on D&I-focused AI for HRM revealed that the application of such AI led to better-structured teams. This was also associated with reduced human bias and fairer decision-making processes at the group level (*"I think it is so crucial to moving any company's mission forward, who it has to be, first of all, of course, a capable team that has to be a really well-fitting team with people who really work together"* [E19: see Table 5.1]).

### 6.2.3 Individual Level

The success of diverse and inclusive workgroups and organizations is fundamentally based on their members' individual capacities and competencies (Bendl et al., 2015). Therefore, in this section, the focus will be placed on the individual level.

Numerous factors can affect the development of individual D&I competencies (Bendl et al., 2015). These can include an individual's learning orientation (mainly when they belong to a dominant group), willingness to learn, openness to new experiences, and interest and motivation to recognize their own unconscious biases and privileges. Additionally, their attitudes toward institutional diversity initiatives, beliefs about whether human traits are fixed or adaptable, and cultural metacognition can also play significant roles.

The research identified key individual-level outcomes, such as better job, culture, and mentor fit, where candidates and employees are matched with jobs, mentors, teams, and organizational cultures based on their values, skills, or preferences. It also highlighted reduced bias, leading to a perception of equal opportunities in HRM practices, where individuals are recruited, assessed, or paid mainly based on their skills and abilities (*"We are trying to divide candidates based on things that are not solely their education, work performance, or something like this. The technology is blind to the bias, so to a bias where I do not know if we staff people like this, but if there is a recruitment manager who sees two people that are different and he or she chooses one based on their own discrimination of the other, this does not exist at all because the tool is nicely blind to differences between people except the ones that are actually relevant to the team and the role. So I think in that way, it is blind to race or gender or ethnicity"* [E19: see Table 5.1]).

Customization/personalization outcomes at the individual level also emerged, which resonates with the uptake of the "me economy" (Scudamore, 2018) and confirms its arrival at HRM. Such HRM practices-tailored to individual employees and varying across organizations-have already been projected to outperform standardized HRM in terms of productivity, favorable HR climate, flexibility, return on investment of HRM, and firm financial performance (Huang et al., 2020). However, such claims are still mostly abstract as they are not grounded in comprehensive empirical evaluations of AI use cases. Indeed, it has been noted in other sectors, such as education, that such personalization approaches could backfire. For instance, the proposed AI-enabled personalized learning, intended to solve challenges like low motivation and achievement gaps, has been observed to potentially hinder students' self-actualization, ultimately leading to more uniform learning outcomes (Holmes, 2023).

## 6.3 Insights on Diversity Attributes with Artificial Intelligence

The definition of diversity-"differences in perspectives resulting in potential behavioral differences among cultural groups as well as identity differences among group members in relation to other groups" (Roberson, 2006)-suggests that diversity can have many dimensions. Around 60 years ago, diversity in the workplace focused primarily on employees from protected classes of gender and race. Since then, the interpretation of diversity has expanded to include a wide range of demographic (e.g., mental and physical abilities) and individual (e.g., educational background) characteristics to reflect that organizational staff is also characterized by great culture, ethnic background, and lifestyles mix (Langdon et al., 2002). Today, diversity is often clustered into observable or promptly detectable (i.e., surface level) and non-observable (i.e., deep level) (Milliken & Martins, 1996). The former, for example, can include race or ethnic background, age, or gender, while the latter includes socioeconomic background, personality characteristics, or values. The main reason for this differentiation (Roberson, 2006) is that when differences between people are visible, they are particularly likely to evoke responses due directly to stereotypes, prejudices, or biases and consequently can impact employees' inclusion or perception of this in organizations. A recent literature review on the evolution of diversity management and dimensions of diversity followed this surface and deep-level classification of diversity attributes. It concluded that age, gender, and racial diversity have been repeatedly covered in diversity management research, while other forms of diversity have been chiefly overlooked (Yadav & Lenka, 2020). The adoption of AI has reinvigorated the discussions around the attributes that can be used to profile and classify people, resulting in consciously or unconsciously discriminatory classifications and potentially unfair, unlawful, or ethically inappropriate consequences (Borgesius, 2020). There are already attempts to explore the dynamic ways diversity dimensions and digitalization intertwine in the work context (e.g., Kelan, 2024). However, these focused on some specific diversity attribute or dimensions. Meanwhile, a myriad of diversity attributes are envisioned or capable of being detected by AI (see Table 6.2) across different HRM practices. Knowing the attributes that AI can detect throughout employee life cycles is imperative to understand how the use of AI for D&I could be maximized by preventing or mitigating discriminatory mechanisms, ensuring the inclusion of employees with different characteristics, as well as increasing awareness about the emerging diversity attributes that need to be protected.

Similar to the findings in the general diversity literature (Yadav & Lenka, 2020), the attributes most frequently mentioned to be detected by AI were relation-oriented surface attributes, such as sex and race/ethnicity. Overall, descriptions of AI solutions analyzed seldom specify what kind of diversity attributes such applications can consider. Indeed, many solutions frequently refer to attributes such as employees' demographics or personal information. At the same time, literature often does not distinguish between attributes that AI can spot unambiguously. Consequently, in

**Table 6.2** Diversity attributes that can be detected by AI

| Diversity attribute | Perf. management | T&D | R&S | C&B | Others |
|---|---|---|---|---|---|
| **Surface** | | | | | |
| **Job-oriented** | | | | | |
| Educational background | | | AI; S | S | |
| Functional/occupational background | | | S | S | |
| Organizational tenure | | | S | S | |
| Employment status[a] | | | E | | |
| Performance[a] | AI; S | | AI; S | | |
| Office location[a] | E | | | | |
| Union membership[a] | S | | | | |
| **Relations-oriented** | | | | | |
| Sex | AI; S | AI; E | AI; S | AI; S | AI |
| Age | S | | E | | |
| Race/ethnicity | S | | AI; S; E | | AI |
| Name[a] | | | AI | | |
| Religion | S | | S; E | | |
| Sexual identity[a] | S | | AI; S | | AI |
| Location/housing[a] | S | | S; E | | |
| Civil status[a] | | | S | | |
| Physical appearance[a] | | | S | | |
| Health[a] | | | S | | |
| Disabled family member[a] | | | S | | |
| Veteran status[a] | | | | | AI |
| **Deep** | | | | | |
| **Job-oriented** | | | | | |
| Language/voice[a] | AI | AI | | | AI |
| Knowledge | | | | AI | S |
| Skills | | AI | AI | AI; E | |
| Behavior | | AI | AI | AI | |
| **Relations-oriented** | | | | | |
| Digital reputation[a] | | S | | | |
| Political opinion[a] | | S | | S | |
| Social/income/credit status | | | | S | |
| Network/s[a] | | | AI | S; E | |
| Values | | | | S | |

[a] New diversity attributes that emerged from the findings. Others include HRM practices such as HR Analytics and employee engagement. AI: Vendor solutions from Garr and Jackson (2019); S: Scholarly perspectives. E: Industry experts' perspectives (See Table 5.1)

such cases, it was not possible to classify the attributes of the vendor tools (Garr & Jackson, 2019). In contrast, all the attributes mentioned in the qualifying literature were included in the analysis (see Table 5.1).

Many of the attributes that emerged were aligned with those that humans could spot, including sex, age, organizational tenure, knowledge, or skills, though additional categories such as performance, union membership, or health also emerged. Existing AI descriptions and experts (see Table 6.2) rarely nominated job-oriented surface-level attributes (e.g., employment status or organizational tenure) while commonly discussing those of deep levels such as language/voice, both verbal and written, employee skills, and experiences. Experts and scholars discussed these attributes both in positive and negative light. For instance, the former discussed the potential of AI to protect candidates/employees from human bias by "blinding" their specific attributes from humans. The latter discussed more critically the generic potential of AI to introduce additional biases (e.g., machine) to HRM decision-making.

As seen from Table 6.2, the research revealed a myriad of the diversity attributes that AI can detect, thus enriching the framework on the attributes from generic diversity literature (Yadav & Lenka, 2020) by suggesting additional categories both at the surface and deep levels. The fact that most of the prevalent attributes that AI can detect are primarily aligned with those of generic diversity literature confirms the trustworthiness of the findings. The emergence of new attributes such as disability resonates with recent developments in the business world, such as the strategic alliances of firms that are being made to tackle prejudice toward disabled people at work (Salmon, 2021). Interestingly, the findings of this study have not revealed the AI's ability to detect people's emotions (e.g., from a face), as has already been reported in news reports (e.g., Murgia, 2021), or identified as a valid AI-related research opportunity (e.g., Benbya et al., 2021). It is worth mentioning that, overall, different attributes reported in this research are not mutually exclusive (e.g., Milliken & Martins, 1996). Furthermore, people can be discriminated against not only on these attributes but also on proxy parameters (the phenomenon known as masking) (Žliobaitė & Custers, 2016). For example, individuals can be discriminated against based on the educational institutions they graduated from, which can be considered as a proxy for social class, or a postcode, which can be viewed as a proxy for socio-economic status.

## 6.4 Insights on Employee Behavior with Convergent Neuroscience Tools

The field of HRM has experienced a prolonged period of stability in its concepts, methods, and tools. However, the recent integration of advanced technologies and big data into every facet of our lives has enabled the adoption of innovative approaches, like NT, within organizational settings, offering a practical means to augment HRM through profound, actionable insights. Specifically, this evolution has paved the way for methodologies and tools from other disciplines, such as Marketing (e.g., consumer neuroscience or neuromarketing) (Alvino et al., 2020) and Strategy (Kaur, 2024), to arrive also in the field of HRM. The price of such tools is expected to become more affordable shortly, thus facilitating their wider adoption (Everett, 2018). Consequently, it would be possible to uncover individuals' thoughts, emotions, and behavior by studying their brain functions and structures to cognitive processes (Poeppel et al., 2020), as well as to address the longstanding question of "What's going on in this person's head that makes them think or act the way they do?" (Waldman et al., 2017) both metaphorically and realistically.

Conceptually, the ascent of neuroscience-related methods in organizational settings is driven by a desire to expand the understanding of constructs such as leadership/management qualities and to examine various facets of organizational behaviors (Waldman et al., 2017). Methodologically, NTs permit the inclusion of physiological and neurophysiological measurements that can help to understand employees' behavior in organizations, bridge the limitations of existing organizational research methods such as surveys with their retrospective nature, and empower managers to obtain real-time results (Waldman et al., 2017). For instance, it can help organizations provide support and tailored professional development for employees with autism, dyslexia, and other cognitive differences. Indeed, EY already operates 23 Neurodiverse Centers of Excellence worldwide, focusing on this (Carroll, 2024). Andre Vermeulen, an international expert in the neuroscience of learning, declared that neuroscience and its tools will become increasingly important in the age of AI: "Mankind will need to out-think, out-learn and out-innovate AI…But while AI is good at pattern recognition, it's not good at complex problem-solving. Its memory is big, but it's not good at innovating, and that's where neuroscience comes in, to help optimise our learning and creative practices" (Everett, 2018).

The notion of integrating organizational HRM with neuroscience has been advocated for some time (Waldman et al., 2019), positing that such integration can enhance our comprehension of individuals in work settings and their management (Waldman et al., 2017). Numerous NTs can be utilized to explore employee decision-making and behavior. These tools often encompass devices capable of measuring essential physiological functions (e.g., respiration rate, heartbeat, blood pressure) and reflexes (e.g., facial expression, gaze fixation, pupil dilation). NTs such as functional magnetic resonance imaging (fMRI) and electroencephalogram (EEG) can offer real-time measurements of brain activity to inform, for instance, understanding of a leader's complexity and predicting adaptive leadership decision-making, as exemplified by research on the topic (Hannah et al., 2013).

Recently, discussions regarding the potential applications of NT have gained prominence within organizational contexts (Farahany, 2023). Thus, there is brainstorming on how NT can enhance employee focus, information processing, and meaningful interactions with management and colleagues (Fitzell, 2021). Microsoft, for instance, conducted a study of brainwave activity employing EEG among 14 volunteers participating in video meetings to measure changes in stress levels during task performance (Rogers, 2021). Their research demonstrated that breaks between meetings allow the brain to "reset," reducing a cumulative buildup of stress across meetings. They also suggested that back-to-back meetings can decrease the ability to focus and engage. Finally, they also concluded that transitioning between meetings can be a source of high stress. These insights encouraged Microsoft to rearrange its meeting schedules.

The diffusion of NT is also driven by the increased awareness of neurodiversity and how not accounting for it in HRM processes, such as job interviews, can challenge employers on dismissals and conditions (Hennekam et al., 2023). The UK's Michelin star chef Blumenthal commissioned research on neurodiversity, which revealed that 11% of people surveyed had been officially diagnosed as neurodivergent, with 21% of them not engaged in full or part-time employment. A separate study he commissioned found that many companies feel they still have work to do to be more inclusive of neurodivergent individuals. Specifically, 37% of Financial Times Stock Exchange Group 350 board directors and HRM professionals rated their company's understanding of neurodivergent employees as average or poor (Saker-Clark, 2024).

Indeed, the adoption of NT in HRM and across different HRM practices so far is poorly understood compared to the application of neuroscience in other organizational functions such as marketing (Alvino et al., 2020) or, more recently also, strategic management (Kaur, 2024). Neuromarketers have already been experimenting with facial coding software through webcams for some time to analyze consumers' expressions and understand their emotional responses to marketing and advertising (Everett, 2018). Moreover, research on utilizing NT in HRM tends to be distributed across interdisciplinary literature. Below is a brief overview of how NTs can be applied or augment different HRM practices by collecting and analyzing previously unavailable insights across the employee life cycle.

In R&S, NT, such as EEG, could become helpful for job profiling and design and streamlining the adaptation process for new employees (Kasperiuniene & Zydziunaite, 2019). At the same time, there are claims that using specialized software like Affectiva (www.affectiva.com) during recruitment can improve candidate selection accuracy (Sandoval & Castillo, 2021).

In T&D, NTs could be helpful in enhancing organizational learning and development. NTs like facial expression recognition or EEG can be used to evaluate employee knowledge, emotional states, and engagement (Rejón-Guardia et al., 2019). Real-time neurofeedback could help train specific competencies (Waldman et al., 2017). NTs also aid in strategic planning by understanding cognitive activities and attention mechanisms (Li et al., 2023). Measuring physiological and neurophysiological aspects in team management can enhance cooperative behavior and identify effective team processes (Hałgas et al., 2023) and effective leadership behaviors (Waldman et al., 2011).

In Performance management, NTs show promise in improving employee retention by focusing on rewards, performance coaching, and personalization (Zito et al., 2021). Studies have utilized Galvanic Skin Response to study emotional responses (Chong et al., 2022) in decision-making contexts and fMRI to understand counterproductive work behaviors (Waldman et al., 2017) and gender differences in neurological responses (Dulebohn et al., 2016). NTs were also helpful in studying work focus, investment performance (Kalgotra et al., 2019), team dynamics, and leadership communication, highlighting the potential of such insights for enhancing team collaboration and employee retention.

In job design, using NTs has been explored for optimizing task allocation (Saedi et al., 2022), studying brain and cognitive processes in teamwork distribution (Riva et al., 2021), and understanding employees' emotions to improve performance and engagement.

Overall, all these examples illustrate that using NTs across the employee life cycle is an emerging innovation in organizations that can augment HRM through emotional and cognitive insights. Though Alison Maitland, research and product director at performance management consultancy Lane4it, also noted that neuroscience insights should always be considered within a broader (psychological) context: "Neuroscience is a means of helping you understand what you're doing and why, but it's up to psychology to interpret that by looking at how someone becomes engaged, for example," she says. "In other words, neuroscience is informing psychology and the two disciplines are now coming together to provide a more rounded view" (Everett, 2018).

## 6.5 Artificial Intelligence for Sustainable Human Resource Management Practices

Sustainability is one of the big questions of the twenty-first century, which affects societies, organizations, and individuals. There are multiple reasons behind the increased concern and demands for sustainability, including, among others, climate change, overpopulation, environmental problems, poverty, social inequalities, and unequal access to resources. UN has been a major proponent of preventing growing environmental degradation and increasing social inequalities (Kramar, 2022). The term Sustainable HRM first appeared almost 20 years ago. Since then, extensive literature has been published on the topic (Ehnert et al., 2016). Today, there are many definitions of sustainability and sustainable development. It can also be analyzed at national, regional, and organizational levels. Organizational sustainability, defined by Dyllick and Hockerts (2002), involves meeting the needs of current stakeholders without compromising future stakeholders' needs. It is considered a competitive strategy that embodies an organization's philosophy and strategy (Samant & Sangle, 2016). Given that a company's performance, including sustainability goals, hinges on its employees (Piwowar-Sulej, 2021), there is increasing focus on new HRM concepts such as sustainable HRM (Piwowar-Sulej, 2021), green HRM (Renwick et al., 2013; Tang et al., 2018), socially responsible HRM (Zhao et al., 2021), and common good HRM (Aust et al., 2020). All these concepts are related, though they emphasize different aspects and approaches to integrating sustainability into HRM (see Table 6.3). For instance, Sustainable HRM integrates financial, social, and ecological goals with a long-term perspective and controls for unintended adverse effects. Green HRM focuses on environmental aspects, such as pollution prevention and eco-friendly practices within the organization. Socially Responsible HRM prioritizes

**Table 6.3** Sustainable HRM-related concepts and definitions

| Concept | Definition |
|---|---|
| Sustainable HRM | *"The adoption of HRM strategies and practices that enable the achievement of financial, social, and ecological goals, with an impact inside and outside of the organization and over a long-term time horizon while controlling for unintended side effects and negative feedback"* (Ehnert et al., 2016, p. 90) |
| Green HRM | *"Green HRM reflects the HRM aspects of environmental management, and its focus is on the role of HRM in pollution prevention through the operational processes of firms"* (Renwick et al., 2013) |
| Socially responsible HRM | *"Policies that companies integrate into their HRM area in a voluntary way and with a dual purpose: (1) to meet the ethical, social, labour and human concerns of their employees, promoting their employees' satisfaction and proper development in the company; and (2) to confer added value to the businesses in regard to their human capital"* (Barrena-Martínez et al., 2019) |
| Common good HRM | *"A common good approach assumes that it is the fundamental responsibility of business to "make an effective contribution to resolving the sustainability challenges we are collectively facing"* (Dyllick & Muff, 2016: 156) *and that business organizations' long-term self-interest lies in sustaining our collective livelihood* (see Ehnert, 2009). *Thus, Common Good HRM places collective interests above - or more realistically equal to - individual (including organizational) wishes, needs, and desires"* (Aust et al., 2020) |

employees' ethical, social, and labor concerns to enhance employee satisfaction and human capital. Finally, Common Good HRM emphasizes the responsibility of businesses to address broader societal sustainability challenges, prioritizing collective interests alongside organizational goals. Thus, despite efforts to establish these new HRM approaches, they lack consensus on their core definitions and specific applications (Brewster & Brookes, 2024).

As awareness of the importance of sustainability has grown, the demand for proactive measures has increased accordingly. This demand has been significantly amplified by the UN's establishment of the 17 SDGs in 2015, which urge organizations to tackle various issues such as poverty, education, gender equality, health, and well-being (Stafford-Smith et al., 2017). The SDGs are interconnected and measurable goals designed to address intertwined challenges and create a more sustainable future (Mio et al., 2020; Yamaguchi et al., 2023). Each SDG is accompanied by targets addressing the most urgent issues within that category. While the 169 targets identify the specific problems to tackle, 230 indicators measure progress (Redman, 2018). Previous literature has recognized the critical role businesses play in achieving the SDGs, noting their contributions through innovation, skills, and resources (García-Sánchez & García-Sánchez, 2020; Buhmann et al., 2018).

Organizations can leverage AI to contribute to sustainability by analyzing workforce-related data (Stankevičiūtė et al., 2024). For instance, AI can help in sustainability (Balusamy & Chilamkurti, 2023) by reporting and evaluating the impact of initiatives on SDGs such as health and well-being (SDG 3), quality education (SDG 4), gender equality (SDG 5), and decent work (SDG 8). By providing insights into metrics like employee satisfaction, retention, and productivity, AI can enable organizations to identify improvement areas, set goals, and assess the effectiveness of their sustainability efforts. This data-driven approach can strengthen their commitment to sustainability, transparency, and responsible business practices, building stakeholder trust (Lazazzara et al., 2024). However, although these topics are currently active and widely discussed in HRM, the related SDGs are distant from being realized (Brewster & Brookes, 2024).

Below, a brief discussion is provided on HRM practices observed by previous scholars to contribute to SDGs, along with some illustrative examples of the role of AI in these efforts.

### 6.5.1 Recruitment and Selection

AI has been reported to be helpful for R&S processes for matching candidates to jobs (Montuschi et al., 2014) and collecting information about candidates' personality characteristics (Kaushal et al., 2021), skills, or job performance (Giermindl et al., 2022). Thus, AI could help match pro-sustainable candidates with organizations that prioritize sustainability and assist in evaluating candidates' sustainability knowledge and skills during R&S and performance appraisals (Stankevičiūtė et al., 2024). Indeed, some organizations already incorporate sustainability criteria into their selection processes and emphasize sustainability aspects in job descriptions to find candidates aligned with these values (Zibarras & Coan, 2015).

It has also been observed that more sustainable HRM practices and sustainability-focused organizational culture can increase employer attractiveness (Willness & Jones, 2013) and employer branding. Indeed, recent research has revealed significant shift in employee preferences within the workplace (Schaefer et al., 2024). The "Employees' Expectations 2022" study by Workday, which surveyed 1.8 million employees globally (The Workday® Human Capital Management, 2022), highlighted these changes. It discovered that although work flexibility and employee development are still key priorities, there is an increasing emphasis on companies' CSR practices. In particular, employees pay closer attention to environmental, social, and governance practices when considering their current or potential employers. This trend is especially pronounced among younger generations, who are more purpose-driven and look for employers that align with their personal values (Schaefer et al., 2024). Schaefer et al. (2024) also discussed the relationship between the sustainability focus of organizations and their employer attractiveness, considering two contrasting cases: Volkswagen and Patagonia. They describe that Volkswagen faced significant fallout from the 2015 emissions scandal, leading employees to view its CSR efforts as inauthentic. This resulted in feelings of betrayal and guilt among employees, who subsequently spoke less favorably about the company and exhibited lower trust, engagement, and commitment (Pontefract, 2016). Conversely, since its inception in 1973, Patagonia company has successfully balanced responsibility and profit, adhering to values such as quality, integrity, environmentalism, and justice (Hansen & Chouinard, 2023). The company pays its global employees a living wage (Patagonia, n.d.), boasting a low % turnover rate of 4% in the fashion industry (Rock, 2020). Unsurprisingly, 91% of its over 1000 employees consider it a great workplace and 94% are proud to be associated with Patagonia (Great Place to Work Institute, 2019).

Some AI recruitment tools promise organizations to reduce bias in hiring and candidate evaluation by analyzing, for instance, language in job advertisements to ensure they are gender-neutral. Thus, these tools directly contribute to SDG 5, or Gender equality. Other AI tools can contribute to this SDG by ensuring a broader reach in job postings and promoting equal employment opportunities regardless of gender, socioeconomic background, or age.

### 6.5.2 Training and Development

Effective training enhances employee awareness and drives behavior change (Stankevičiūtė et al., 2024). The UK CIPD/KPMG survey found that 42% of organizations in the UK provide sustainability-related training (Zibarras & Coan, 2015). However, the success of such training is often compromised by factors like inadequate needs analysis, low trainee readiness, poor transfer of training to the job, and employee cynicism (Jackson et al., 2011). AI promises to address such shortages by identifying current and future skills gaps and personalized training recommendations (Tursunbayeva et al., 2022) and enabling proactive upskilling and reskilling initiatives on sustainable practices and responsible consumption/production, as well as permitting advanced and actionable learning and development analytics. Thus, it can help to contribute to SDG 4-Quality Education and SDG 9-Industry, Innovation, and Infrastructure, among others.

### 6.5.3 Performance Management

Sustainability indicators are increasingly included in performance appraisals to hold employees accountable for sustainability efforts (Stankevičiūtė et al., 2024). However, there are ongoing debates about this approach's validity, reliability, and fairness, particularly regarding the distribution of sustainability responsibilities within the organization. Studies show that involving employees in environmental management can enhance sustainability performance, but successful implementation of new behaviors or changes requires full employee involvement and empowerment as key stakeholders (Del Brío et al., 2007; Leitch et al., 1995).

AI can also assist organizations in "shaping" employees" behavior through "nudging" to induce changes in context-specific behavior. Such nudging is often seen as a complement to traditional policy instruments rather than a substitute for laws, regulations, and economic tools (Lehner et al., 2016).

### 6.5.4 Job Design

Technologies such as AI and AI-related collaboration tools also promise to facilitate remote or hybrid work (Todisco et al., 2023), reducing the need for commuting and contributing to sustainable urban living (SDG 11 or Sustainable Cities and Communities). To fully understand the implications of such emerging forms of work (Bronzini et al., 2022), a recent Harvard Business Review article recommends that organizations consider multiple parameters (Shreedhar et al., 2022). For instance, the evidence on the energy impact from such work arrangements is mixed and depends on employees' characteristics (e.g., awareness, family size), home infrastructure (e.g., building energy rating, energy supplier), and situational factors (geographic location or season). Remote work arrangements reduce commuting but were found to increase non-travel-related short trips. For instance, a study in California during the COVID-19 pandemic found a decrease in vehicle miles traveled but a 26% increase in the number of trips taken (Riggs, 2020). With fewer in-person interactions, more online communication and collaboration can increase digital footprints (Shreedhar et al., 2022). However, the impact on waste footprint seems to be primarily positive. For instance, research on recycling in the UK during the first lockdown revealed that employees are more sustainable with waste practices at home than in the office (Sharman, 2020).

### 6.5.5 Compensation and Benefit

Organizations have successfully promoted pro-sustainability commitment and practices using effective monetary and nonmonetary reward-focused HRM practices (Berrone & Gomez-Mejia, 2009). AI has the potential to offer personalized reward and recognition programs that can further support pro-sustainability behaviors and enhance sustainable reporting (Kaushal et al., 2021). At the same time, there are also concerns related to the "one size fits all" approach of reward systems, which may not address individual differences and could lead to adverse outcomes, such as withdrawal from sustainability activities due to punitive measures (Handgraaf et al., 2013; Renwick et al., 2013).

## References

Abiew, G. E., Okyere-Kwakye, E., & Ellis, F. Y. A. (2021). Examining the effect of functional diversity on organizational team innovation. *International Journal of Innovation Science, 14*(2), 193–212. https://doi.org/10.1108/IJIS-02-2021-0027

Alvino, L., Pavone, L., Abhishta, A., & Robben, H. (2020). Picking your brains: Where and how neuroscience tools can enhance marketing research. *Frontiers in Neuroscience, 14*. https://www.frontiersin.org. https://doi.org/10.3389/fnins.2020.577666

Arunachalam, D., Kumar, N., & Kawalek, J. P. (2018). Understanding big data analytics capabilities in supply chain management: Unravelling the issues, challenges and implications for practice. *Transportation Research Part E: Logistics and Transportation Review, 114*, 416–436. https://doi.org/10.1016/j.tre.2017.04.001

Aust, I., Matthews, B., & Muller-Camen, M. (2020). Common good HRM: A paradigm shift in sustainable HRM? *Human Resource Management Review, 30*(3), 100705. https://doi.org/10.1016/j.hrmr.2019.100705

Balusamy, B., & Chilamkurti, N. (2023). In A. Pandey (Ed.), *Disruptive artificial intelligence and sustainable human resource management: Impacts and innovations—the future of HR*. River Publishers. https://ieeexplore.ieee.org/book/10198741

Barrena-Martínez, J., López-Fernández, M., & Romero-Fernández, P. M. (2019). Towards a configuration of socially responsible human resource management policies and practices: Findings from an academic consensus. *The International Journal of Human Resource Management, 30*(17), 2544–2580. https://doi.org/10.1080/09585192.2017.1332669

Benbya, H., Pachidi, S., & Jarvenpaa, S. (2021). Special issue editorial: Artificial intelligence in organizations: Implications for information systems research. *Journal of the Association for Information Systems, 22*(10). https://doi.org/10.17705/1jais.00662

Bendl, R., Bleijenbergh, I., Henttonen, E., & Mills, A. J. (2015). *The Oxford handbook of diversity in organizations*. Oxford University Press.

Berrone, P., & Gomez-Mejia, L. R. (2009). Environmental performance and executive compensation: An integrated agency-institutional perspective. *Academy of Management Journal, 52*(1), 103–126. https://doi.org/10.5465/amj.2009.36461950

Borgesius, F. J. Z. (2020). Strengthening legal protection against discrimination by algorithms and artificial intelligence. *The International Journal of Human Rights, 24*(10), 1572–1593. https://doi.org/10.1080/13642987.2020.1743976

Brewster, C., & Brookes, M. (2024). Sustainable development goals and new approaches to HRM: Why HRM specialists will not reach the sustainable development goals and why it matters. *German Journal of Human Resource Management: Zeitschrift Für Personalforschung, 38*(2), 183–201. https://doi.org/10.1177/23970022241229037

Bronzini, M., Torre, T., Sarti, D., & Cori, E. (2022). Isolamento professionale e inclusione nell'esperienza del lavoro da remoto durante la pandemia in Italia. *Prisma: economia, società, lavoro, 1/2*, 68–89. https://doi.org/10.3280/PRI2022-001005

Buhmann, K., Jonsson, J., & Fisker, M. (2018). Do no harm and do more good too: Connecting the SDGs with business and human rights and political CSR theory. *Corporate Governance: The International Journal of Business in Society, 19*(3), 389–403. https://doi.org/10.1108/CG-01-2018-0030

Carroll, L. (2024). EY is focusing on neurodiverse talent BBC. *BBC*. https://www.bbc.com/worklife/article/20240320-ey-karyn-twaronite-neurodiversity-bbc-executive-interview

Catalyst. (2004). The bottom line: Connecting corporate performance and gender diversity (Report).

Chong, D., Yu, A., Su, H., & Zhou, Y. (2022). The impact of emotional states on construction workers' recognition ability of safety hazards based on social cognitive neuroscience. *Frontiers in Psychology, 13*, 895929. https://doi.org/10.3389/fpsyg.2022.895929

Confetto, M. G., Ključnikov, A., Covucci, C., & Normando, M. (2023). Diversity and inclusion in employer branding: An explorative analysis of European companies' digital communication. *Employee Relations: The International Journal, 45*(7), 121–139. https://doi.org/10.1108/ER-11-2022-0522

Del Brío, J. Á., Fernández, E., & Junquera, B. (2007). Management and employee involvement in achieving an environmental action-based competitive advantage: An empirical study. *The International Journal of Human Resource Management, 18*(4), 491–522. https://doi.org/10.1080/09585190601178687

Di Lauro, S., Tursunbayeva, A., Sarti, D., Antonelli, G., & Torre, T. (2024). Demystifying People Analytics Adoption: Insights from Italy. In T. A. Adisa (Ed.), *HRM 5.0: Unpacking the Digitalisation of Human Resource Management* (pp. 191–214). Springer Nature Switzerland. . https://doi.org/10.1007/978-3-031-58912-6_9

Dulebohn, J. H., Davison, R. B., Lee, S. A., Conlon, D. E., McNamara, G., & Sarinopoulos, I. C. (2016). Gender differences in justice evaluations: Evidence from fMRI. *The Journal of Applied Psychology, 101*(2), 151–170. https://doi.org/10.1037/apl0000048

Dyllick, T., & Hockerts, K. (2002). Beyond the business case for corporate sustainability. *Business Strategy and the Environment, 11*(2), 130–141. https://doi.org/10.1002/bse.323

Dyllick, T., & Muff, K. (2016). Clarifying the meaning of sustainable business: Introducing a typology from business-as-usual to true business sustainability. *Organization & Environment, 29*(2), 156–174. https://doi.org/10.1177/1086026615575176

Ehnert, I. (2009). Sustainable human resource management. *Springer*. https://link.springer.com. https://doi.org/10.1007/978-3-7908-2188-8

Ehnert, I., Parsa, S., Roper, I., Wagner, M., & Muller-Camen, M. (2016). Reporting on sustainability and HRM: A comparative study of sustainability reporting practices by the world's largest companies. *The International Journal of Human Resource Management, 27*(1), 88–108. https://doi.org/10.1080/09585192.2015.1024157

Ely, R. J., & Thomas, D. A. (2020, November 1). Getting Serious About Diversity: Enough Already with the Business Case. *Harvard Business Review*. https://hbr.org/2020/11/getting-serious-about-diversity-enough-already-with-the-business-case

Everett, C. (2018). *What neuroscience can teach you about engaging your employees*. World Economic Forum. https://www.weforum.org/agenda/2018/06/neuroscience-offers-insights-into-employee-engagement/#:~:text=%E2%80%9CNeuroscience%20helps%20individuals%20to%20understand%20who%20they%20are,difference%20%E2%80%93%20and%20this%20means%20they%E2%80%99re%20naturally%20engaged.%E2%80%9D.

Farahany, N. A. (2023). *The Battle for your brain: Defending the right to think freely in the age of neurotechnology*. St. Martin's Press.

Fitzell, S. (2021). How to maximize employees' brain power (and why it's worth the investment). *LinkedIn*. https://www.linkedin.com/pulse/how-maximize-employees-brain-power-why-its-worth-susan

García-Sánchez, I.-M., & García-Sánchez, A. (2020). Corporate social responsibility during COVID-19 pandemic. *Journal of Open Innovation: Technology, Market, and Complexity, 6*(4), 126. https://doi.org/10.3390/joitmc6040126

Garr, S. S., & Jackson, C. (2019). *Diversity & inclusion technology: The rise of a transformative market*. Mercer. https://www.mercer.com/our-thinking/career/diversity-and-inclusion-technology.html.

Giermindl, L. M., Strich, F., Christ, O., Leicht-Deobald, U., & Redzepi, A. (2022). The dark sides of people analytics: Reviewing the perils for organisations and employees. *European Journal of Information Systems, 31*(3), 410–435. https://doi.org/10.1080/0960085X.2021.1927213

Great Place to Work Institute. (2019). Patagonia. https://www.greatplacetowork.com/certified-company/1000745.

Hałgas, E. A., Van Eijndhoven, K. H. J., Gevers, J. M. P., Wiltshire, T. J., Westerink, M., Westerink, J. H. D. M., & Rispens, S. (2023). A review of using wearable technology to assess team functioning and performance. *Small Group Research, 54*(1), 41–76. https://doi.org/10.1177/10464964221125717

Handgraaf, M. J. J., De Jeude, V. L., van Lidth de Jeude, M., & Appelt, K. C. (2013). Public praise vs. private pay: Effects of rewards on energy conservation in the workplace. *Ecological Economics, 86*, 86–92. https://doi.org/10.1016/j.ecolecon.2012.11.008

Hannah, S. T., Balthazard, P. A., Waldman, D. A., Jennings, P. L., & Thatcher, R. W. (2013). The psychological and neurological bases of leader self-complexity and effects on adaptive decision-making. *The Journal of Applied Psychology, 98*(3), 393–411. https://doi.org/10.1037/a0032257

Hanappi-Egger, E. (2012). "Shall I stay or shall I go"? On the role of diversity management for women's retention in SET professions. *Equality, Diversity and Inclusion: An International Journal, 31*(2), 144–157. https://doi.org/10.1108/02610151211202790

Hansen, T., & Chouinard, Y. (2023). *Patagonia shows how turning a profit doesn't have to cost the earth*. McKinsey & Company. https://www.mckinsey.com/industries/agriculture/our-insights/patagonia-shows-how-turning-a-profit-doesnt-have-to-cost-the-earth?stcr=81DF2CA6D6884AF09A539278BC5A6DA9%26cid=other-eml-dre-mip-mck%26hlkid=c8d7c1acd51e46cc88108d5fbb79ee6b%26hctky=11665003%26hdpid=bb

Harvey, B. H. (1999). Technology diversity and work culture—key trends in the millennium. *HR Magazine, 44*, 58–59.

Hennekam, S., Volpone, S., & Pullen, A. (2023). Special issue: Neurodiversity at work: Challenges and opportunities for human resource management. *Human Resource Management*.

Holmes, W. (2023). The unintended consequences of artificial intelligence and education. *Education International*. https://www.ei-ie.org/en/item/28115:the-unintended-consequences-of-artificial-intelligence-and-education

Horwitz, H., & Horwitz, H. (2007). The effects of team diversity on team outcomes: A meta-analytic review of team demography. *Journal of Management, 33*(6), 987–1015. https://doi.org/10.1177/0149206307308587

Huang, X., Zhang, L., & Feng, C. (2020). Personalized human resource management: Theory and implications. *Academy of Management Proceedings, 2020*(1), 12029. https://doi.org/10.5465/AMBPP.2020.12029abstract

Hur, H. (2020). The role of inclusive work environment practices in promoting LGBT employee job satisfaction and commitment. *Public Money & Management, 40*(6), 426–436. https://doi.org/10.1080/09540962.2019.1681640

Jackson, S. E., Renwick, D. W. S., Jabbour, C. J. C., & Muller-Camen, M. (2011). State-of-the-art and future directions for green human resource management: Introduction to the special issue. *German Journal of Human Resource Management: Zeitschrift Für Personalforschung, 25*(2), 99–116. https://doi.org/10.1177/239700221102500203

Jerónimo, H. M., Henriques, P. L., & Carvalho, S. I. (2021). Being inclusive boosts impact of diversity practices on employee engagement. *Management Research: Journal of the Iberoamerican Academy of Management, 20*(2), 129–147. https://doi.org/10.1108/MRJIAM-05-2021-1175

Jonsen, K., Point, S., Kelan, E. K., & Grieble, A. (2021). Diversity and inclusion branding: A five-country comparison of corporate websites. *The International Journal of Human Resource Management, 32*(3), 616–649. https://doi.org/10.1080/09585192.2018.1496125

Kasperiuniene, J., & Zydziunaite, V. (2019). A systematic literature review on professional identity construction in social media. *SAGE Open, 9*(1), 215824401982884. https://doi.org/10.1177/2158244019828847

Kalgotra, P., Sharda, R., & McHaney, R. (2019). Don't disturb me! Understanding the impact of interruptions on knowledge work: An exploratory neuroimaging study. *Information Systems Frontiers, 21*(5), 1019–1030. https://doi.org/10.1007/s10796-017-9812-9

Kaur, V. (2024). Neurostrategy: A scientometric analysis of marriage between neuroscience and strategic management. *Journal of Business Research, 170*, 114342. https://doi.org/10.1016/j.jbusres.2023.114342

Kaushal, N., Kaurav, R. P. S., Sivathanu, B., & Kaushik, N. (2021). Artificial intelligence and HRM: Identifying future research agenda using systematic literature review and bibliometric analysis. *Management Review Quarterly*. https://doi.org/10.1007/s11301-021-00249-2

Kelan, E. (2024). *Patterns of inclusion: How gender matters for automation, artificial intelligence and the future of work*. Routledge. https://doi.org/10.4324/9781003427100

Kramar, R. (2022). Sustainable human resource management: Six defining characteristics. *Asia Pacific Journal of Human Resources, 60*(1), 146–170. https://doi.org/10.1111/1744-7941.12321

Kundu, S. C., & Mor, A. (2017). Workforce diversity and organizational performance: A study of IT industry in India. *Employee Relations, 39*(2), 160–183. https://doi.org/10.1108/ER-06-2015-0114

Langdon, D., McMenamin, T. M., & Krolik, T. J. (2002). U.S. labor market in 2001: Economy enters a recession. *Monthly Labor Review*. https://www.bls.gov/opub/mlr/2002/article/us-labor-market-in-2001-economy-enters-a-recession.htm

Lazazzara, A., Reina, R., & Za, S. (2024). Digital transformation and sustainability goals: Advancing the "Twin Transition". In A. Lazazzara, R. Reina, & S. Za (Eds.), *Towards digital and sustainable organisations* (pp. 1–7). Springer Nature. https://doi.org/10.1007/978-3-031-52880-4_1

Lehner, M., Mont, O., & Heiskanen, E. (2016). Nudging—a promising tool for sustainable consumption behaviour? *Journal of Cleaner Production, 134*, 166–177. https://doi.org/10.1016/j.jclepro.2015.11.086

Leitch, J., Nieves, D., Burke, G., Little, M., & Gorin, M. J. (1995). Strategies for involving employees. *The Journal for Quality and Participation, 18*(5), 68–74.

Li, Y., Zhang, L., Shiau, W.-L., Xu, L., & Liu, Q. (2023). Psychophysiological responses to mobile reading: Evidence from frontal EEG signals under a distracting reading environment and different text genres. *Information Technology & People, 36*(3), 1048–1075. https://doi.org/10.1108/ITP-02-2021-0111

Linnehan, F., & Konrad, A. M. (1999). Diluting diversity: Implications for intergroup inequality in organizations. *Journal of Management Inquiry, 8*(4), 399–414. https://journals.sagepub.com. https://doi.org/10.1177/105649269984009

Malik, A., Budhwar, P., & Kazmi, B. A. (2023). Artificial intelligence (AI)-assisted HRM: Towards an extended strategic framework. *Human Resource Management Review, 33*(1), 100940. https://doi.org/10.1016/j.hrmr.2022.100940

Milliken, F. J., & Martins, L. L. (1996). Searching for common threads: Understanding the multiple effects of diversity in organizational groups. *The Academy of Management Review, 21*(2), 402–433. https://doi.org/10.5465/amr.1996.9605060217

Mio, C., Panfilo, S., & Blundo, B. (2020). Sustainable development goals and the strategic role of business: A systematic literature review. *Business Strategy and the Environment, 29*(8), 3220–3245. https://doi.org/10.1002/bse.2568

Montuschi, P., Gatteschi, V., Lamberti, F., Sanna, A., & Demartini, C. (2014). Job recruitment and job seeking processes: How technology can help. *IT Professional, 16*(5), 41–49. https://doi.org/10.1109/MITP.2013.62

Murgia, M. (2021, May 12). Emotion recognition: Can AI detect human feelings from a face? *Financial Times*. https://www.ft.com/content/c0b03d1d-f72f-48a8-b342-b4a926109452

Parry, E., & Tyson, S. (2011). Desired goals and actual outcomes of e-HRM. *Human Resource Management Journal, 21*(3), 335–354. https://doi.org/10.1111/j.1748-8583.2010.00149.x

Patagonia. (n.d.). *Patagonia social responsibility*. https://www.patagonia.ca/social-responsibility/

Petrou, F., & Rammata, M. (2021). The emerging impact of neuroscience in human resource management and in the public sector. *SCIREA Journal of Management, 7*(1), 89–106. https://doi.org/10.54647/management63082

Piwowar-Sulej, K. (2021). Core functions of sustainable human resource management. A hybrid literature review with the use of H-classics methodology. *Sustainable Development, 29*(4), 671–693. https://doi.org/10.1002/sd.2166

Poeppel, D., Mangun, G. R., & Gazzaniga, M. S. (2020). *The cognitive neurosciences*. The MIT Press. https://doi.org/10.7551/mitpress/11442.001.0001

Pontefract, D. (2016). Faking corporate social responsibility does not fool employees. *Forbes*. https://www.forbes.com/sites/danpontefract/2016/09/24/faking-corporate-social-responsibility-does-not-fool-employees/

Redman, A. (2018). Harnessing the sustainable development goals for businesses: A progressive framework for action. *Business Strategy & Development, 1*(4), 230–243. https://doi.org/10.1002/bsd2.33

Rejón-Guardia, F., García-Sastre, M. A., & Alemany-Hormaeche, M. (2019). Electroencephalographic response of e-learning tasks on a learning management system: An emotional and cognitive approach. In *11th international conference on education and new learning technologies proceedings* (pp. 6675–6680). https://doi.org/10.21125/edulearn.2019.1604

Renkema, M., Meijerink, J., & Bondarouk, T. (2017). Advancing multilevel thinking in human resource management research: Applications and guidelines. *Human Resource Management Review, 27*(3), 397–415. https://doi.org/10.1016/j.hrmr.2017.03.001

Renwick, D. W. S., Redman, T., & Maguire, S. (2013). Green human resource management: A review and research agenda*. *International Journal of Management Reviews, 15*(1), 1–14. https://doi.org/10.1111/j.1468-2370.2011.00328.x

Riggs, W. (2020). Telework and sustainable travel during the COVID-19 Era (SSRN Scholarly Paper No. 3638885). https://doi.org/10.2139/ssrn.3638885.

Riva, G., Wiederhold, B. K., & Mantovani, F. (2021). Surviving COVID-19: The neuroscience of smart working and distance learning. *Cyberpsychology, Behavior, and Social Networking, 24*(2), 79–85. https://doi.org/10.1089/cyber.2021.0009

Roberson, Q. M. (2006). Disentangling the meanings of diversity and inclusion in organizations. *Group & Organization Management, 31*(2), 212–236. https://doi.org/10.1177/1059601104273064

Rock, D. (2020). The NLI interview: Patagonia's dean Carter on how to treat employees like people. *Forbes*. https://www.forbes.com/sites/davidrock/2020/01/09/the-nli-interview-patagonias-dean-carter-on-how-to-treat-employees-like-people/?sh=303392f6188c

Rogers, B. (2021). Our brains need breaks from virtual meetings. *Forbes*. https://www.forbes.com/sites/brucerogers/2021/04/20/our-brains-need-breaks-from-virtual-meetings/

Romanelli, M., & Ferrara, M. (2024). Liberare i talenti nelle organizzazioni inclusive. *Prospettive in Organizzazione*. https://ricerca.uniparthenope.it/handle/11367/129176?mode=full

Saedi, S., Fini, A. A. F., Khanzadi, M., Wong, J., Sheikhkhoshkar, M., & Banaei, M. (2022). Applications of electroencephalography in construction. *Automation in Construction, 133*, 103985. https://doi.org/10.1016/j.autcon.2021.103985

Saker-Clark, H. (2024, May 20). Workplaces must change attitudes to neurodiversity, says chef Heston Blumenthal. *The Independent*. https://www.independent.co.uk/business/workplaces-must-change-attitudes-to-neurodiversity-says-chef-heston-blumenthal-b2547734.html

Salmon, J. (2021, May 19). *Insolvencies down, inflation up*. The Credit Protection Association. https://cpa.co.uk/insolvencies-down-inflation-up-business-news-190521/.

Samant, S. M., & Sangle, S. (2016). A selected literature review on the changing role of stakeholders as value creators. *World Journal of Science, Technology and Sustainable Development, 13*(2), 100–119. https://doi.org/10.1108/WJSTSD-01-2016-0002

Sandoval, A. V., & Castillo, L. C. Z. (2021). A theoretical approach to neuroscience technologies' contributions to administration in the digital transformation context. *Cuadernos de Administración, 37*(69), e4010691. https://doi.org/10.25100/cdea.v37i69.10691

Schaefer, S. D., Cunningham, P., Diehl, S., & Terlutter, R. (2024). Employees' positive perceptions of corporate social responsibility create beneficial outcomes for firms and their employees: Organizational pride as a mediator. *Corporate Social Responsibility and Environmental Management, 31*(3), 2574–2587. https://doi.org/10.1002/csr.2699

Sharman, L. (2020). Household recycling "soared" during pandemic. https://www.localgov.co.uk/Household-recycling-soared-during-pandemic/51261.

Scudamore, B. (2018, June 18). How to grow your business in the "Do It For Me" economy. *Forbes*.

Shen, J., Chanda, A., D'Netto, B., & Monga, M. (2009). Managing diversity through human resource: An international perspective and conceptual framework. *International Journal of Human Resource Management, 20*(2), 235–251. https://doi.org/10.1080/09585190802670516

Sherbin, L., & Rashid, R. (2017). Diversity doesn't stick without inclusion. *Harvard Business Review*.

Shreedhar, G., Laffan, K., & Giurge, L. M. (2022, March 7). Is remote work actually better for the environment? *Harvard Business Review*. https://hbr.org/2022/03/is-remote-work-actually-better-for-the-environment

Stafford-Smith, M., Griggs, D., Gaffney, O., Ullah, F., Reyers, B., Kanie, N., Stigson, B., Shrivastava, P., Leach, M., & O'Connell, D. (2017). Integration: The key to implementing the sustainable development goals. *Sustainability Science, 12*(6), 911–919. https://doi.org/10.1007/s11625-016-0383-3

Stankevičiūtė, Z., Tursunbayeva, A., & Moschera, L. (2024). Linking people analytics, HRM practices and sustainable development goals reporting: An interpretative framework. In R. Agrifoglio, A. Lazazzara, & S. Za (Eds.), *Navigating digital transformation: Organizational change, digital work, and individual behavior*. Springer Nature.

Tang, G., Chen, Y., Jiang, Y., Paillé, P., & Jia, J. (2018). Green human resource management practices: Scale development and validity. *Asia Pacific Journal of Human Resources, 56*(1), 31–55. https://doi.org/10.1111/1744-7941.12147

The Workday® Human Capital Management. (2022). Employee expectations report 2022. Heartbeat by Workday. https://heartbeat.peakon.com/reports/employee-expectations-2022/.

Thomas, K. M., Tran, N. M., & Dawson, B. L. (2010). An inclusive strategy of teaching diversity. *Advances in Developing Human Resources, 12*(3), 295–311.

Todisco, L., Tomo, A., Canonico, P., & Mangia, G. (2023). The bright and dark side of smart working in the public sector: Employees' experiences before and during COVID-19. *Management Decision, 61*(13), 85–102. https://doi.org/10.1108/MD-02-2022-0164

Tursunbayeva, A., Di Lauro, S., & Pagliari, C. (2018). People analytics—a scoping review of conceptual boundaries and value propositions. *International Journal of Information Management, 43*, 224–247. https://doi.org/10.1016/j.ijinfomgt.2018.08.002

Tursunbayeva, A., Pagliari, C., Di Lauro, S., & Antonelli, G. (2022). The ethics of people analytics: Risks, opportunities and recommendations. *Personnel Review, 51*(3), 900–921. https://doi.org/10.1108/PR-12-2019-0680

Waldman, D. A., Balthazard, P. A., & Peterson, S. J. (2011). Social cognitive neuroscience and leadership. *The Leadership Quarterly, 22*(6), 1092–1106. https://doi.org/10.1016/j.leaqua.2011.09.005

Waldman, D. A., Ward, M. K., & Becker, W. J. (2017). Neuroscience in organizational behavior. *Annual Review of Organizational Psychology and Organizational Behavior, 4*(1), 425–444. https://doi.org/10.1146/annurev-orgpsych-032516-113316

Waldman, D. A., Wang, D., & Fenters, V. (2019). The added value of neuroscience methods in organizational research. *Organizational Research Methods, 22*(1), 223–249. https://doi.org/10.1177/1094428116642013

Willness, C. R., & Jones, D. A. (2013). Corporate environmental sustainability and employee recruitment: Leveraging "Green" business practices to attract talent. In *Green organizations*. Routledge.

Wittenberg-Cox, A. (2020). What do countries with the best coronavirus responses have in common? Women leaders. *Forbes*. https://www.forbes.com/sites/avivahwittenbergcox/2020/04/13/what-do-countries-with-the-best-coronavirus-reponses-have-in-common-women-leaders/?sh=7ec37c253dec

Yadav, S., & Lenka, U. (2020). Diversity management: A systematic review. *Equality, Diversity and Inclusion: An International Journal, 39*(8), 901–929. https://doi.org/10.1108/EDI-07-2019-0197

Yamaguchi, N. U., Bernardino, E. G., Ferreira, M. E. C., de Lima, B. P., Pascotini, M. R., & Yamaguchi, M. U. (2023). Sustainable development goals: A bibliometric analysis of literature reviews. *Environmental Science and Pollution Research, 30*(3), 5502–5515. https://doi.org/10.1007/s11356-022-24379-6

Zhao, H., Zhou, Q., He, P., & Jiang, C. (2021). How and when does socially responsible HRM affect employees' organizational citizenship behaviors toward the environment? *Journal of Business Ethics, 169*(2), 371–385. https://doi.org/10.1007/s10551-019-04285-7

Zibarras, L. D., & Coan, P. (2015). HRM practices used to promote pro-environmental behavior: A UK survey. *The International Journal of Human Resource Management, 26*(16), 2121–2142. https://doi.org/10.1080/09585192.2014.972429

Zito, M., Bilucaglia, M., Fici, A., Gabrielli, G., & Russo, V. (2021). Job assessment through bioelectrical measures: A neuromanagement perspective. *Frontiers in Psychology, 12*. https://doi.org/10.3389/fpsyg.2021.673012

Žliobaitė, I., & Custers, B. (2016). Using sensitive personal data may be necessary for avoiding discrimination in data-driven decision models. *Artificial Intelligence and Law, 24*(2), 183–201. https://doi.org/10.1007/s10506-016-9182-5

# Chapter 7
# Artificial Intelligence for Human Resource Management: Organizational Enlightenment or an Ethical Minefield?

## 7.1 Challenges of Artificial Intelligence

As the previous book chapters described, there is much hype around the transformative potential of AI across various HRM practices and configurations. AI promises to streamlines routine administrative tasks through automation and algorithmic management. Moreover, AI can enhance relational HRM throughout the employee life cycle. The integration of AI can also augment HRM practices and functions by providing invaluable insights on diversity attributes, employee emotions, feelings, and thoughts for strengthening D&I and contributing to organizational sustainability actions. All these sound like organizational enlightenment. However, the fear perspective suggests that such advanced tools can also generate previously unseen concerns, risks, and challenges. Below, the reasons why AI in HRM can be considered an ethical, if not legal, minefield are explored by separately addressing the challenges AI presents for both employees and organizations.

## 7.2 Challenges for Employees

AI can collect and analyze employee data throughout their life cycle. All of us here are very excited about this, aren't we? This is because such data promise to generate actionable insights different HRM practices, including onboarding, HR development, performance appraisal, or HR retention. The challenge lies in these data's highly sensitive, granular, and personal nature (Tursunbayeva et al., 2022). Unlike most other forms of business analytics, such as supply chain analysis, money flows, or financial performance, where humans are not the direct focus, using AI and



A. Tursunbayeva, *Augmenting Human Resource Management with Artificial Intelligence*, Contributions to Management Science,
https://doi.org/10.1007/978-3-031-75266-7_7

analytics in HRM can have direct implications on employees (Giermindl et al., 2022). Indeed, employees are only marginally affected by analytics in other organizational functions. For instance, employing business analytics to highlight inefficiencies in business processes and subsequently cutting costs based on those insights is generally accepted. However, applying similar analytics or AI algorithms to analyze, evaluate, and manage employees raises ethical and moral concerns (Tursunbayeva et al., 2022).

What makes some people particularly worried is that the types of data organizations can collect and analyze on their employees are increasing. These types of data go beyond the traditional sources of HRM data, such as the ones coming from CVs or employee reports. An example often mentioned here is the data from wearables provided to employees by employers (Gauttier, 2019), social media data, data from emails (Charbonneau & Doberstein, 2020), or, more recently also data on COVID-19 vaccinations or test results (Tursunbayeva & Pagliari, 2023) which many organizations had started to collect since the start of the COVID-19 emergency, and which specifically could fall under employees' sensitive health data category.

The types of data that organizations can collect on employees are also getting, in a sense, more unusual, or some call it even "creepier." Indeed, today, such data can include data on diversity dimensions or attributes, or even neuroscience-related data, as discussed in a previous chapter, that can challenge "neuro privacy"-our last privacy fortress (Farahany, 2023). From one side, in the era of AI and analytics, organizations are reported to be turning all such data into insights for increasing employees' health, safety, and engagement, predicting how to identify and attract suitable candidates, or even protecting employees during the pandemic by mitigating the risks of workplace COVID-19 infections. However, from another side, such data also allows organizations to generate deep individual-target insights about employees' professional and personal lives (Tursunbayeva et al., 2022).

Another concern raised frequently about AI for HRM is the potential pervasive nature of the methods that can be adopted. Such debates comprise, for example, employee monitoring, surveillance, and tracking and how these encounter issues related to privacy, data protection, or employees' autonomy. AI is frequently positioned as a tool for managers and organizations to track and monitor their employees, both in the workplace and, sometimes, in their personal lives, such as through mobile phones or social media accounts. Excessive monitoring can encroach on personal privacy and intrude into private lives. Gartner recently discovered that more than 50% of the 239 large corporations surveyed employ "nontraditional" monitoring methods, such as tracking meetings, analyzing emails and social media, or examining automated phone transcripts (Wartzman, 2019). Other research supports these findings, showing that prominent performance appraisal systems use employee data from sources like surveys (76%), integrated HRM and financial systems (87%), and social media (17%) (Agarwal et al., 2018). A 2017 survey by Career Builder of 2300 hiring managers also found that 70% used social media to screen candidates, and 54% discovered content on social media that led them to decide against hiring a candidate (Mann et al., 2018). The primary reason was candidates posting provocative or inappropriate content. Most employees accept digital monitoring (Tursunbayeva et al., 2022). A blog for the Academy to Innovate HR by Mann et al. (2018) highlighted a survey by ExecuNet, which found that 82% of employees expect potential employers to "Google" them, while only 33% have Googled themselves. This expectation is attributed to organizations effectively convincing employees that sharing personal information is beneficial, thus transforming the perception of workplace monitoring from "authoritarian" to "participatory surveillance" (Marchant, 2019; Wartzman, 2019).

Employee monitoring and surveillance is a topic that has been discussed previously. However, it has received a massive increase since the COVID-19 pandemic, when many employees moved to hybrid or fully remote working arrangements. Many organizations have started adopting experimental monitoring methods to navigate the risk of, for example, infections among their workforce (Tursunbayeva & Pagliari, 2023). Research commissioned by the Information Commissioner's Office (2023) revealed that one in five UK adults believe their employer has monitored them. However, 70% of the surveyed public found it intrusive to be monitored at/for work.

Indeed, compared to the methods already widely used on personal data for other purposes (e.g., marketing), the use of data in HRM could be different. Firstly, in the case of the former, people are usually aware that their personal details, such as their private social media activities or cell phone usage, are stored and transformed for further use (Giermindl et al., 2022). Meanwhile, in the organizational context, employees are usually less aware of the extent to which employers can harvest and evaluate their data (Giermindl et al., 2022). Secondly, in private lives, people can also opt out of using specific websites or sharing information about specific aspects of their lives. Contrarily, at work, people are financially dependent on their employers. Thus, they might only sometimes be able to object to their data being analyzed or shared with external analytics providers (Giermindl et al., 2022). Finally, employees might not even know that their data is being collected or analyzed at specific times or for some specific purposes. An extreme allegory/metaphor that is used to represent employee surveillance is the Panopticon. The Panopticon is a prison design conceived in 1791 by philosopher and jurist Jeremy Bentham. This structure allows a single observer in a central tower to monitor all prisoners without them knowing if they are being watched at any given moment. Inspired by Argo Panoptes from Greek mythology, the design symbolizes invisible power and has inspired science fiction novels such as WE by Yevgeny Zamyatin and 1984 by George Orwell, among others. The Panopticon setup encourages prisoners to self-regulate their behavior, fostering discipline and order. Over time, the concept has evolved to represent the broader relationship between individuals and societal rules. Mustafa Suleyman (2023), the co-founder of Deepmind-one of the leading AI companies-and Infection AI, in his "The Coming Wave" book co-written with Michael Bhaskar, has stated that what in the past was a part of science fiction today is already implemented in practice at homes, streets, and workplaces in many contexts. He referred to these new monitoring methods as a high-tech panopticon.

One of the main expected benefits of AI in HRM is to assist humans in decision-making (Rodgers et al., 2023), augmenting their capabilities by, for example, enabling them to draw on different sources and quantities of data to detect patterns and correlations. In some cases, AI can even substitute humans in decision-making processes, including those related to HRM practices such as R&S or performance management. Such algorithmic decision-making offers strategic opportunities for organizations and individuals (Newell & Marabelli, 2015). For instance, a meta-analysis of 136 studies found that, on average, algorithms were 10% more accurate than human judgment (Grove et al., 2000). A recent study investigating factors contributing to group success examined the ability of humans and machines to predict success from group photos. Analyzing over 43,000 photos, the study found that humans could guess success with 58.3% accuracy, which improved to around 67% with some training, while machine learning algorithms had an accuracy of up to 71.6% (Saveski et al., 2021).

At the same time, assisted, augmented, or even purely algorithmic decision-making has also raised discussions around (unintended) outcomes for individuals, organizations, and society. For example, who is responsible for the decision made by an algorithm? Human or algorithm? There are also concerns that such decision-making could marginalize human reasoning or even erode managerial competencies. Moreover, with the increasing analytical power, the decisions made by AI are expected to become increasingly opaque, inaccessible, and untraceable regarding their underlying assumptions, mechanisms, and processes (Ozmen Garibay et al., 2023). This implies that some decisions could be hard to understand or explain, even for line or HRM managers, without the actual technology designers. In extreme cases, it is even mentioned that if/when advanced self-learning algorithms are applied also, their designers would have a hard time explaining the rationale behind the outcomes of such algorithms due to their unpredictability (Ozmen Garibay et al., 2023).

However, the rationale for utilizing AI algorithms in decision-making hinges on the belief that they are objective; many are indeed crafted with genuine intentions to support HRM decisions through data rather than potentially biased human judgment (Tursunbayeva et al., 2022). Despite this, because humans create these systems, there remains a risk that prejudice, misunderstandings, and biases could be embedded in these algorithms. An illustrative example of this concern is Amazon's case. In 2015, Amazon found that its recruitment system, designed to screen software developers, was biased against female candidates due to being trained on resumes predominantly from men, leading the system to favor male applicants. Despite attempts to address the bias, Amazon abandoned the system in 2018 (Dastin, 2018). Similarly, Facebook's ad-targeting algorithms faced a lawsuit from the Communications Workers of America, which alleged that Facebook's platform was used for age-discriminatory job ads. The lawsuit began when a jobseeker noticed she received different ads from her daughter, leading to a broader class action against companies using Facebook's advertising tools (Fernández Campbell, 2018).

Thus, it is evident that AI for HRM can have unintended consequences in different HRM practices. Below are some illustrative examples of reported backfired AI for/in R&S, T&D, and performance management that made it to the headlines and generated significant public debates (Table 7.1).

**Table 7.1** Examples of reported backfired AI for HRM

| HRM practice | Example |
|---|---|
| R&S | *"The American Civil Liberties Union* [ACLU] *alleged in a complaint to regulators that a large consulting firm* [Aon Consulting, Inc.] *is selling AI-powered hiring tools that discriminate against job candidates on the basis of disability and race, despite marketing these services to businesses as "bias free"...*<br>*In its complaint, the ACLU said Aon's algorithmically driven personality test, ADEPT-15, relies on questions that adversely impact autistic and neurodivergent people, as well as people with mental health disabilities. Aon also offers an AI-infused video interviewing system and a gamified cognitive assessment service that are likely to discriminate based on race and disability, according to the complaint."* (Alba & Yin, 2024) |
| R&S | *"Amazon had to withdraw a machine learning system for sorting through job applications. It was designed to replicate existing hiring practices, using 10 years of past data, but "learned" a bias against women applicants based on that data (acquisition)."* (Dastin, 2018) |
| R&S | *"Woman are less likely than men to be shown ads for high paid jobs on Google and LinkedIn. The models built for displaying these adds used information such as personal information, browsing history and internet activity."* (Gibbs, 2015) |
| T&D | *"Back in 1988, the UK Commission for Racial Equality found a British medical school guilty of discrimination. The computer program it was using to determine which applicants would be invited for interviews was determined to be biased against women and those with non-European names. However, the program had been developed to match human admissions decisions, doing so with 90 to 95 percent accuracy. What's more, the school had a higher proportion of non-European students admitted than most other London medical schools."* (Selimi, 2021) |
| Performance management | *"Teachers in Houston, Texas, US have challenged the legality of the use of Education Value-Added Assessment System (EVAAS) scores to judge individual teachers (including dismissing them from their positions), on the grounds that teachers had no way to ensure that EVAAS was correctly calculating their performance score, nor was there a way to promptly correct a mistake. The latter point has much wider significance: because of the comparative nature of the method used in EVAAS, any error (in data or in the algorithm) in calculating the score for one teacher would potentially affect the scores for all other teachers in that district."* (Edwards & Rodriguez, 2019) |

(continued)

**Table 7.1** (continued)

| HRM practice | Example |
|---|---|
| Performance management | *"The [IBM] company introduced an algorithm that used points to evaluate workers' performance. The more points an employee received, the more protected that employee was from the risk of termination (www.reddit.com). However, the algorithm was poorly constructed - it gave more points to employees who were relatively new to the job. In other words, employees who had worked for IBM for only a few years received more points than those who had been there longer. As a result, those with no points had worked for IBM for an average of 30 years, while those with the most points had an average tenure of 15 years. The points did not reflect employees' skills. Notably, 80% of the more experienced, older workers were evaluated by the company itself as 'good enough to stay at current job levels or be promoted'."* (Minbaeva, 2021) |
| Generic | *"People are not ready for "digital workers" just yet. That's the lesson learned by Sarah Franklin, the CEO of Lattice, a human resources and performance management platform that offers performance coaching, talent reviews, onboarding automation, compensation management and a host of other HR tools to more than 5000 organizations around the world* [that was suspended after three days due to intense pushback on Sarah's company's plans on social media]." (Marks, 2024) |

Data on individual employees' performance patterns, combined with information from emails and questionnaires, is being utilized to "feed" algorithms that send personalized messages to influence or "nudge" behavior (Tursunbayeva et al., 2022). Drawing on principles from behavioral economics and persuasive psychology (Thaler & Sunstein, 2021), these messages aim to help individuals, teams, or organizations achieve work-related goals. An example of such an AI for HRM tool could be Humu, founded by former Google executive Laszlo Bock. Humu's "nudge engine" can set up reminders, prompt questions during meetings, and encourage employee-centric activities like retirement savings or healthier snacks (Wakabayashi, 2018; High, 2019). While the company has been keen to show its ethical credentials by emphasizing its respect for privacy and its ability to influence employees' job satisfaction (High, 2019), critics have pointed to a lack of transparency around the purposes of nudges and uncertainties over whether employees know they are being nudged, raising ethical questions around users' information rights, effects on their autonomy and protection from manipulation (Wakabayashi, 2018). The company was acquired by Perceptyx in 2023. In announcing the acquisition, Perceptyx CEO John Borland highlighted the importance of listening to employees (Moody, 2023). "By adding Humu's ground-breaking nudge technology to our AI-powered platform, we can help all employees influence positive change at every level, improving both the employee experience and business results" (Moody, 2023).

Indeed, AI algorithms are currently widely used to monitor and measure the performance of individuals, teams, and organizational workforce (Tursunbayeva et al., 2022). At the individual level, in the era of AI for HRM, it is possible to quantify and profile performance and time usage even at a distance. Proponents argue that this can provide workers with objective insights about their performance, optimize their development, and improve the objectivity of promotion decisions (Chowdhury, 2018). Despite these worthy goals, human performance can be too complex. Indeed, as concluded by a world-famous psychologist and winner of the Nobel Prize in Economics, a significant portion of human behavior is not entirely rational (Kahneman, 2013). For instance, people often delay tasks, overspend, and make poor choices in various areas of life. Thus, reducing employee performance to numbers can devalue other essential characteristics that are harder to measure and have also been criticized for lacking context (O'Neil, 2016a, b). A notable example supporting this claim is the tennis match between Nadal and Medvedev, where an algorithm predicted Nadal had only a 4% chance of winning, while Medvedev was given a 96% likelihood of victory. Just a few hours later, Nadal emerged as the champion of his second Australian Open (Ezra, 2022). The potential risks of miscalculation and misinterpretation of data can, overall, weigh very heavily in organizational HRM practices in comparison to other business settings, as these can determine employees' future career prospects, thus directly impacting not only their professional lives but also their private sphere (Tursunbayeva et al., 2022).

At the team level, AI offers insights that could enhance productivity and engagement by analyzing team performance and mistakes, as seen with companies like Microsoft (Hogan, 2016). Even NASA deployed AI technology on the International Space Station. Their CIMON robot was sent as an intelligent assistant to aid astronauts with various tasks during their space missions (Shaikh & Cruz, 2023). However, the lab experiment on AI within human teams indicated that there could be unforeseen effects on cognitive abilities related to problem-solving, the development of group cohesion, creativity, and team interdependency (Shaikh & Cruz, 2023). Moreover, treating teams like machines where "suboptimal" members might be replaced and potentially overlooking the importance of diversity and collaborative synergy were also highlighted as potential ethical concerns in analyzing team performance with AI (O'Neil, 2016a, b).

At a broader level, some projects have been criticized for focusing on organizational populations rather than individuals or teams. This approach can lead to data and machine learning systems prioritizing idealized traits, potentially resulting in a uniform workforce that lacks the advantages of individual diversity (O'Neil, 2016a, b). A significant factor driving homogenization is the "winner-takes-all" mindset frequently associated with AI-driven optimization (Würzburg, 2023). Algorithms designed to maximize specific outcomes-such as profit or engagement-tend to favor only the most efficient solutions. This can result in a feedback loop where the most popular products, ideas, or cultural phenomena are continuously reinforced and amplified. At the same time, those that deviate from the norm are ignored or discarded (Würzburg, 2023).

Specific AI-driven HRM tools have been criticized for causing disruptions to employees, especially by automatically changing work schedules in industries with fluid workforces (Samaan & Tursunbayeva, 2024). Such algorithms often prioritize business needs, resulting in inconsistent weekly schedules that disrupt employees' personal planning. For example, Starbucks incorporated various data sources, such as weather and pedestrian patterns, into its scheduling software, leading to uncertainty regarding shift work availability (O'Neil, 2016a, b). The variability in work hours can lead to fluctuating paychecks, causing financial stress for those relying on stable income. Additionally, algorithms can implement short-notice schedule changes, further inconveniencing employees. The lack of employee input in algorithmic scheduling can result in work schedules disregarding individual needs or preferences. For example, a study of Uber drivers found that while they are theoretically in control of their work, deviating from the company's algorithms could result in being banned from the platform (Mohlmann & Henfridsson, 2019).

Finally, trust in AI within the workplace is a significant concern. A comprehensive MIT database of risks from AI captured more than 700 risks, which they categorized into seven domains, including Discrimination and Toxicity; Privacy and security; Misinformation; Malicious actors and misuse; Human–computer interaction; Socioeconomic and environmental harms; and AI system safety, failure and limitations (MIT Future Tech, 2024). At the same time, the Workday Global Survey found that only 62% of C-suite executives and 52% of employees trust AI, with 23% of employees doubting that their organizations prioritize their interests when deploying AI (Workday, 2024). Additionally, 63% of employees suspect their employers are tracking sensitive data about them, and 72% believe their companies are not transparent about data collection (Pease, 2018). This lack of transparency and constant surveillance can lead to employees gaming the system (Jacobs, 2017).

## 7.3 Challenges for Organizations

The risks associated with AI in HRM are challenging also for organizations. Successful implementation of AI innovations in HRM relies heavily on addressing privacy concerns, maintaining a human-centered approach, and ensuring employee acceptability (Tursunbayeva et al., 2022). A survey by Insight222 revealed that 81% of companies face issues with data ethics and privacy in their workforce analytics projects, and 84% require guidance on the fair use and privacy of new data sources (Petersen, 2018). Since AI for HRM is relatively new, there is a lack of historical legal, ethical, or risk management precedents, and existing strategies may not be fully applicable, making it difficult for organizations to identify potential failures (Calvard & Jeske, 2018).

Organizations are also reportedly putting AI projects on hold due to uncertainty over their regulatory compliance, particularly with the EU General Data Protection Regulation (GDPR) and emerging AI regulations (Ryan-Mosley et al., 2024). However, while the EU GDPR and AI Act represent significant advancements in employee rights in the digital era, they only apply to EU citizens, albeit also to companies processing their data overseas. Nevertheless, there is a lack of regulatory frameworks in other areas, especially in numerous developing countries (Ryan-Mosley et al., 2024).

Determining what is acceptable versus feasible is a significant challenge for HRM professionals. This echoes the quote from the Jurassic Park movie: "Scientists were so preoccupied with whether or not they could, they didn't stop to think if they should" (Scott & Dargis, 2020). Similarly, it is central to consider legal, moral, and ethical dilemmas in AI projects. This was effectively discussed in Deloitte's 2017 Human Capital Trends report.

Technologies are developing at an exponential rate. Individuals quickly adopt innovations. For instance, in January 2023, a study by professional social network Fishbowl revealed that 30% of 4500 professionals working for Amazon, Bank of America, JPMorgan, Google, Twitter, and Meta reported they had used OpenAI's ChatGPT or another AI in their work (Bloomberg, 2023). Nearly 70% of these respondents have said they do not disclose usage to their bosses (Christian, 2023). Conversely, organizations evolve slower due to corporate planning, organizational structure, job design, goal-setting, and management practices that originated in the first industrial age. For instance, Citigroup, Bank of America, Deutsche Bank, Goldman Sachs, and Wells Fargo have restricted their employees' use of ChatGPT. These institutions were joined by JPMorgan Chase, Amazon, and several major public school districts to limit the use of OpenAI's new chatbot due to raised concerns about sharing sensitive information (Bushard, 2023). Lastly, public policy directly impacts businesses through regulation, taxes, and legislation and adapts even more slowly. The current regulation on AI is currently behind real-world practices. This disparity between public policy and the other three domains (i.e., the level of technological development and individual and organizational adoption levels) creates imbalances and challenges for business and HRM leaders. These gaps, referred to as grey zones, should be addressed by implementing ethical guidelines within organizations.

Finally, the agenda in AI for HRM projects is often accused of being left to technologists, computer scientists, or vendors when what is really needed are experts in human behavior and ethics (Calvard & Jeske, 2018). The lack of diversity in the profiles of such AI-related professionals was also associated with some human biases that can be embedded in AI. For example, minority groups are underrepresented in the AI industry. The statistics at leading technology companies are particularly disheartening: Black employees comprise only 2.5% of Google's workforce and 4% of Facebook's and Microsoft's workforces, as reported in MIT Sloan Management Review paper (Howard & Isbell, 2020). Gender disparities are also pronounced, with only 22% of AI professionals being female globally, compared to 78% being male. This lack of diversity extends to academia, which is concerning since universities are the primary training grounds for AI professionals (Howard & Isbell, 2020).

## References

Agarwal, D., Bersin, J., Lahiri, G., Schwartz, J., & Volini, E. (2018). People data: How far is too far? *Deloitte Insights*. https://www2.deloitte.com/insights/us/en/focus/human-capital-trends/2018/people-data-analytics-risks-opportunities.html.

Alba, D., & Yin, L. (2024). ACLU says in FTC complaint that Aon's AI tools discriminatory. *Bloomberg News*. https://news.bloomberglaw.com/artificial-intelligence/aclu-says-in-ftc-complaint-that-aons-ai-tools-discriminatory

Bloomberg, J. C. (2023). Survey reveals 30% of professionals have tried ChatGPT at work. *TIME*. https://time.com/6248707/survey-chatgpt-ai-use-at-work/

Bushard, B. (2023). Workers' ChatGPT use restricted at more banks—Including Goldman, Citigroup. *Forbes*. https://www.forbes.com/sites/brianbushard/2023/02/24/workers-chatgpt-use-restricted-at-more-banks-including-goldman-citigroup/

Calvard, T. S., & Jeske, D. (2018). Developing human resource data risk management in the age of big data. *International Journal of Information Management, 43*, 159–164. https://doi.org/10.1016/j.ijinfomgt.2018.07.011

Charbonneau, É., & Doberstein, C. (2020). An empirical assessment of the intrusiveness and reasonableness of emerging work surveillance technologies in the public sector. *Public Administration Review, 80*(5), 780–791. https://doi.org/10.1111/puar.13278

Chowdhury, R. (2018). How human-centric AI can help your employees love Mondays again. *Forbes*. https://www.forbes.com/sites/rummanchowdhury/2018/03/16/how-human-centric-ai-can-help-your-employees-love-mondays-again/#61944ac63f45

Christian, A. (2023). The employees secretly using AI at work. *BBC*. https://www.bbc.com/worklife/article/20231017-the-employees-secretly-using-ai-at-work

Dastin, J. (2018). Amazon scraps secret AI recruiting tool that showed bias against women. *Reuters*. https://www.reuters.com/article/us-amazon-com-jobs-automation-insight/amazon-scraps-secret-ai-recruiting-tool-that-showed-bias-against-women-idUSKCN1MK08G.

Edwards, J. S., & Rodriguez, E. (2019). Remedies against bias in analytics systems. *Journal of Business Analytics, 2*(1), 74–87. https://doi.org/10.1080/2573234X.2019.1633890

Ezra. (2022). *During a moment of the match, Nadal had a 4% chance of winning. It was a milestone against AI*. Bullfrag. https://www.bullfrag.com/during-a-moment-of-the-match-nadal-had-a-4-chance-of-winning-it-was-a-milestone-against-ai/.

Farahany, N. A. (2023). *The Battle for your brain: Defending the right to think freely in the age of neurotechnology*. St. Martin's Press.

Fernández Campbell, A. (2018). Facebook, Amazon, and hundreds of companies post targeted job ads that screen out older workers. *Vox*. https://www.vox.com/policy-and-politics/2018/5/31/17408884/facebook-amazon-job-ads-age-discrimination-lawsuit

Gauttier, S. (2019). Modifying consent procedures to collect better data: The case of stress-monitoring wearables in the workplace. In W. Abramowicz & R. Corchuelo (Eds.), *Business information systems* (pp. 350–360). Springer International Publishing. https://doi.org/10.1007/978-3-030-20485-3_27

Gibbs, S. (2015, July 8). Women less likely to be shown ads for high-paid jobs on Google, study shows. *The Guardian*. https://www.theguardian.com/technology/2015/jul/08/women-less-likely-ads-high-paid-jobs-google-study

Giermindl, L. M., Strich, F., Christ, O., Leicht-Deobald, U., & Redzepi, A. (2022). The dark sides of people analytics: Reviewing the perils for organisations and employees. *European Journal of Information Systems, 31*(3), 410–435. https://doi.org/10.1080/0960085X.2021.1927213

Grove, W. M., Zald, D. H., Lebow, B. S., Snitz, B. E., & Nelson, C. (2000). Clinical versus mechanical prediction: A meta-analysis. *Psychological Assessment, 12*(1), 19–30. https://doi.org/10.1037/1040-3590.12.1.19

High, P. (2019). Former Google HR chief Laszlo bock aims to revolutionize people management with Humu. *Forbes*. https://www.forbes.com/sites/peterhigh/2019/09/09/former-google-hr-chief-laszlo-bock-aims-to-revolutionize-people-management-with-humu/

Hogan, K. (2016). *Empower your employees to leverage their own data* [LinkedIn]. https://www.linkedin.com/pulse/empower-your-employees-leverage-own-data-kathleen-hogan/

Howard, A., & Isbell, C. (2020). Diversity in AI: The invisible men and women. *MIT Sloan Management Review*. https://sloanreview.mit.edu/article/diversity-in-ai-the-invisible-men-and-women/

Information Commissioner Office. (2023). *ICO publishes guidance to ensure lawful monitoring in the workplace*. Information Commissioner Office. https://ico.org.uk/about-the-ico/media-centre/news-and-blogs/2023/10/ico-publishes-guidance-to-ensure-lawful-monitoring-in-the-workplace/

Jacobs, K. (2017). The ethics of gathering employee data. *HR Magazine*. https://www.hrmagazine.co.uk/article-details/the-ethics-of-gathering-employee-data?utm_content=buffer54f95&utm_medium=social&utm_source=twitter.com&utm_campaign=buffer

Kahneman, D. (2013). *Thinking, fast and slow*. FSG Adult.

Mann, H., Neale, C., & Tajinder, K. (2018). *People analytics: Ethical considerations* [analytics in HR]. https://www.analyticsinhr.com/blog/people-analytics-ethical-considerations/?utm_source=twitter&utm_medium=social&utm_campaign=social-share

Marchant, G. E. (2019). What are best practices for ethical use of nanosensors for worker surveillance? *AMA Journal of Ethics, 21*(4), E356–E362. https://doi.org/10.1001/amajethics.2019.356

Marks, G. (2024, July 21). The world is not quite ready for 'digital workers.' *The Guardian*. https://www.theguardian.com/technology/article/2024/jul/21/ai-digital-workers-employment

Minbaeva, D. (2021). Disrupted HR? *Human Resource Management Review, 31*(4), 100820. https://doi.org/10.1016/j.hrmr.2020.100820

MIT Future Tech. (2024). *The AI risk repository*. https://airisk.mit.edu/#Repository-Overview

Mohlmann, M., & Henfridsson, O. (2019). What people hate about being managed by algorithms, according to a study of Uber drivers. *Harvard Business Review*. https://hbr.org/2019/08/what-people-hate-about-being-managed-by-algorithms-according-to-a-study-of-uber-drivers

Moody, K. (2023). *Humu, 'nudging' tool founded by ex-Google CHRO, acquired by Perceptyx. HR Dive*. https://www.hrdive.com/news/Perceptyx-acquires-humu-nudging-tool/690124/.

Newell, S., & Marabelli, M. (2015). Strategic opportunities (and challenges) of algorithmic decision-making: A call for action on the long-term societal effects of 'datification'. *The Journal of Strategic Information Systems, 24*(1), 3–14. https://doi.org/10.1016/j.jsis.2015.02.001

O'Neil, C. (2016a). 'Rogue algorithms' and the dark side of big data. *Knowledge at Wharton*. https://knowledge.wharton.upenn.edu/article/rogue-algorithms-dark-side-big-data/

O'Neil, C. (2016b). How algorithms rule our working lives. *The Guardian*. https://www.theguardian.com/science/2016/sep/01/how-algorithms-rule-our-working-lives

Ozmen Garibay, O., Winslow, B., Andolina, S., Antona, M., Bodenschatz, A., Coursaris, C., Falco, G., Fiore, S. M., Garibay, I., Grieman, K., Havens, J. C., Jirotka, M., Kacorri, H., Karwowski, W., Kider, J., Konstan, J., Koon, S., Lopez-Gonzalez, M., Maifeld-Carucci, I., Xu, W., et al. (2023). Six human-centered artificial intelligence grand challenges. *International Journal of Human–Computer Interaction, 39*(3), 391–437. https://doi.org/10.1080/10447318.2022.2153320

Pease, G. (2018). People analytics—Privacy vs. transparency. *Best Practice in Human Resources*. http://www.bestpracticeinhr.com/people-analytics-privacy-vs-transparency-2/

Petersen, D. (2018). *Data ethics: 6 steps for ethically sound people analytics* [Visier]. https://www.visier.com/clarity/six-steps-ethically-sound-people-analytics/

Rodgers, W., Murray, J. M., Stefanidis, A., Degbey, W. Y., & Tarba, S. Y. (2023). An artificial intelligence algorithmic approach to ethical decision-making in human resource management processes. *Human Resource Management Review, 33*(1), 100925. https://doi.org/10.1016/j.hrmr.2022.100925

Ryan-Mosley, T., Heikkilä, M., & Yang, Z. (2024). What's next for AI regulation in 2024? *MIT Technology Review*. https://www.technologyreview.com/2024/01/05/1086203/whats-next-ai-regulation-2024/

Samaan, D., & Tursunbayeva, A. (2024). Fluid workforce management in the health sector: Navigating the changing face of workforces and their management. *International Journal of Public Sector Management*, ahead-of-print(ahead-of-print). https://doi.org/10.1108/IJPSM-10-2023-0311

Saveski, M., Awad, E., Rahwan, I., & Cebrian, M. (2021). Algorithmic and human prediction of success in human collaboration from visual features. *Scientific Reports, 11*(1), 2756. https://doi.org/10.1038/s41598-021-81145-3

Scott, A. O., & Dargis, M. (2020, July 2). 'Jurassic Park': Where the wild things are. *The New York Times*. https://www.nytimes.com/2020/07/02/movies/jurassic-park.html

Selimi, S. (2021). *Is artificial intelligence discriminatory or simply reflective of humans?* https://www.helvetas.org/en/eastern-europe/about-us/follow-us/helvetas-mosaic/article/September2021/Is-Artificial-Intelligence-Discriminatory-or-Simply-Reflective-of-Humans-

Shaikh, S. J., & Cruz, I. F. (2023). AI in human teams: Effects on technology use, members' interactions, and creative performance under time scarcity. *AI & SOCIETY, 38*(4), 1587–1600. https://doi.org/10.1007/s00146-021-01335-5

Suleyman, M., & Bhaskar, M. (2023). *The coming wave: Technology, power, and the twenty-first century's greatest dilemma*. Crown.

Thaler, R. H., & Sunstein, C. R. (2021). *Nudge: Improving decisions about health, wealth, and happiness*. Penguin Books.

Tursunbayeva, A., & Pagliari, C. (2023). COVID-19 "passports" and the safe return to work: Consideration for HR professionals on how to navigate this new responsibility. In S. Bergum, P. Peters, & T. Vold (Eds.), *Virtual management and the new normal: New perspectives on HRM and leadership since the COVID-19 pandemic* (pp. 333–357). Springer International Publishing. https://doi.org/10.1007/978-3-031-06813-3_17

Tursunbayeva, A., Pagliari, C., Di Lauro, S., & Antonelli, G. (2022). The ethics of people analytics: Risks, opportunities and recommendations. *Personnel Review, 51*(3), 900–921. https://doi.org/10.1108/PR-12-2019-0680

Wakabayashi, D. (2018). Firm led by Google veterans uses A.I. To 'nudge' workers toward happiness. *The New York Times*. https://www.nytimes.com/2018/12/31/technology/human-resources-artificial-intelligence-humu.html

Wartzman, R. (2019). *Workplace tracking is growing fast. Most workers don't seem very concerned*. Fast Company. https://www.fastcompany.com/90318167/workplace-tracking-is-growing-fast-most-workers-dont-seem-very-concerned

Workday. (2024). *Workday Global Survey Reveals AI Trust Gap in the Workplace*. https://investor.workday.com/2024-01-10-Workday-Global-Survey-Reveals-AI-Trust-Gap-in-the-Workplace

Würzburg, T. (2023). *The power of AI: Is everything moving towards homogeneity?* https://www.linkedin.com/pulse/power-ai-everything-moving-towards-homogeneity-tom-w%C3%BCrzburg

# Chapter 8
# A Multilevel Responsible Artificial Intelligence Approach

## 8.1 The Need for a Multilevel Responsible Artificial Intelligence Approach

The complexity of AI integration in work and organizations, including the robustness and validity of AI-powered applications for HRM practices, poses significant challenges. Interdisciplinary researchers studying technologies and work raise concerns about these issues and the potential of AI to transform professions and their knowledge. They emphasized the need to examine the dynamic manifestations of these phenomena at different levels and within increasingly complex institutional contexts characterized by conflicting values, norms, and behaviors. Indeed, proactive steps are being taken at multiple levels to ensure AI deployment is more ethical, referred often to as Responsible AI RAI. In what follows, drawing on original research results, RAI activities occurring at macro (analysis of RAI guidelines), meso (analysis of AI for HRM vendor solutions), and micro (analysis of RAI competencies) levels are discussed.

## 8.2 Responsible Artificial Intelligence at Macro Level

At a macro level, the employment law is remarkably behind real-world practices, leaving many workers managed with the assistance of AI vulnerable to exploitation and discrimination (Kelly-Lyth & Thomas, 2023). In response to mounting concerns regarding AI a wide array of institutional actors at (inter)national fronts have taken proactive steps by establishing specialized expert committees such as the High-Level Expert Group on AI (appointed by the EU Commission), or the expert group on AI in Society within the Organization for Economic Cooperation and



A. Tursunbayeva, *Augmenting Human Resource Management with Artificial Intelligence*, Contributions to Management Science,
https://doi.org/10.1007/978-3-031-75266-7_8

Development Co-operation dedicated to addressing AI-related issues. These committees have either already produced or are actively in the process of generating the so-called RAI reports and guidance documents. There is now even an ISO standard (i.e., ISO/IEC 42001) for AI management systems, aiming to provide organizations with a structured approach to managing the risks and opportunities of AI, ensuring a balance between innovation and effective governance (ISO, 2024).

Adhering to these guiding principles, which refer to normative statements regarding the development, deployment, and governance of AI, is believed to mitigate or prevent any adverse effects that AI may bring to society (Wang & Siau, 2019). Professional associations and non-profit organizations, such as the Association of Computing Machinery, Access Now, and Amnesty International, have also joined this effort by issuing declarations and recommendations on AI ethics. The Catholic Church has partnered with Microsoft, IBM, the Food and Agriculture Organization of the UN, and the Italian Ministry for Innovation (part of the Italian Government) to launch the Rome Call for AI Ethics in February 2020 (RenAIssance Foundation, 2024). The objective of the call, as per the description of Vincenzo Paglia, the president of the Pontifical Academy for Life, is "to recognize and then to assume the responsibility that comes from the multiplication of options made possible by new digital technologies" (RenAIssance Foundation, 2024).

Algorithm Watch, an organization that tracks the effects of increased digitalization of everyday activities, identified over 170 AI guidelines in various stages of development as part of its AI Ethics Guidelines Global Inventory as of 2021. These guidelines cover various topics, such as artifacts and their development, implementation, use, and assessment guidelines (Deshpande & Sharp, 2022).

However, while there were numerous attempts to analyze "hard" AI laws or regulations in different contexts (Roberts et al., 2021) or for different industries (Shahlaei & Berente, 2024), a comprehensive and more importantly recent analysis of the global landscape of "soft" RAI guidelines containing non-legal norms issued by organizations is currently mostly missing. An exploratory attempt to analyze such international AI guidelines in 2018 identified 84 relevant documents in English, German, French, Italian, or Greek (Jobin et al., 2019). A more recent, ILO funded, research aims to refresh this knowledge by understanding which types of organizations have issued various RAI guidelines, their focus, and the principles to which they adhere (Di Lauro et al., 2024). Although still in progress, this research has already revealed 198 relevant ethical guidelines, of which 169 were included in the analysis. These come from 33 different countries or jurisdictions (see Fig. 8.1), most of which are economically developed countries such as the US (26%), UK (16%), EU (6%), Canada (3%), or are international (18%).

By drawing on the categorization proposed by Jobin et al. (2019), the analysis revealed (see Fig. 8.2) that existing guidelines come from private companies (24%); governmental agencies (21%); non-profit organizations, professional associations, and scientific societies (15%); academic and research institutions (13%); intergovernmental or supranational organizations (10%); private sector alliance (3%); religious organizations; political parties; federations of workers unions; science foundations; research alliances (all with 1%); and documents issued by

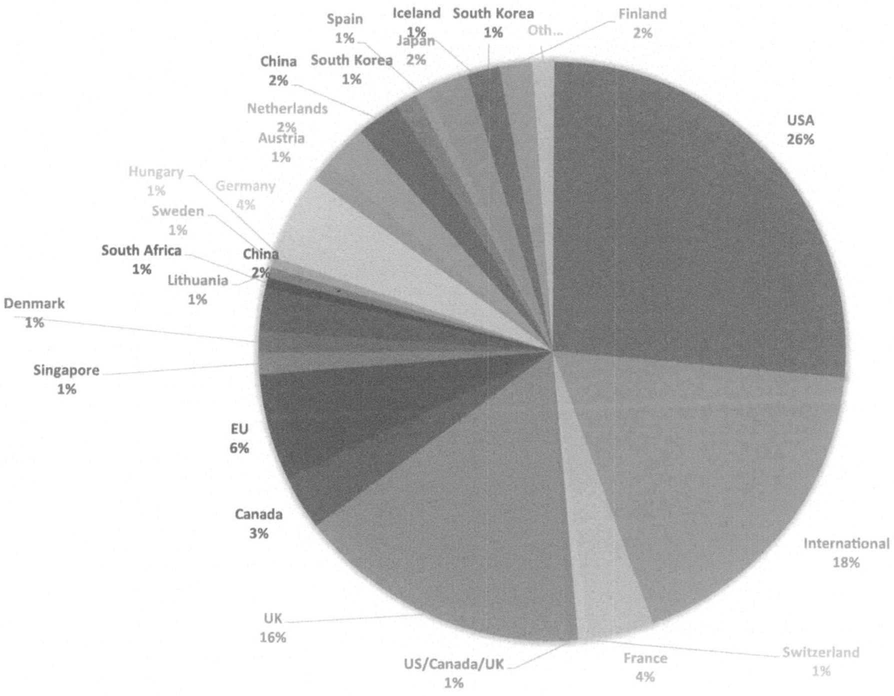


**Fig. 8.1** Geographical provenance of RAI guidelines

organizations belonging to more than one of the above categories or that could not be classified (9%).

The guidelines were published between 2011 and 2023. The data reveal a significant increase over time in the number of RAI guidelines, with 50% released in 2018 (see Fig. 8.3).

The increasing number and diversity of guidance documents reflect a growing interest in RAI principles globally. The surge in publications of RAI guidelines, peaking in 2018 and 2019, suggests a critical juncture where stakeholders have started recognizing the urgency of establishing ethical norms concerning AI development, implementation, and use. This could also be associated with the reported backfired AI cases discussed in the previous chapter (see Table 7.1), such as Amazon's gender-biased algorithm, which attracted the attention of the major public and regulators. Moreover, this could also be associated with enforcing GDPR in Europe. The varied contributions from private companies, non-profits, government, and intergovernmental organizations highlight the collaborative effort required to shape RAI. The engagement of a wide range of stakeholders also reflects the need for a well-rounded approach that considers different perspectives and expertise in RAI. The distribution of documents from both the public sector (governmental and intergovernmental organizations) and the private sector (companies and private sector alliances) indicates that RAI principles are relevant to both public and private

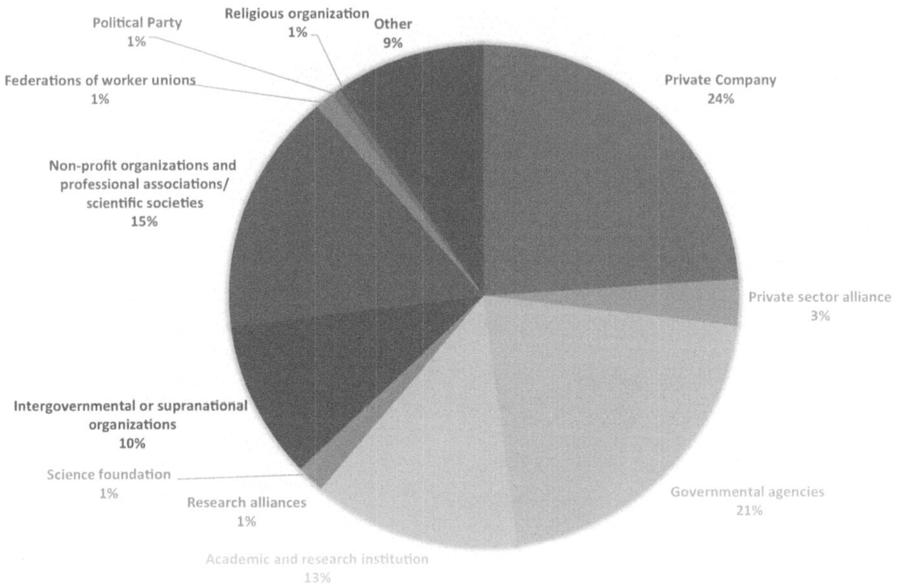


**Fig. 8.2** RAI guidelines by issuing organization

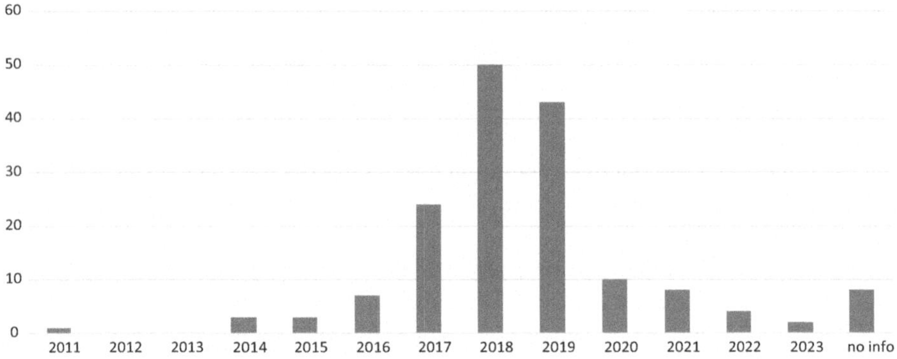


**Fig. 8.3** RAI guidelines by publication year

organizations. Additionally, the lack of representation from geographical areas such as Africa, South and Central America, the Middle East, and Central Asia potentially highlights unequal participation in the RAI discourse, revealing a power disparity in the international conversation. More economically developed countries seem to disproportionately influence this debate, raising concerns about the potential neglect of local knowledge, cultural diversity, and the imperative of global fairness. However, this lack of representation might also relate to the fact that the study reported above analyzes only the RAI guidelines in English.

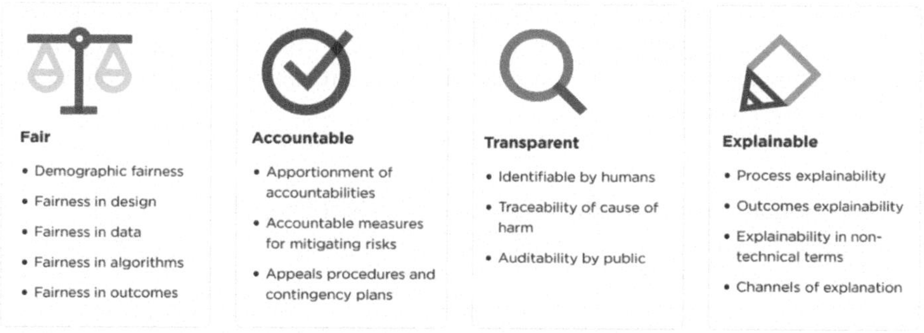


**Fig. 8.4** AI ethics principles by The Public Voice

The RAI principles in the analyzed guidelines are usually generic and comprise four to six principles. For example, the RAI principles proposed by the Public Voice Coalition established in 1996 for promoting public participation in decisions concerning the future of the Internet, included four key principles: Fair, Accountable, Transparent, and Explainable (The Public Voice, n.d.). See Fig. 8.4 for a brief description of these principles.

## 8.3 Responsible Artificial Intelligence at Meso Level

The development of the guidelines above is usually a multi-disciplinary effort that involves the integration of inputs from such fields as economics, law, ethics, computer science, and many others. However, the multiplicity of actors across different institutional fields, characterized by different sets of norms, values, and expectations (i.e., institutional logics) with respect to AI in general and what RAI means in particular, introduces significant complexity in explaining how these multiple and sometimes incompatible logics shape the emergence of a shared understanding of what RAI means in general, and specifically in the context of HRM.

Among the guidelines reported in the study above, none seem specific for developing, implementing, or using AI for HRM. Similarly, recent research has acknowledged no consensus on the definition and applications of RAI in the HRM domain (Bujold et al., 2023). Indeed, the same study followed the broad definition of RAI from Barredo Arrieta et al. (2020), which states that it is "[…] a series of AI principles to be necessarily met when deploying AI in real applications" (Barredo Arrieta et al., 2020, p. 83).

Meanwhile, useful ethical recommendations were proposed by an earlier scholarly study on AI-related People Analytics projects in/for HRM (Tursunbayeva et al., 2022). The results of this research published in 2022 in the Personnel Review journal concluded that the main recommendations for AI-related projects in HRM concerned transparency and diverse stakeholder inclusion, respecting privacy rights, fair and proportionate use of data, fostering a systemic culture of ethical practice, delivering benefits for employees, including ethical outcomes in business models, ensuring legal compliance and using ethical charters (Tursunbayeva et al., 2022). See the textbox below for a brief description of these recommendations, contextualized for AI for HRM projects.

**Recommendations for (ethical) AI-related HRM Projects**

Adopted from Tursunbayeva et al. (2022)

*Transparency and fairness*

Transparency is important in projects to ensure employee acceptance and avoid perceptions of unfairness (Manyika et al., 2019). Thus, organizations should clearly communicate the reasons for such projects and the benefits they bring to employees.

*Legal compliance*

Adherence to laws (Kim, 2017), such as GDPR, is essential.

*Ethical guidelines and charters*

Organizations must navigate rapidly evolving technologies "bearing in mind that what may be legal is not automatically ethical." Developing (Petersen, 2018) and aligning ethical charters with social norms (Guenole et al., 2018) and professional standards (e.g., CIPD) is recommended. This ensures that AI practices respect cultural differences and uphold ethical standards (Green, 2019).

*Proportionality and protection*

AI projects should focus on job-related data (Bersin, 2019), use aggregated and non-identifying data (Kumar, 2018) when possible, and ensure that data that is not permitted or no longer helpful is deleted (Jacobs, 2017). Transparency and security are critical as employee awareness grows (Haim, 2018).

*Data rights and consent*

Employees should be informed of their data rights and allowed to opt out of data collection (Kaupins & Minch, 2005). Consent should be renewed regularly, and participation should be voluntary (Mann et al., 2018).

*Inclusion of stakeholders*

Involving diverse stakeholders, including HRM professionals, legal and compliance officers, and employees (Leong, 2017), is essential for the success of the projects (Calvard & Jeske, 2018). However, the project control should be within internal HRM teams, who should carefully monitor AI decisions (Agarwal et al., 2018). New roles like Chief Data Officer can help protect privacy while aligning with corporate goals (Leong, 2017).

*People skills and culture*

AI stakeholder roles should ideally be filled internally to leverage company knowledge (Fleming et al., 2018). Ethics should be integrated into AI training and daily practices to ensure that ethical considerations are operationalized (West, 2018).

*Evaluation*

Continuous monitoring and evaluation of projects are essential for their potential risks and unintended outcomes (Pease, 2018), focusing on ethical impacts and people outcomes.

*Ethical business models*

There is a growing recognition that ethical considerations, alongside financial profits, are crucial in business models (Bersin, 2018).

Overall, the multiplicity and complexity of existing RAI frameworks have created significant challenges for vendors and users of AI for HRM in figuring out how to implement these frameworks within their products (for vendors) and HRM practices (for users). For instance, Clarke (2019), after synthesizing AI principles presented by 30 different organizations, has put forth a set of 50 RAI principles. Such complexity will likely reflect the institutional complexity that characterized its emergence and introduce further complexity regarding how these frameworks are translated into practice. Organizations adopting such principles need to balance conflicting and potentially incompatible logics (e.g., market, corporation, or professions), different RAI principles (e.g., accountability, trustworthiness, transparency, or fairness), and various requirements for efficiency and effectiveness in developing (for vendors) or adopting (for users) AI. Successful organizations, both developers and adopters, can embrace the inherent tensions within such paradoxes and strive to uphold all their constituent elements concurrently rather than responding or opting for only one. For example, selecting an appropriate set of adequate RAI principles for processes and products to respond to both the AI Act and Industry RAI standards is important.

Also, while such frameworks have laid out the expectations of what AI vendors have to adhere to, what these principles mean for them, in terms of how to translate them into their HRM tools, is still unclear (Khan, 2021). For instance, how should principles such as fairness be operationalized in practice in a specific AI HRM tool? For whom? In what context? To what extent? Finally, it is unclear whether all these principles are concurrently achievable, as they may reflect conflicting norms and values (for instance, interpretability and fairness), especially in relation to the concurrent promises for improved efficiency and effectiveness that AI deployments hold for their users. For example, most of the workplace outcomes associated with the use of AI in HRM are defined around improvement in employee performance (which may be related to model accuracy), productivity (where cost may be important), satisfaction (where speed of execution may be relevant), and capabilities (where ease of use matters) (Pereira et al., 2023), rather than trustworthiness and accountability. Thus, AI HRM vendors may need to figure out how to balance (Khan, 2021) between which RAI principles to embed in their AI tools and how to improve the utility of their tools for their clients.

In developing AI tools for HRM, there is thus a variety of demands that vendors have to adhere to, including institutional-based expectations of what is moral and ethical within the context they and their clients operate and their clients' utility-based expectations for efficiency and effectiveness in their HRM practices. To map this variety of demands that AI HRM tool vendors should respond to, there are, however, already attempts to investigate the adoption of RAI principles by AI for HRM vendors. One such effort departed from an assumption that vendors must respond to the utility-based expectations associated with AI HRM tools, such as clients' demands for improved effectiveness and efficiency in their HRM practices, and to the institutional, normative-based expectations associated with responsibly deploying such tools. This longitudinal netnography research (Kozinets, 2019) draws on a database of 215 verified vendors of AI tools for HRM identified through scholarly research, online searches, industry reports, participation at industry conferences, and networking with HRM professionals.

Tursunbayeva and Bunduchi, (2024) have adopted here legitimacy as a suitable theoretical lens to examine the utility and institutional factors that explain the adoption of technology by its users (Bunduchi et al., 2021), such as the adoption of AI by AI HRM vendors. The theory distinguishes between three types of legitimacy depending on the basis on which audiences bestow it (Suchman, 1995). Pragmatic legitimacy is based on alignment with self-interest, such as the client's expectations related to the improvements in the effectiveness and efficiency of HRM practices following the adoption of AI for HRM tools. Moral legitimacy is based on alignment with societal values and norms, such as the adoption of RAI frameworks by vendors to develop AI tools that are ethical, trustworthy, and beneficial for society. Finally, cognitive legitimacy involves alignment with existing mental and cultural models, for instance, leveraging AI features that align with characteristics of other technologies already familiar to HRM tools, such as automation (Suchman, 1995). By distinguishing between the three types of legitimacy, the study aims not only to identify the different RAI principles the vendors follow as part of building moral legitimacy but also to examine the trade-offs that such vendors make between pursuing moral legitimacy (the specific RAI principles they embed in their tools), pragmatic legitimacy (the specific efficiency and effectiveness criteria they emphasize as key benefits of their tools) or even cognitive legitimacy (considering alignment with the clients' preexisting cultural models, for instance by noting similarities with technologies which are already familiar to clients). See Table 8.1 for some illustrative examples.

**Table 8.1** Examples of product legitimization approaches used by AI for HRM Vendors

| Legitimacy | Example |
|---|---|
| Pragmatic | "*Personalised learning paths get new employees up to speed and on the floor quicker, with easy access job aids to support on-the-job learning*" (Axonify Learning, n.d.) |
| Moral | "*Our algorithms meet stringent standards for predictive accuracy and bias mitigation*" (Harver, n.d.) |
| Cognitive | "*Pro Search is like a reverse job board. You don't need to post jobs for people to apply to, instead Pros post their profiles and you can message with them if they're a good match for what you need*" (Instawork, n.d.) |

## 8.4 Responsible Artificial Intelligence at Individual Level

At the *individual* level, the institutional complexity that characterizes the emergence of the RAI framework is relevant in how it focuses the attention of individual end-users (e.g., candidates or employees in adopting organizations) on specific problems and issues while obscuring others and, in doing so, it affects their organizational practices and behaviors (e.g., engagement with the AI HRM tool). To understand the consequences of the development of a shared RAI framework at the macro level, it is thus important to consider the patterns characterizing the development and implementation of RAI at the individual level, too. Gasser and Mayer-Schönberger (2024) referred to this as to decisional guardrails, which serve as the bridge between personal choices and societal input. Factors like a user's background, education, experience, personality, values, and even neurophysiological factors such as neurodiversity (e.g., Doyle, 2020) may affect how they understand and appreciate the RAI principles. Nevertheless, as of now, there is limited research exploring individual users' perceptions and strategic responses to RAI principles within AI applications for HRM.

While numerous attempts have been made to investigate (also empirically) RAI governance at the societal and regulatory levels (Jarota, 2021), the concept of responsibility at the individual level has so far been primarily overlooked in scholarly research (Mikalef et al., 2022). This raises many unanswered questions about whether or how organizations internationally value knowledge related to RAI principles in their employees (Crawford, 2021). Thus, recently, there have been scholarly attempts to investigate whether the demand for RAI-related knowledge that AI professionals should possess is recognized and incorporated by organizations in their online job advertisements (Tursunbayeva et al., 2024). To achieve this aim, one such study analyzes around 9000 job advertisements of AI professionals in the US, the UK, and India, drawing on signaling and attention-based view perspectives and using NLP that permits the development of rich (descriptive) empirical insights on how organizations enact RAI principles in practice. The analysis indicates a limited presence of RAI signals across and within the job advertisements analyzed. Where these were present, the analysis suggests variations of RAI signals across different countries, employment statuses, and seniority levels regarding the actual RAI keywords and their combinations. The correlation analysis of RAI principles provides insights into the interconnectedness of some of the principles, emphasizing the multifaceted nature of addressing ethical, legal, and quality considerations in AI development and deployment within the RAI context. The analysis also revealed the disparity between the RAI keywords used in job advertisements and those the most frequently used in existing RAI guidelines (e.g., Jobin et al., 2019). Finally, the research demonstrates that translating RAI principles into practices might be challenging even for companies recognized as the most ethical.

Overall, the findings of this research generate rich insights into the RAI principles organizations actually pay attention to and concrete recommendations for organizations to apply and enact RAI principles in practice. Job advertisements also signal to the external stakeholders the knowledge, skills, and behavior-such as knowledge of RAI principles-that organizations value. Finally, the findings underscore the need for immediate action by management scholars and organizational managers to develop profiles for AI professionals that incorporate socio-centric (i.e., responsibility-related skills), not only those of a techno-centric nature.

## 8.5 Multilevel Responsible Artificial Intelligence

Analyzing RAI for HRM at different levels is crucial. However, it is equally important to investigate cross-level effects. Firstly, integrating multiple levels of analysis can provide insights into how lower-level entities, such as employees, align with higher-level entities like (supra)national guidelines and organizational goals (Renkema et al., 2017). Second, given the hierarchical nature of organizations, most managerial challenges, such as adopting RAI principles or signaling about it to other actors, are rarely isolated at a single level. Since managerial issues often have multiple underlying causes spanning various levels, adopting a multilevel perspective can offer a nuanced view aligned with the HRM reality within organizations. Building on the multilevel perspective, HRM studies have demonstrated that organization-level HRM practices can have a positive, top-down effect on individual-level outcomes and that individual employees' traits, attitudes, and behaviors can aggregate to higher organizational levels, leading to a bottom-up influence on organizational-level outcomes, such as organizational innovation, service quality, and financial performance (see Renkema et al., 2017 for discussion). To navigate this multilevel research landscape, the principles proposed by Kozlowski and Klein (2000) could aid in specifying the what, how, where, when, and why constructs and relationships that span various levels.

For instance, the aforementioned findings of the RAI research at the *individual* level (e.g., Tursunbayeva et al., 2024) hold significant implications at the meso level. They offer practical recommendations on how organizations can strengthen their commitment to RAI principles by explicitly integrating them into (HRM) practices, such as hiring and job advertisement development. At the *macro* level, these findings suggest that policymakers should develop RAI guidelines that account for the multi-dimensional nature of RAI principles and bridge the gap between existing principles and their practical application within organizations. Moreover, regulatory frameworks should mandate more precise and more consistent attention of organizations at *meso* level to RAI principles across various job positions, seniority levels, and employment types, ensuring that ethical, legal, and quality considerations are deeply embedded in AI development and deployment.

## References


Agarwal, D., Bersin, J., Lahiri, G., Schwartz, J., & Volini, E. (2018). *People data: How far is too far?* Deloitte Insights. https://www2.deloitte.com/insights/us/en/focus/human-capital-trends/2018/people-data-analytics-risks-opportunities.html.

Barredo Arrieta, A., Díaz-Rodríguez, N., Del Ser, J., Bennetot, A., Tabik, S., Barbado, A., Garcia, S., Gil-Lopez, S., Molina, D., Benjamins, R., Chatila, R., & Herrera, F. (2020). Explainable artificial intelligence (XAI): Concepts, taxonomies, opportunities and challenges toward responsible AI. *Information fusion, 58*, 82–115. Scopus. https://doi.org/10.1016/j.inffus.2019.12.012

Bersin, J. (2018). *The ethics of artificial intelligence: It's trickier than you think* [Josh Bersin]. https://joshbersin.com/2018/08/the-ethics-of-ai-its-much-trickier-than-you-think/

Bersin, J. (2019). *People analytics and AI in the workplace: Four dimensions of trust* [Josh Bersin]. https://joshbersin.com/2019/05/the-ethics-of-ai-and-people-analytics-four-dimensions-of-trust/.

Bujold, A., Roberge-Maltais, I., Parent-Rocheleau, X., Boasen, J., Sénécal, S., & Léger, P.-M. (2023). Responsible artificial intelligence in human resources management: A review of the empirical literature. *AI and Ethics*. https://doi.org/10.1007/s43681-023-00325-1

Bunduchi, R., Tursunbayeva, A., & Pagliari, C. (2021). Legitimizing disruptive technology: The case of blockchain in the human resources sector. In A. Pathak & S. Rana (Eds.), *Transforming human resource functions with automation*. https://doi.org/10.4018/978-1-7998-4180-7.ch001

Calvard, T. S., & Jeske, D. (2018). Developing human resource data risk management in the age of big data. *International Journal of Information Management, 43*, 159–164. https://doi.org/10.1016/j.ijinfomgt.2018.07.011

Clarke, R. (2019). Principles and business processes for responsible AI. *Computer Law & Security Review, 35*(4), 410–422. https://doi.org/10.1016/j.clsr.2019.04.007

Crawford, K. (2021). *Atlas of AI*. Yale University Press. https://yalebooks.yale.edu/9780300264630/atlas-of-ai

Deshpande, A., & Sharp, H. (2022). Responsible AI systems: Who are the stakeholders? *Proceedings of the 2022 AAAI/ACM Conference on AI, Ethics, and Society*, 227–236. https://doi.org/10.1145/3514094.3534187.

Di Lauro, S., Samaan, D., & Tursunbayeva, A. (2024). *Ethical AI guidelines—Recent developments and implications for the world of work*. European Group for Organizational Studies Colloquium.

Doyle, N. (2020). Neurodiversity at work: A biopsychosocial model and the impact on working adults. *British Medical Bulletin, 135*(1), 108–125. https://doi.org/10.1093/bmb/ldaa021

Fleming, O., Fountaine, T., Henke, N., & Saleh, T. (2018). Ten red flags signaling your analytics program will fail. *McKinsey Analytics*. https://www.mckinsey.com/business-functions/mckinsey-analytics/our-insights/ten-red-flags-signaling-your-analytics-program-will-fail

Gasser, U., & Mayer-Schönberger, V. (2024). *Guardrails: Guiding human decisions in the age of AI*. Princeton University Press.

Green, D. (2019). *Episode 2: driving business performance with people data (Interview with Edward Houghton, Head of research and thought leadership at the CIPD)*, MyHRfuture. Available at: https://www.myhrfuture.com/digital-hr-leaders-podcast/2019/5/20/episode-2-driving-business-performance-with-people-data-interview-with-edward-houghton-head-of-research-and-thought-leadership-at-the-cipd

Guenole, N., Feinzig, S., & Green, D. (2018). The Grey area: Ethical dilemmas in HR analytics. *IBM*. https://www.ibm.com/downloads/cas/O3DLWXBQ

Haim, L. S. (2018). *Will people analysts always be human?* [Littal Shemer Haim]. http://www.littalshemerhaim.com/will-people-analysts-always-be-human/

ISO. (2024). ISO/IEC 42001:2023. ISO. https://www.iso.org/standard/81230.html

Jacobs, K. (2017). The ethics of gathering employee data. *HR Magazine*. https://www.hrmagazine.co.uk/article-details/the-ethics-of-gathering-employee-data?utm_content=buffer54f95&utm_medium=social&utm_source=twitter.com&utm_campaign=buffer

Jarota, M. (2021). Artificial intelligence and robotisation in the EU - should we change OHS law? *Journal of Occupational Medicine and Toxicology, 16*(1), 18. https://doi.org/10.1186/s12995-021-00301-7

Jobin, A., Ienca, M., & Vayena, E. (2019). The global landscape of AI ethics guidelines. *Nature Machine Intelligence, 1*(9), 389–399. https://doi.org/10.1038/s42256-019-0088-2

Kaupins, G., & Minch, R. (2005). Legal and ethical implications of employee location monitoring. *Proceedings of the 38th annual Hawaii international conference on system sciences*, 133a–133a.

Kelly-Lyth, A., & Thomas, A. (2023). Algorithmic management: Assessing the impacts of AI at work. *European Labour Law Journal, 14*(2), 230–252. https://doi.org/10.1177/20319525231167478

Khan, S. (2021). Artificial intelligence for human resources toolkit helps organizations overcome implementation challenges. *World Economic Forum*. https://www.weforum.org/press/2021/12/artificial-intelligence-for-human-resources-toolkit-helps-organizations-overcome-implementation-challenges/

Kim, P. (2017). Data-driven discrimination at work. *William & Mary Law Review, 48*, 857–936.

Kozinets, R. V. (2019). *Netnography. The Essential Guide to Qualitative Social Media Research*. Sage Publications Ltd. https://uk.sagepub.com/en-gb/eur/netnography/book260905

Kozlowski, S. W. J., & Klein, K. J. (2000). A multilevel approach to theory and research in organizations: Contextual, temporal, and emergent processes. In K. J. Klein & S. W. J. Kozlowski (Eds.), *Multilevel theory, research, and methods in organizations: Foundations, extensions, and new directions* (pp. 3–90). Jossey-Bass/Wiley.

Kumar, T. (2018). *Ethics and workforce data: Is legislation enough?* [Analytics in HR]. https://www.analyticsinhr.com/blog/ethics-and-workforce-data-is-legislation-enough/?platform=hootsuite

Leong, K. (2017). Is your company using employee data ethically? *Harvard Business Review*. https://hbr.org/2017/03/is-your-company-using-employee-data-ethically

Mann, H., Neale, C., & Tajinder, K. (2018). *People analytics: Ethical considerations* [analytics in HR]. https://www.analyticsinhr.com/blog/people-analytics-ethical-considerations/?utm_source=twitter&utm_medium=social&utm_campaign=social-share

Manyika, J., Silberg, J., & Presten, B. (2019). What do we do about the biases in AI? *Harvard Business Review*. https://hbr.org/2019/10/what-do-we-do-about-the-biases-in-ai

Mikalef, P., Conboy, K., Lundström, J. E., & Popovič, A. (2022). Thinking responsibly about responsible AI and 'the dark side' of AI. *European Journal of Information Systems, 31*(3), 257–268. https://doi.org/10.1080/0960085X.2022.2026621

Pease, G. (2018). People analytics—Privacy vs. Transparency. *Best Practice in Human Resources*. http://www.bestpracticeinhr.com/people-analytics-privacy-vs-transparency-2/

Pereira, V., Hadjielias, E., Christofi, M., & Vrontis, D. (2023). A systematic literature review on the impact of artificial intelligence on workplace outcomes: A multi-process perspective. *Human Resource Management Review, 33*(1), 100857. https://doi.org/10.1016/j.hrmr.2021.100857

Petersen, D. (2018). *Data ethics: 6 steps for ethically sound people analytics* [Visier]. https://www.visier.com/clarity/six-steps-ethically-sound-people-analytics/.

RenAIssance Foundation. (2024). *Rome call | what is the matter with AI ethics?* https://www.romecall.org/

Renkema, M., Meijerink, J., & Bondarouk, T. (2017). Advancing multilevel thinking in human resource management research: Applications and guidelines. *Human Resource Management Review, 27*(3), 397–415. https://doi.org/10.1016/j.hrmr.2017.03.001

Roberts, H., Cowls, J., Morley, J., Taddeo, M., Wang, V., & Floridi, L. (2021). The Chinese approach to artificial intelligence: An analysis of policy, ethics, and regulation. *AI & SOCIETY, 36*(1), 59–77. https://doi.org/10.1007/s00146-020-00992-2

Shahlaei, C. A., & Berente, N. (2024). An analysis of European data and AI regulations for automotive organizations (no. arXiv:2407.11271). *arXiv*. https://doi.org/10.48550/arXiv.2407.11271

Suchman, M. C. (1995). Managing legitimacy: Strategic and institutional approaches. *The Academy of Management Review, 20*(3), 571–610.

The Public Voice. (n.d.). *AI Universal Guidelines* [The Public Voice: AI Universal Guidelines]. https://unbias.wp.horizon.ac.uk/initiatives-and-research-projects/

Tursunbayeva, A., & Bunduchi, R. (2024). *Legitimizing artificial intelligence (AI) for human resource management (HRM) tools through responsible AI: Insights from a longitudinal analysis of AI for HRM vendors.* 6th edition of European academy of management research Grants scheme. https://euram.academy/euram?service=grants

Tursunbayeva, A., Pagliari, C., Di Lauro, S., & Antonelli, G. (2022). The ethics of people analytics: Risks, opportunities and recommendations. *Personnel Review, 51*(3), 900–921. https://doi.org/10.1108/PR-12-2019-0680

Tursunbayeva, A., Jain, S., Basu, S. N., & Moschera, L. (2024). Signaling the adoption of responsible AI principles: A study of AI job advertisements. *Academy of Management Proceedings, 2024*(1), 18841. https://doi.org/10.5465/AMPROC.2024.18841abstract

Wang, W., & Siau, K. (2019). Artificial intelligence, machine learning, automation, robotics, future of work and future of humanity: A review and research agenda. *Journal of Database Management, 30*(1), 61–79. https://doi.org/10.4018/JDM.2019010104

West, D. M. (2018). The role of corporations in addressing AI's ethical dilemmas. *Brookings*. https://www.brookings.edu/research/how-to-address-ai-ethical-dilemmas/

# Chapter 9
# Artificial Intelligence Adoption and Change Management

## 9.1 Navigating Artificial Intelligence-Driven Transformation

Integrating AI into organizations can significantly alter organizational processes and employee practices. As such, effective change management is key for successful AI adoption. Furthermore, organizational change management practices are increasingly being supported and transformed by AI, challenging established change management models. The narrative below offers a brief overview of how AI can be implemented through the lens of prominent change management models, such as those proposed by Kurt Lewin and John Kotter. It also examines the approaches to AI adoption of leading change management experts and major consulting firms like Prosci and the Big Four (PwC, KPMG, EY, and Deloitte) (De Simone, 2024).

## 9.2 Change Management Models and Artificial Intelligence Adoption

Companies have always faced disruptive "forces of change" (Robbins & Judge, 2023). For example, throughout history, there have been several important events, such as the energy crisis of the 1970s, the financial crisis of 2007–2009, and the COVID-19 pandemic of 2020, which required companies to reorganize the structure and management of work to remain competitive. Also, recent technological advancements have been viewed as a disruptive force that drives change at various levels-from individuals' everyday routines to intense competition between organizations (Bentzen et al., 2020).



A. Tursunbayeva, *Augmenting Human Resource Management with Artificial Intelligence*, Contributions to Management Science,
https://doi.org/10.1007/978-3-031-75266-7_9

Organizational changes aim at improvement, strengthening, and value creation. These are critical to having sustainability over time, as no company would be able to have continuity except through constant adaptation. The ability to manage change is thus becoming the key element for success. Even though companies have always been subjected to countless challenges, a 2016 Harvard Business Review study revealed that 60–70% of business transformation initiatives (still) fail (Carucci, 2016). Thus, it is evident that successfully implementing organizational change is not easy. Meanwhile, according to Gartner (2024), in the past 3 years, the average organization has implemented five significant company-wide changes, and nearly 75% anticipate an increase in the number of major change initiatives they will pursue in the next 3 years. Thus, change is an ever-present feature of organizational life at the operational and strategic levels (Burnes, 2004). In fact, it should be rooted within organizations. That is why there is a rising need for proper change management, defined as continually renewing an organization's direction, structure, and capabilities to meet changing needs (Moran & Brightman, 2000). Change management is also constantly referred to as the approach by which a company plans to execute change from an existing state (how the organization appears at that time) to a desired state (how the organization would like to be) (By, 2005).

The main challenge to successfully implementing change management is resistance to change (Robbins & Judge, 2023), for example, "fear of the unknown." This is especially true in relation to AI, which could disrupt the business-as-usual context in which employees are used to operating, breaking their routines, and requiring the (re)definition of existing approaches to work.

The change that AI integration causes requires individual and organizational values focused on continuous learning, embracing change, and being willing to explore new possibilities. Organizational culture thus must be considered when managing change because this can drive deep support and commitment from employees. Organizational culture creates a feeling of identity between staff and the organization (Tadesse Bogale & Debela, 2024), resulting in a greater willingness to deal with change. A study conducted by MIT Sloan Management Review and the Boston Consulting Group on the cultural benefits of AI in the enterprise analyzed the relationship between AI and organizational models, gathering the testimony of 2200 employees and 20 managers from large companies in various industries. The study defined the ongoing interaction between culture, AI use, and organizational effectiveness as "culture use effectiveness," i.e., how culture influences the use of AI, improving team productivity and improving organizational culture itself (Ransbotham et al., 2021). Other scholars have also noted that AI's benefits will not be fully realized until synergy between AI and the organization is achieved (Brynjolfsson et al., 2018). Thus, it can be deduced that introducing AI undoubtedly requires proper change management, but at the same time, AI can also be a valuable tool for implementing organizational change.

The disruptive or exponential nature of AI can intimidate many managers and leaders. However, if not adapted proactively, they could be passively affected by AI advancements. AI's impact on organizational structure is also expected, changing the variety and scope of work. It is anticipated that task variety can alter depending on the nature of the task and as individuals engage in more complex activities (Leyer

& Schneider, 2021), requiring intuition, thinking, and empathy. Scholars also predict that the future with AI will push managers to revisit organizational spans of control, and the number of middle and top managers. However, the debates around these topics are only heating up. For instance, Baumann and Wu (2023), in their publication on managerial hierarchy in AI-driven organizations, debated such implications through illustrative examples of real organizations. Some of their arguments and examples are presented in Table 9.1.

The innovation caused by AI can be incremental, improving what already exists, or exponential going beyond any existing laws (e.g., Moore's law) or predictions (Berman, 2016). Unlike linear growth, which involves repeatedly adding a constant, the latter exponential growth involves repeatedly multiplying by a constant (Berman, 2016). Linear growth produces a stable, straight line over time, while exponential growth line rapidly increases. For example, exponential growth is explained in a SingularityHub blog post by the number of human steps:

> "*Imagine you are going to walk down a road taking steps a meter in length. You take 6 steps, and you've progressed six meters (1, 2, 3, 4, 5, 6). After 24 more steps, you're 30 meters from where you began. It's easy to predict where 30 more steps will get you - that's the simplicity of linear growth. However, setting anatomy aside, imagine you could double the length of your stride. Now when you take six steps, you've actually progressed 32 meters (1, 2, 4, 8, 16, 32), which is significantly more than the 6 meters you'd move with equal steps. Amazingly, by step number 30, doubling your stride will put you a billion meters from where you started, a distance equal to twenty-six trips around the world.*" (Berman, 2016)

This exponential growth is expected to lead to what is known as the Singularity, a concept in mathematics referring to a point at which an object ceases to behave in a predictable manner. In the context of exponential growth, the Singularity concept is used metaphorically to represent the moment when machine intelligence surpasses human intelligence. Ray Kurzweil, an inventor, thinker, futurist, and Principal Researcher and AI Visionary at Google, has predicted that humanity will reach this point by 2045 (Karakas, 2021).

Many organizational change models have been proposed to support organizations in implementing innovations such as AI. These models guide managers and leaders, helping them to monitor, evaluate, and plan changes (Van Oosten, 2006). Below, a brief overview is provided of how AI adoption could be implemented through the lens of the most prevalent and taught change management models. These include Kurt Lewin's model of planned change, which emphasizes transition and gradual adaptation suitable for incremental change (Burnes, 2004), and John Kotter's model, which provides a more employee-centered perspective and is suitable for radical innovation involving significant changes (Kotter, 2012).

**Table 9.1** Organizational (structure) changes due to the adoption of AI

| Category | Description |
|---|---|
| Human role in organizational design | *"In the automotive industry, for instance, companies like Tesla have used AI to optimize their supply chain and production processes. However, human decision-making is still required to address challenges such as labor relations, regulatory compliance, and strategic partnerships. AI can support these efforts but cannot entirely replace the need for human judgment and understanding in translating them into organization design choices."* (Baumann & Wu, 2023) |
| Organizational structure | *"In a software development company like GitHub, for instance, AI-powered tools can automate routine tasks, such as code review and issue tracking, enabling developers to collaborate more effectively. With AI facilitating collaboration, the organization might adopt a flatter structure that encourages cross-functional collaboration and empowers developers to make decisions with reduced managerial oversight."* (Baumann & Wu, 2023) |
| Hierarchy | *"The software company Adobe, for example, has embraced a more flexible hierarchy to adapt in a rapidly evolving industry. Combining elements of hierarchy with a more decentralized decision-making process, Adobe's "kickbox" innovation program empowers employees at all levels to develop and pitch new ideas, providing them with resources and support to bring these ideas to fruition."* (Baumann & Wu, 2023) |

### 9.2.1 Kurt Lewin's Model of Change

Lewin's change model consists of three stages: unfreezing, changing, and refreezing. If AI is considered an element of change to *unfreeze* the status quo, at this stage, change agents must present a plan that accounts for both the investment required to implement the new tool and their strategy for managing the resulting changes. In addition, addressing employees' fears of job displacement-one of the most significant and debated concerns-could assist in maintaining a change-oriented environment (Hillyer, 2024). Positive incentives in the form of a shorter work week, which are currently piloted in many contexts (Autonomy, 2019), without reducing salary and productivity, could, for instance, motivate employees to "change" their initial state. This approach can shift employees' perception of AI from a job threat to a potential enabler of improved work–life balance that allows for more time for personal interests without compromising financial stability or productivity.

In Lewin's second change phase, it is essential to provide employees with the necessary training and skills to manage the changes caused by AI (Dahlbom et al., 2020; Tursunbayeva & Chaluz-Ben Gal, 2024). This acquired knowledge should be disseminated throughout the organization to ensure long-term sustainability and competitiveness (Foss & Pedersen, 2002), aiming to achieve a "democratization" of AI (Taulli, 2021) that aligns with organizational strategy and goals (Di Vaio et al., 2022). The change agents are responsible here for ensuring that correct information is input into AI systems, as anything omitted will not be considered (Vincent, 2021). Additionally, this process must adhere to the company's principles and values, particularly in managing AI inputs, to avoid "the alignment problem" with AI or the outcomes that contradict the intended direction (Christian, 2023). For instance, if a word embedding model accurately predicts that few women will be hired in a sexist corporate culture, it may be deployed in a way that leads to the hiring of fewer women (Christian, 2023). Finally, the change agents must keep the organization's members engaged and informed about how AI systems function to prevent reluctance and resistance (Jarrahi, 2018).

In Lewin's third phase-refreezing-the newly established equilibrium must be stabilized to prevent regression to previous behaviors. The new behaviors must align with the members' organizational norms and acceptable standards (Tadesse Bogale & Debela, 2024).

### *9.2.2 John Kotters's Model for Change*

John Kotter, a leadership professor at Harvard Business School, developed his "8-step model for change" based on observing over 100 companies. These included large organizations like Ford, smaller ones like Landmark Communications, US-based companies like General Motors, international firms like British Airways, and profitable companies such as Bristol-Myers Squibb (Kotter, 1995).

The first step of his model is *creating a sense of urgency*. When introducing AI, it is essential to emphasize that it could assist with all three HRM configurations ranging from automation to augmentation. The industry projections could support this urgency. By 2025, AI is projected to generate nearly $90 billion in profits, up from just $7 billion in 2018 (Wamba-Taguimdje et al., 2020). AI also promises most benefits to the early adopters (Agrawal et al., 2022). According to the Digital Transformation 2020 survey, companies that executives recognized as being well advanced (or digitally mature) in their digital transformation journey were three times more likely to have experienced revenue growth in the past year (Marr, 2020). Thus, companies that do not embrace AI could risk their continuity and the security of their employees' jobs, making the urgency clear.

The second step is *building a guiding coalition*. The coalition should work together to integrate AI tools. Its goal should be continuous improvement, promoting experimentation and learning, and empowering employees to explore and implement various AI solutions across organizational processes (Tursunbayeva & Chaluz-Ben Gal, 2024). Encouraging collaboration and cross-functional teams here can foster innovation and creativity (Guckelsberger, 2020).

The third step is *forming a strategic vision*. The importance of creating a cohesive organizing vision for HR technologies is well-recognized (Bunduchi et al., 2019). Similarly, with AI, this organizing vision should leverage its efficiency opportunities while adhering to organizational conduct norms and relevant governmental and soft regulations (see previous chapter). This will help to establish a clear path to achieve the set strategy, with all efforts unified toward this goal.

The fourth step is *communicating the vision*: delivering a clear and compelling message to all organization members about AI adoption (Tursunbayeva &

Chaluz-Ben Gal, 2024). This communication should outline the overall direction, motivate employees, and coordinate their actions effectively.

The fifth step is to *empower others to act on the vision*: engaging employees' ideas and increasing their motivation can increase the chances of success by mitigating resistance to change. Employee motivation is crucial in AI adoption, though little is known about it in relation to AI, as most studies focus on employee competencies (Tursunbayeva & Chaluz-Ben Gal, 2024). Some existing literature advises establishing a recognition and rewards program to acknowledge employees who significantly contribute to AI initiatives and demonstrate exceptional skills. Moreover, setting up feedback channels to gather employee input on AI initiatives, processes, and tools could help to timely address concerns and incorporate feedback, thus fostering a sense of ownership and involvement in the organization's AI adoption journey (Chalutz-Ben Gal, 2023; Kellogg et al., 2020).

The sixth step is *planning and creating short-term wins*. Monitoring and evaluation are critical for AI (for HRM projects), and sharing "quick wins" can help gain support (Tursunbayeva et al., 2022). It is advised that, beyond their benefits for addressing strategic challenges and broader organizational changes, future AI investment decisions should consider their effects on "people outcomes" to ensure ethical practices. These decisions should be made together by HRM professionals and company management rather than only by suppliers. When making these choices, it is essential to assess potential negative impacts on employees and develop strategies to manage risks and prevent unintended consequences (Pease, 2018).

The seventh step involves *consolidating improvements* and implementing further changes. It is useful here to analyze the results achieved to identify areas needing enhancement and address errors. To support this sensitive phase, engaging a wide range of stakeholders and conducting pilot projects can be beneficial (Tursunbayeva et al., 2022). Learning from previous experiments in the field can also help minimize costs and manage risks effectively.

The eighth step is *institutionalizing new approaches*: it is important to solidify the change and connect it to business success to ensure that the improvements are sustainable. The implemented changes must be integrated into the organizational practices and processes. However, it is still currently unknown whether and how RAI principles are actually institutionalized (Schultz & Seele, 2023) or implemented in practice (Crawford, 2021). Additionally, it is strategic to formalize the stakeholders and roles for (Responsible) AI change management projects (Deshpande & Sharp, 2022) to make AI a stable and enduring aspect of the organization.

## 9.3 Artificial Intelligence as a Tool to Support Change Management Processes

The role of AI in organizational change management is only beginning to be explored. In what follows, a brief overview will be provided on how change leaders utilize AI tools in change management, the ways these tools are being employed, and the initial benefits being experienced. To do so, industry insights will be drawn upon, an approach frequently utilized among scholars to explore innovative topics (Tursunbayeva et al., 2022). Specifically, research insights by Prosci, positioning itself as the Global Leader in Change Management, will be discussed, along with approaches employed by the Big Four consulting and audit companies, including PwC, KPMG, EY, and Deloitte.

### *9.3.1 Prosci Insights on the Current State of Artificial Intelligence in Change Management*

A recent Prosci study revealed that 84% of change professionals surveyed were moderately to very familiar with AI, but only 48% said they employ it in change management (Anderson, 2024). However, the actual number of survey respondents is not clear from the report. Professionals who do not use AI tools reported that this happens due to uncertainty and inexperience (20%); lack of relevance and use cases (17%); lack of understanding (16%); limited access and resources (16%); time constraints and priorities (15%); data security and privacy concerns (8%); and finally the organizational maturity reasons (8%) (Anderson, 2024). The report also indicates that seasoned change management professionals with over 5 years of experience utilize AI more frequently than newcomers. Additionally, professionals with dual roles, such as strategy consultants, business leaders, project managers, or executive sponsors, also report a higher usage of AI in their work.

The study also revealed several approaches to applying AI in change management projects. For instance, AI can assist in *supporting communications* by creating new content or refining existing content to enhance efficiency. Anderson (2024) claims that it can improve the quality of communications by addressing grammatical issues and tailoring text for different audiences for maximum impact. It is also believed to establish a starting point by facilitating goal-setting, strategy planning, and resource identification. Additionally, it can control the tone of messages, which is crucial for how the audience perceives them, as an inappropriate tone can obscure the intended message. Finally, AI can enable the reuse of original content for various formats and audience segments, such as converting a written report into a presentation slide, thereby maximizing content utilization.

AI can facilitate *content creation* through training guides, industry-specific case studies, and presentations and accelerate communication processes overall. It could break down complex topics into manageable parts, enabling employees to focus on their specific roles and impacts. AI can also generate typical user profiles (i.e., personas), summarize communications, and assist in brainstorming sessions.

In terms of *strategy and planning*, AI is claimed to analyze vast amounts of data to help determine a company's most effective tactics or predict the success of different strategies based on historical data and current trends. It could also be valuable for conducting simulations to forecast the impact of various change strategies, allowing for scenario planning and preparation for potential challenges. Additionally,

AI could assist in creating specific plans, such as managing resistance to change by identifying potential obstacles and proposing strategies to overcome them.

AI can also enable *automation and efficiency*. A prime example is the deployment of internal chatbots. These chatbots can enable organizations to offer personalized training and respond to questions promptly and accurately. They can be programmed to address frequently asked questions, provide links to relevant resources, and gather user feedback.

AI can be utilized to *analyze data* such as survey results, including aggregate data and business cases, and provide real-time insights. This can help change agents understand emerging trends and make informed decisions. The analyzed data can also be segmented to personalize content and offer targeted services. Additionally, AI can allow for testing various hypotheses, serving as a valuable tool for change management to validate ideas and identify areas for improvement.

AI seems to offer substantial potential for enhancing change management. According to the Prosci study (Anderson, 2024), respondents who have adopted AI reported increased efficiency (30%), experienced improved communication (19%), found it helpful for content creation (19%), noted that AI can facilitate idea generation (14%), and saw better workload management (10%). At the same time, 8% reported limited impact. However, the respondents also noted AI's imperfections and lack of reliability and feared for their job security. Finally, research indicated that while 65% of professionals believe AI will contribute to their future success, 37% identified a gap in AI capabilities within change management practices.

### 9.3.2 PwC: Embracing Artificial Intelligence with Human-Centric Approach

PwC, employing 364,000 people in 151 countries, stands out as a key player in professional services such as Assurance, Tax, and Advisory. Its purpose is "Building trust in society and solving important problems" (PwC, 2024). In 2023, it announced a chatbot experiment with Harvey's start-up chatbot, aimed at speeding up the work of its 4000 lawyers (O'Dwyer et al., 2023). In 2024, PwC declared a $1 billion partnership with OpenAI in which PwC became the largest OpenAI enterprise customer and the first reseller of its enterprise product. As a part of this deal, PwC will provide ChatGPT to its 75,000 employees in the US and 26,000 in the UK (Reuters, 2024).

PwC reports to be committed to ethics and legal compliance (PwC Global, 2024). PwC Germany, for instance, has partnered with Monitaur (www.monitaur.ai), an AI governance software company, to meet the demands of EU AI Regulatory Compliance (Business Wire, 2022). PwC Germany also proposed to embrace AI with a human-centric approach, advocating synergy between technology and human expertise (Hufnagel et al., 2024). The proposal mentions that organizations aim to embrace AI to gain a competitive advantage through cost savings and productivity gains and that the success of AI projects hinges on employee acceptance. PwC proposes to address such potential employee resistance-especially fear-by focusing on welcoming and motivating employee concerns, an approach aligned with the initial stage of Kurt Lewin's change model. They also suggest a systems approach to AI integration, aligned with Lewin's second transition phase, stressing the importance of harmonizing technology with human skills to ensure sustainable and robust growth. Here, they also highlight the need for transparency and open communication to transform fear into a catalyst for change. Furthermore, they underline the necessity of involving various organizational levels-executive, managerial, and staff-to create a trusting and open environment that mitigates fear and makes members active contributors to success. They also emphasize the importance of identifying supporters and skeptics, encouraging the former, and carefully addressing the latter.

PwC has its own RAI principles (PwC, n.d.). In 2023, the Chairman of PwC UK also highlighted the importance of urgently equipping people with responsibility skills: "The [technological] acceleration came with challenges…This will in turn require more coaching to equip people for more responsibility sooner, and impart knowledge that would typically be acquired over a longer period" (Jones, 2023).

### 9.3.3 *KPMG's Business-Led Approach*

KPMG, operating in 143 countries and territories and employing more than 270,000 people, offers audit, tax, and advisory services (KPMG, 2024). For years, KPMG has also been experimenting with and deploying AI aspects across its business. In 2023, the company took another step forward by announcing an alliance with Canada-based MindBridge that was planned to bring "the tech firm's statistical, machine learning and rules-based analytics technology into KPMG Clara and existing digital audit platform" (Webber Sadovi, 2023).

KPMG's approach to AI, data, and other emerging digital technologies is business-led, emphasizing the specific needs of the market and industry in which a company operates (KPMG Global, 2024a). KPMG promises companies to optimize the value of AI tools by guiding them through the entire change process, from design to execution. KPMG stresses the capabilities and skills of their professional teams to transfer to their clients the right skills and knowledge to adopt AI tools, deploying them correctly within the value chain and providing technical support to address internal and external needs. For instance, the companies undergoing the change process are promised to progress more swiftly from one phase to the next, supported by the KPMG professional's expertise and RAI framework comprising principles like fairness, transparency, or explainability that the company considers throughout the technology life cycle (KPMG Global, 2024b).

### *9.3.4 EY: Bringing Together Human Capabilities and Artificial Intelligence*

EY is a global network operating in over 150 countries, employing 400,000 people, and offering professional services in Assurance, Consulting, Strategy and Transactions, and Tax. EY aims to "build a better working world" (EY Global, 2024). Recently, the company announced the launch of the EY AI platform, supported by a $1.4 billion investment (Lloyd, 2024). This platform integrates human capabilities with AI, leveraging EY's experience in strategy, change, and risk management, and is supported by a comprehensive AI ecosystem comprising partnerships with tech leaders like Microsoft, Dell Technologies, IBM, and Thomson Reuters, among others.

Carmine Di Sibio, EY Global Chairman and CEO, emphasized that the time for AI is now and that the challenge is more than just technological (Lloyd, 2024). EY aims to help clients harness AI's transformative power responsibly, unlocking new economic values. This integration involves enhancing employees' potential through AI. They claim that relying on reputable third-party companies like EY, for instance, for training can ensure organizational security and effectiveness (Lloyd, 2024). Looking at their proposal through the lens of the change management models proposed by Kurt Lewin and John Kotter, it could be deduced that partnering with EY can provide organizations willing to implement AI comfort and a clear trajectory for acquiring the necessary skills. However, companies should also maintain careful internal planning to navigate their AI journey, which overall requires both external support and internal strategy.

EY follows a "responsible AI by design" approach, supported by a governance framework and operating model that balances risk management with flexibility throughout the AI development life cycle (EY, 2024).

### *9.3.5 Deloitte: A New Data-Driven Change Management*

Deloitte is another leading consulting firm that operates in over 150 countries and leverages local knowledge and international expertise from more than 450,000 professionals (Deloitte Italia, 2024). In 2023, Deloitte announced an expansion of its strategic alliance with NVIDIA to help enterprises worldwide use generative AI to reinvent how they conduct business (Deloitte Consulting, 2023).

The firm's culture emphasizes integrity, a strong focus on the market and clients, commitment to colleagues, and the value of differences. Deloitte's purpose is to "make an impact every day" (Deloitte, 2024). The firm acts across various business areas, including AI, where it has developed new data-driven change management using a transformational intelligence model. The proposal for this new, what they refer to as a "prototype" model, highlights that the company clients "are testing new solutions not yet found in dated books on change, nor Master of Business Administration programs, nor even in academic research." To support this argument, they bring the results of their research, concluding that "high-performing organizations are 3.5 times more likely to use data to inform change efforts and four times more likely to gain worker input when shaping changes" (Deloitte Consulting, 2020).

Deloitte refers to AI as the "why," the "what," and the "how" of change underlying, especially the importance of the latter. The model consists of four stages, including Intelligent Sensing (where AI is envisioned to help organizations clarify change management goals and readiness for change, assessing the environment, and aligning the organization to establish the necessary effort for achieving desired results); Intelligent Blueprint (where data is used to allocate resources efficiently, creating customized change plans tailored to individual needs, analyzing resistance areas, monitoring change adoption, and ensuring targeted communications); Intelligent Delivery (where AI promises to enable continuous monitoring of the complex interdependencies of people and processes, and ensuring the focus on prioritized activities); and finally Intelligent Sustain (where AI is used to help adopt and integrate new technologies over time, fostering group norms around technology and creating a virtuous cycle of improved adoption).

Despite the initial assertion that old change models are incompatible with today's challenges, the foundational models by experts like Kurt Lewin seem to align with the stages proposed by Deloitte. For instance, similar to Lewin's unfreeze phase, Intelligent Sensing also focuses on clarifying goals, aligning leadership, and creating a shared understanding of the need for change. Intelligent Blueprint and Delivery, focusing on the execution and monitoring of change activities, seem to align with Lewin's second phase, where new behaviors and processes are implemented. Finally, the Intelligent Sustain phase, which focuses on sustaining change in organizations, seems to be aligned with Lewin's refreeze phase, where new ways of working are reinforced. The differences between the preexisting and new emerging change models may lie in the details, but what is clearly illustrated by Deloitte's new model is that the approach to change management is now data-driven and can be supported by technology.

Deloitte, like its fellow Big Four firms, is claimed to be dedicated to Ethical AI, which it calls Trustworthy AI. Their ethical AI principles are based on the insights from Beena Ammanath's (2022) *Trustworthy AI* book.

## 9.4 Shared Principles and Unique Approaches

All of the Big Four consulting companies have made substantial investments in AI, reflecting their commitment to integrating advanced technologies into their services and their clients' interest and acceptance of change management with AI. This is also confirmed by the findings of the Prosci research (Anderson, 2024). While their approaches to change management for AI adoption differ slightly, they all emphasize the critical intersection of human and technological factors. Despite nuanced variations in their methodologies, each of these companies has established RAI frameworks, highlighting their shared commitment to balancing innovation with ethical considerations.

## References


Agrawal, A., Gans, J., & Goldfarb, A. (2022). *Power and prediction: The disruptive economics of artificial intelligence* (Unabridged ed.). Ascent Audio and Blackstone Publishing.

Ammanath, B. (2022). *Trustworthy AI: A business guide for navigating trust and ethics in AI.* Wiley.

Anderson, J. (2024). AI in change management: Early findings, challenges and opportunities. *Prosci.* https://www.prosci.com/blog/ai-in-change-management-early-findings

Autonomy. (2019). *The shorter working week: A radical and pragmatic proposal.* Autonomy Research Ltd. https://autonomy.work/portfolio/the-shorter-working-week-a-report-from-autonomy-in-collaboration-with-members-of-the-4-day-week-campaign/

Baumann, O., & Wu, B. (2023). Managerial hierarchy in AI-driven organizations. *Journal of Organization Design, 12*(1), 1–5. https://doi.org/10.1007/s41469-023-00147-9

Bentzen, N., Boucher, P. N., Latici, T., Madiega, T. A., Schmertzing, L., & Szczepanski, M. (2020). Disruption by technology: Impacts on politics, economics and society. *European Parliament.* https://www.europarl.europa.eu/thinktank/en/document/EPRS_IDA(2020)652079

Berman, A. E. (2016, April 5). How to think exponentially and better predict the future. *Singularity Hub.* https://singularityhub.com/2016/04/05/how-to-think-exponentially-and-better-predict-the-future/

Brynjolfsson, E., Hui, X., & Liu, M. (2018). *Does machine translation affect international trade? Evidence from a large digital platform* (working paper no. 24917). National Bureau of Economic Research. https://doi.org/10.3386/w24917

Bunduchi, R., Tursunbayeva, A., & Pagliari, C. (2019). Coping with institutional complexity: Intersecting logics and dissonant visions in a nation-wide healthcare IT implementation project. *Information Technology & People, 33*(1), 311–339. https://doi.org/10.1108/ITP-08-2018-0373

Burnes, B. (2004). Kurt Lewin and the planned approach to change: A re-appraisal. *Journal of Management Studies, 41*(6), 977–1002. https://doi.org/10.1111/j.1467-6486.2004.00463.x

Business Wire. (2022). *PwC Germany and Monitaur Form Strategic Partnership to Advance AI Governance.* https://www.businesswire.com/news/home/20220907005341/en/PwC-Germany-and-Monitaur-Form-Strategic-Partnership-to-Advance-AI-Governance.

By, R. T. (2005). Organisational change management: A critical review. *Journal of Change Management, 5*(4), 369–380. https://doi.org/10.1080/14697010500359250

Carucci, R. (2016, October 24). Organizations can't change if leaders can't change with them. *Harvard Business Review.* https://hbr.org/2016/10/organizations-cant-change-if-leaders-cant-change-with-them

Chalutz-Ben Gal, H. (2023). Person–skill fit: Why a new form of employee fit is required. Academy of Management Perspectives, 37(2), 117–137. https://doi.org/10.5465/amp.2022.0024.

Christian, A. (2023). The employees secretly using AI at work. *BBC.* https://www.bbc.com/worklife/article/20231017-the-employees-secretly-using-ai-at-work

Crawford, K. (2021). *Atlas of AI: Power, politics, and the planetary costs of artificial intelligence.* Yale University Press.

Dahlbom, P., Siikanen, N., Sajasalo, P., & Jarvenpää, M. (2020). Big data and HR analytics in the digital era. *Baltic Journal of Management, 15*(1), 120–138. https://doi.org/10.1108/BJM-11-2018-0393

Deloitte. (2024). *Who we are.* https://www.deloitte.com/global/en/about.html

Deloitte Consulting. (2020). *High-impact workforce architecture study.* Deloitte.

Deloitte Consulting. (2023). Deloitte expands strategic Alliance with NVIDIA to unlock value of generative AI across Enterprise software platforms. *PR Newswire.* https://www.prnewswire.com/news-releases/deloitte-expands-strategic-alliance-with-nvidia-to-unlock-value-of-generative-ai-across-enterprise-software-platforms-301901977.html

Deloitte Italia. (2024). Chi siamo Deloitte Italy. *Deloitte Italia.* https://www2.deloitte.com/it/it/legal/about-deloitte-italy.html

Deshpande, A., & Sharp, H. (2022). Responsible AI systems: Who are the stakeholders? *Proceedings of the 2022 AAAI/ACM conference on AI, ethics, and society*, 227–236. https://doi.org/10.1145/3514094.3534187

Di Vaio, A., Hassan, R., & Alavoine, C. (2022). Data intelligence and analytics: A bibliometric analysis of human–artificial intelligence in public sector decision-making effectiveness. *Technological Forecasting and Social Change, 174*, 121201. https://doi.org/10.1016/j.techfore.2021.121201

De Simone, L. (2024). *Sinergia tra Intelligenza Artificiale e Cambiamento Organizzativo: un'analisi approfondita* [Bachelor thesis]. University of Naples Parthenope.

EY. (2024). *Responsible AI*. EY. https://www.ey.com/en_us/services/ai/responsible-ai

EY Global. (2024). *About us—Who we are* [EY]. https://www.ey.com/en_gl/about-us

Foss, N. J., & Pedersen, T. (2002). Transferring knowledge in MNCs: The role of sources of subsidiary knowledge and organizational context. *Journal of International Management, 8*(1), 49–67. https://doi.org/10.1016/S1075-4253(01)00054-0

Gartner. (2024). Organizational change management. Deliver on complex organizational change management initiatives. *Gartner*. https://www.gartner.com/en/human-resources/insights/organizational-change-management

Guckelsberger, C. (2020). *Intrinsic motivation in computational creativity applied to videogames* [PhD Thesis, Aalto University]. https://research.aalto.fi/en/publications/intrinsic-motivation-in-computational-creativity-applied-to-video

Hillyer, R. (2024). Council post: Overcoming barriers to AI adoption: Addressing organizational challenges. *Forbes*. https://www.forbes.com/sites/forbescoachescouncil/2024/05/22/overcoming-barriers-to-ai-adoption-addressing-organizational-challenges/

Hufnagel, W., Blank, D., Heyder, L., & Rautauoma, K. (2024). *The people side of AI: Embracing technology with a human-centric approach*. PwC Germany.

Jarrahi, M. H. (2018). Artificial intelligence and the future of work: Human-AI symbiosis in organizational decision making. *Business Horizons, 61*(4), 577–586. https://doi.org/10.1016/j.bushor.2018.03.007

Jones, O. (2023). Will AI kill off WFH? *Mail Online*. https://www.dailymail.co.uk/news/article-12135837/AI-kill-WFH-Workers-return-office-differentiate-robot.html

Karakas, F. (2021, January 26). Why you should read "The Singularity is Near: When Humans Transcend Biology." *Medium*. https://medium.com/predict/why-you-should-read-the-singularity-is-near-when-humans-transcend-biology-f8066b5921ed

Kellogg, K., Valentine, M., & Christin, A. (2020). Algorithms at work: The new contested terrain of control. *Academy of Management Annals, 14*(1), 366–410.

Kotter, J. P. (1995, May 1). Leading change: Why transformation efforts fail. *Harvard Business Review*. https://hbr.org/1995/05/leading-change-why-transformation-efforts-fail-2.

Kotter, J. P. (2012, November 1). Accelerate! *Harvard Business Review*. https://hbr.org/2012/11/accelerate

KPMG. (2024). About - KPMG global. *KPMG*. https://kpmg.com/xx/en/home/about.html

KPMG Global. (2024a, May 17). Data, AI & emerging technologies. *KPMG*. https://kpmg.com/xx/en/home/services/advisory/management-consulting/data-artificial-intelligence-emerging-technologies.html

KPMG Global. (2024b, May 7). KPMG Trusted AI framework. *KPMG*. https://kpmg.com/xx/en/home/services/kpmg-trusted-ai/trusted-ai-framework.html

Leyer, M., & Schneider, S. (2021). Decision augmentation and automation with artificial intelligence: Threat or opportunity for managers? *Business Horizons, 64*(5), 711–724. https://doi.org/10.1016/j.bushor.2021.02.026

Lloyd, R. (2024). EY announces launch of artificial intelligence platform EY.ai following US$1.4b investment. https://www.ey.com/en_gl/newsroom/2023/09/ey-announces-launch-of-artificial-intelligence-platform-ey-ai-following-us-1-4b-investment

Marr, B. (2020). Deloitte survey finds digital maturity is critical to business success. *Forbes*. https://www.forbes.com/sites/bernardmarr/2020/05/27/digital-maturity-is-critical-to-business-success%2D%2Dnow-more-so-than-ever%2D%2Dsurvey-finds/

Moran, J. W., & Brightman, B. K. (2000). Leading organizational change. *Journal of Workplace Learning, 12*(2), 66–74. https://doi.org/10.1108/13665620010316226

O'Dwyer, M., Murgia, M., & Neil Alim, A. (2023). PwC experiments with chatbots to speed up its lawyers. *Financial Times*. https://www.ft.com/content/463f8cc1-9feb-46ac-a14e-7826c87e2bf4

Pease, G. (2018). People analytics – Privacy vs. Transparency. *Best Practice in Human Resources*. http://www.bestpracticeinhr.com/people-analytics-privacy-vs-transparency-2/

PwC. (2024). About us. *PwC*. https://www.pwc.com/gx/en/about.html

PwC. (n.d.). *Responsible AI at PwC*. PwC. Retrieved July 31, 2024, from https://www.pwc.com/gx/en/issues/artificial-intelligence/what-is-responsible-ai.html

PwC Global. (2024). Ethics and compliance. *PwC*. https://www.pwc.com/gx/en/about/ethics-business-conduct.html

Ransbotham, S., Candelon, F., Kiron, D., LaFountain, B., & Khodabandeh, S. (2021). The cultural benefits of artificial intelligence in the enterprise. *MIT Sloan Management Review*. https://sloanreview.mit.edu/projects/the-cultural-benefits-of-artificial-intelligence-in-the-enterprise/

Reuters. (2024, May 29). PwC to become OpenAI's largest enterprise customer amid genAI boom. *Reuters*. https://www.reuters.com/technology/pwc-become-openai-largest-enterprise-customer-wsj-reports-2024-05-29/

Robbins, S. P., & Judge, T. (2023). *Organizational behavior* (19th ed.). Pearson. https://www.pearson.com/en-us/subject-catalog/p/organizational-behavior/P200000007044/9780137687206

Schultz, M. D., & Seele, P. (2023). Towards AI ethics' institutionalization: Knowledge bridges from business ethics to advance organizational AI ethics. *AI and Ethics, 3*(1), 99–111. https://doi.org/10.1007/s43681-022-00150-y

Tadesse Bogale, A., & Debela, K. L. (2024). Organizational culture: A systematic review. *Cogent Business & Management, 11*(1), 2340129. https://doi.org/10.1080/23311975.2024.2340129

Taulli, T. (2021). Artificial intelligence: Should you teach it to your employees? *Forbes*. https://www.forbes.com/sites/tomtaulli/2021/09/10/ai-artificial-intelligence-should-you-teach-it-to-your-employees/

Tursunbayeva, A., & Chaluz-Ben Gal, H. (2024). Adoption of artificial intelligence: A TOP framework-based checklist for digital leaders. *Business Horizons, 67*, 357. https://doi.org/10.1016/j.bushor.2024.04.006

Tursunbayeva, A., Pagliari, C., Di Lauro, S., & Antonelli, G. (2022). The ethics of people analytics: Risks, opportunities and recommendations. *Personnel Review, 51*(3), 900–921. https://doi.org/10.1108/PR-12-2019-0680

Van Oosten, E. B. (2006). Intentional change theory at the organizational level: A case study. *Journal of Management Development, 25*(7), 707–717. https://doi.org/10.1108/02621710610678508

Vincent, V. U. (2021). Integrating intuition and artificial intelligence in organizational decision-making. *Business Horizons, 64*(4), 425–438. https://doi.org/10.1016/j.bushor.2021.02.008

Wamba-Taguimdje, S.-L., Fosso Wamba, S., Kala Kamdjoug, J. R., & Tchatchouang Wanko, C. E. (2020). Influence of artificial intelligence (AI) on firm performance: The business value of AI-based transformation projects. *Business Process Management Journal, 26*(7), 1893–1924. https://doi.org/10.1108/BPMJ-10-2019-0411

Webber Sadovi, M. (2023). KPMG's Stöckle on auditing's 'human-machine' connection. *CFO Dive*. https://www.cfodive.com/news/kpmgs-stockle-auditings-human-machine-connection/649457/

# Chapter 10
# Artificial Intelligence and the Future of Human Resource Management Work

## 10.1 Exploring the Future of HRM

The role of HRM functions and professionals in shaping the Future of Work and organizations is frequently debated. However, discussions about the Future of HRM work are less common, reflecting the proverb that "the cobbler's children have no shoes." Despite the extensive exploration of various worker categories and professions, the Future of HRM as a distinct field remains underexplored. For instance, there are already books and studies on the future of specific professions (Susskind & Susskind, 2017), but they do not consider the future of the HRM profession. Below the Future of HRM work is examined through three specific lenses: the Future of Work, Knowledge Work, and Responsible AI. Finally, it also discusses the influence of sociotechnical factors in shaping the Future of HRM.

## 10.2 Future of Work Perspective

The concept of the Future of Work has gained growing attention across various scientific disciplines, primarily focusing on how employees will work in the future and how they will be managed. As a result, numerous definitions of the concept have been proposed. For example, a report by Deloitte defines the Future of Work as "a result of many forces of change affecting three deeply connected dimensions of an organization: work (the what), the workforce (the who), and the workplace (the where)" (Schwartz et al., 2019). According to the OECD, the Future of Work is related to how digitalization and globalization influence how we live and work, raising questions about job precarity, retirement, skills, quality of jobs, and employee voice (OECD, n.d.). Balliester and Elsheikhi (2018) define "the Future of Work along five dimensions in which current changes will impact the world of work: the future of jobs; their



A. Tursunbayeva, *Augmenting Human Resource Management with Artificial Intelligence*, Contributions to Management Science,
https://doi.org/10.1007/978-3-031-75266-7_10

quality; wage and income inequality; social protection systems; and social dialogue and industrial relations." McKinsey (2023) refers to the Future of Work as an "informed perspective on what businesses and other organizations need to know about how work could shift (given digitization and other trends), plus how workforces and workplaces can prepare for those changes, big and small." Based on a literature review, Schulte et al. (2020) concluded that the Future of Work exists of labor market changes, societal values, and type of work (cognitive vs. manual), whereby technology is identified as the main driver of the Future of Work (Schulte et al., 2020).

The numerous definitions of the Future of Work present a challenge, as they contribute to the fragmentation of research and hinder the advancement of the field. Despite this, these varied definitions reveal several important characteristics of the Future of Work.

Firstly, it is evident that the Future of Work research is about studying how macro-level trends such as digitalization and globalization affect the quality and number of jobs and how these changes in jobs, in turn, affect individuals, organizations, and society in general. Therefore, the Future of Work is inherently multilevel, consisting of aspects related to the individual level (e.g., job quality), the organization level (e.g., workplace configurations), and the societal level (e.g., number and types of jobs, social protection) outcomes (Balliester & Elsheikhi, 2018; OECD, n.d.). Secondly, the Future of Work results from those above-mentioned forces, which affect three connected dimensions of an organization: the what, the who, and where (Minbaeva, 2021; Schwartz et al., 2019). The "What" dimension pertains to the nature of the tasks employees perform and the level of autonomy they possess in deciding which tasks to undertake and how to execute them. The "Where" dimension concerns work's physical or virtual location, encompassing telework and remote work, particularly emphasized during the COVID-19 pandemic. The "When" dimension involves the timing aspects of work, such as flexible hours, shift work, and work pace. As highlighted by Bolino et al. (2021), traditional 9-to-5, 5-day workweeks are becoming obsolete.

Finally, technology is the primary driver of the Future of Work, which affects labor market changes, societal values, and the type of work people perform (Schulte et al., 2020). AI is a technology that has been most frequently discussed in relation to the Future of Work (Bohr & Memarzadeh, 2020), mainly because it envisions automating activities historically considered difficult to automate due to their reliance on tacit knowledge and skills, such as flexibility and judgment (Autor, 2015). This potential distinguishes AI from the previous generation of technologies.

Building on the concept of the Future of Work, AI has the potential to reshape the roles and functions of HRM professionals across three essential dimensions: What, Where, and When. Predicting the future is a complex task, but researchers are increasingly utilizing Generative AI tools to aid in this effort. For instance, recent studies have utilized ChatGPT to generate scenarios related to the Future of (knowledge) Work (Renkema & Tursunbayeva, 2024). In this book, a similar methodology is employed to explore the future landscape of HRM. Specifically, ChatGPT was tasked with creating scenarios for each dimension of the Future of Work-What, Where, and When-while presenting both optimistic and pessimistic viewpoints to reflect the dual nature of future possibilities (see Table 10.1).

**Table 10.1** Scenarios on the Future of Work of HRM professionals

| Future of work dimension | Positive scenario | Negative scenario |
|---|---|---|
| What | In this scenario, AI assists HRM professionals by automating routine tasks like payroll processing, candidate screening, and performance evaluations. Employees have higher autonomy to focus on strategic, creative, and complex problem-solving tasks, as AI takes over repetitive and mundane work | In this scenario, AI systems are used to monitor and control every aspect of employee performance, leading to a significant reduction in employee autonomy. Tasks are dictated by AI algorithms, leaving little room for creativity or personal decision-making |
| Where | With AI-driven tools, HRM professionals and employees can work from anywhere, increasing the prevalence of telework and remote work. Advanced virtual collaboration platforms ensure seamless communication and coordination across geographies, making physical office spaces less critical | Although remote work is possible, the constant surveillance and monitoring by AI tools create a sense of being perpetually watched, which can erode trust and increase stress among employees. The virtual workspace becomes a digital panopticon, where every move is scrutinized |
| When | Flexible work hours become standard as AI systems monitor and manage productivity and project timelines. Employees have the freedom to work at their own pace, accommodating personal schedules and promoting a better work-life balance | Work hours become rigidly structured as AI systems enforce strict schedules and productivity metrics. Flexibility in work timing is minimal, and employees are expected to adhere to AI-generated schedules, leading to a potentially unhealthy work environment and burnout |
| Prompt | *As a specialist in developing future scenarios, your task is to develop three scenarios for the future role of HRM professionals, where they are influenced by Artificial Intelligence (AI). Develop one positive and one negative scenario, and discuss them across the following dimensions:*<br>*– "What" dimension pertaining to the nature of the tasks employees perform and the level of autonomy they possess in deciding which tasks to undertake and how to execute them.*<br>*– "Where" dimension concerning the physical or virtual location where work is conducted, encompassing telework and remote work, particularly emphasized during the Covid-19 pandemic.*<br>*– "When" dimension involving the timing aspects of work, such as flexible hours, shift work, and work pace.*<br>*Develop the three scenarios of about 150 words each in one paragraph* (Renkema & Tursunbayeva, 2024) | |

Created with ChatGPT, personal communication, September 01, 2024

The scenarios proposed by ChatGPT align with the arguments discussed in the previous chapters of this book, also in relation to the future of HRM professionals work itself. Thus, they reflect the enthusiasm (i.e., hype perspective) among HRM professionals regarding AI's potential to support and enhance their roles across various work configurations. However, they also echo fears or concerns about AI presenting ethical challenges for HRM professionals.

## 10.3 Knowledge Work Perspective

Cherry (2020) conducted a historical analysis of the relationship between work and technology. She observed that the discussion about automation and the Future of Work has been recurring throughout the twentieth century. However, whereas in the 1960s, blue-collar and factory workers were primary targets for mechanization and automation, AI has recently impacted knowledge and service workers (Cherry, 2020). Gartner recently estimated that the global number of such workers reached 1 billion (Roth, 2019).

Knowledge workers are defined as a new class of employees (Wuthnow & Shrum, 1983) who apply theoretical and analytical knowledge from formal education (Janz et al., 1997) and generate new knowledge at work, challenging traditional organizational structures (Drucker, 1993). They are categorized broadly into professional occupations such as scientists, engineers, and doctors (Nomikos, 1989) and those in high-tech industries (Kelloway & Barling, 2000). "Knowledge" can help occupational groups protect their status (Abbott, 1988). Additionally, knowledge workers are identified by their traits, such as creativity, innovation (Harris & Vining, 1987), and critical thinking (Larson et al., 2024), and by the nature of their work, which involves a balance between intellectual and manual tasks (Fox, 1990).

HRM professionals fit all of the definitions above. Thus, they can be considered knowledge workers. Below is an explanation of why this is the case, along with the potential future of HRM professionals based on these definitions and existing evidence.

Firstly, HRM professionals apply theoretical and analytical knowledge from formal education. They use this knowledge to develop and implement HRM strategies, policies, and practices that challenge traditional organizational structures, such as introducing flexible work arrangements or promoting a more inclusive workplace culture. A recent research study of 5648 HRM practitioners revealed that only 21% believe they have the competencies to tackle current and future workforce challenges (Verlinden, 2023). Many individuals today turn to massive online courses, such as those on the Coursera platform, to advance their knowledge and skills. A quick search of Coursera for HRM courses reveals that while the most popular options remain generic HRM courses, many new offerings now incorporate a technological component, such as IBM's "Generative AI for HR Professionals" and "Generative AI: Advance Your HR Career." This trend suggests that HRM functions and professionals will need to continue strengthening their data literacy and digital proficiency skills alongside business acumen and functional competencies (Vulpen, 2021) as exponential technologies and advanced data analytics become indispensable parts of their work. This trend aligns with the broader labor market, as highlighted in the Digital Skills Opportunity for All report from Randstad and the OECD. The report analyzed over 400 million job postings published in the last 10 years across ten countries and found that jobs requiring digital skills already comprise 6–12% of all vacancies posted online (Van't Noordende & Scarpetta, 2022).

Secondly, HRM is an "organizational profession," and its practitioners are "organizational professionals" (Roper & Higgins, 2020). The professionalization of HRM is progressing, with organizations like the UK's CIPD or WorldatWork and Society for Human Resource Management (SHRM) in the US striving to model themselves after more established occupational or collegial professions (Syrigou & Williams, 2023).

Thirdly and relatedly, like other knowledge workers, HRM professionals aim to protect their occupational status by obtaining professional certifications from such associations. Professional certifications were reported to enhance an individual's reputation by decreasing uncertainty related to performance standards and addressing technical uncertainty (Graffin & Ward, 2010). In a 2018 PayScale survey of over 102,000 HRM professionals, 34% reported having earned at least one certification, and their salaries showed that these certifications were becoming increasingly valuable over time (Rowley, 2020). The generic predictions for professional certifications suggest that the demand for HRM certifications will continue to be actual due to the demand for upskilling and reskilling (of HRM professionals themselves) caused by rapid technological changes, making certifications essential for job market competitiveness (PeopleCert, n.d.). The shift to online learning will likely continue, increasing global access to certifications. Certifications in emerging technologies like AI and cybersecurity could continue gaining popularity, while micro-credentials and stackable certifications will offer more focused, flexible learning options (PeopleCert, n.d.).

Fourthly, HRM professionals must exhibit creativity and innovation in their work. Indeed, their role requires them to think strategically and adapt to changing organizational needs, making creativity and innovation essential traits. According to a Statista survey of 11.3 million employees across 803 organizations conducted between November 2022 and February 2023, over 70% of companies expect creative and analytical thinking skills to become increasingly important between 2023 and 2027 (Wells, 2024). This is because they can help navigate and resolve complex organizational challenges, stay ahead of competitors, lead to continuous improvement, and, most importantly, are currently irreplaceable by AI (Wells, 2024). Thus, creativity could be critical to the future-proofing of an HRM career.

Finally, HRM work involves a blend of intellectual tasks, such as designing HRM strategies or policies, and more practical tasks, such as handling employee relations issues or managing payroll. This balance mirrors the definition of knowledge workers who engage in both "thinking" and "doing" activities. Preexisting HRM literature indicated that, currently, 65–75% of HRM activities involve operational "doing" tasks, 15–30% involve relational activities, and only 5–15% involve transformational "thinking" tasks (Johnson et al., 2020; Ruël et al., 2004). In the future, achieving the right balance between automation and algorithmic management activities, performing essential tasks to strengthen stakeholder relationships, and augmenting others will be crucial. This balance is key to maintaining human-centered HRM practices while also meeting the constraints of HRM budgets. HRM leaders and professionals are constantly pressured to "do more with less" (Zielinski, 2023). Gartner reports that HR receives one of the lowest investments of all organizational support functions. The average HRM functional spend as a percentage of revenue is 0.74% (Berger-Böcker, 2022). Companies prefer to keep HRM department budgets flat or reduce them (Tubbs, 2022), forcing HRM professionals to make difficult decisions regularly. This concept seems to affect HRM more than other business functions, partly due to its non-revenue-generating nature, which continually compels HRM to prove its strategic importance. Additionally, HRM departments often face accusations of being overstaffed, with an average HR-to-staff ratio of 2.57. This ratio varies by company size, being 3.4 for small organizations and dropping to 1.22 and 1.03 for medium and large organizations, respectively (Snyder et al., 2023). The optimal target for HRM departments is commonly viewed as a one to one hundred ratio, considered the "standard" ratio of HRM staff to employees (Indeed Editorial Team, 2023).

HRM departments' strategics also need to evolve alongside the HRM professionals and their roles. This is one of the biggest challenges they will face in their frequently "linear" organizations in the era of the "exponential" growth in technology. Historically, a similar trend was observed during World War I, where rapid advancements in military technology, such as airplanes and machine guns (Department of Veterans' Affairs, 2021), far outpaced the evolution of military strategy that remained unchanged from the Franco-Prussian War of 1870. The exponential growth of technologies today is outstripping the ability of organizations to adapt their strategies and structures. This lag can create vulnerabilities and inefficiencies as organizations struggle to keep pace with the rapid technological advancements that are reshaping industries and society at large. Addressing this gap is crucial for ensuring that AI is effectively integrated into organizational and then HRM strategies.

To conclude, research on the management of knowledge workers and their Future of Work has extensively focused on occupations such as accountants, lawyers, consultants (Løwendahl, 2005; Susskind & Susskind, 2017), and healthcare professionals. Interestingly, research focused on the jobs of HRM professionals is limited. Nevertheless, with the growing importance of the knowledge economy and the pervasive role of information technology (Richthofen et al., 2022), it is becoming increasingly important to understand the distinct work needs, attitudes, and behavior of such knowledge workers as HRM professionals. This is also because HRM professionals shape the future of work for all other people at work (CIPD, 2021).

## 10.4 Responsible Artificial Intelligence Perspective

While the debate continues about AI's impact on the future of HRM, some innovators suggest a different perspective: that HRM may actually shape the future of AI rather than the other way around. This, for instance, was proposed by Christopher J. Fernandez (2024), Corporate VP of HR at Microsoft, in his recent LinkedIn post. Reflecting on his 18-month journey to lead Microsoft's AI transformation within the HR function, he emphasized that his background was in traditional HRM and not in technology. Thus, he underlines that technological skill was not the most critical in driving such large-scale digital transformations in HRM. The journey involved collaboration with HRM leaders, technologists, and engineers to enhance HRM services globally through AI. The approach was rooted in Microsoft's six RAI Standards: Accountability, Inclusiveness, Reliability and Safety, Fairness, Transparency, and Privacy and Security. The key initiatives included leveraging AI to create better employee experiences and empowering HRM professionals with practical AI applications. HRM professionals here were empowered as "citizen developers" using low-code tools like Microsoft Power Apps to create custom business applications that automate (previously) workflows. The introduction of AI-powered tools, such as Power Virtual Agents and then Copilot, further revolutionized HRM operations by improving employee experiences and enabling HR professionals to focus on high-value tasks. He labeled these initiatives as successful, attributing it to integrating human judgment in AI processes and creating an AI community of practice across HRM. This community fostered innovation and collaboration, driving AI adoption across the organization. He emphasized the need for HRM leaders to develop a clear AI adoption plan grounded in RAI and prepare their HRM team for successfully leading such projects:

> The HR profession is in a unique position to lead the AI transformation in organizations as the human experience itself changes. The work of HR leaders will shape how the employee experience continues to benefit from this transformation. How we approach AI as HR professionals now will define the world of work over the next century and beyond (Fernandez, 2024).

Given Microsoft's leadership in technology development and its influential role in shaping the global discourse on RAI, its approach is poised to set a precedent for companies worldwide. Microsoft was among the first eight global tech companies to commit to applying UN Educational, Scientific and Cultural Organization's Recommendations in developing AI solutions (O'Hagan, 2024). Furthermore, they are leading the expansion of the Trustworthy and RAI Network into Europe (Balasubramanian, 2024). As a result, Microsoft's RAI approach is likely to be seen as futuristic and aspirational for HRM professionals in various countries and sectors still in the early stages of their AI journeys and aiming to navigate the complexities of AI integration while ensuring that ethical standards are upheld.

## 10.5 Human Agency and Technology: Co-Creating the Future of HRM

Numerous approaches can be utilized to envision the potential future of HRM. This chapter has considered three of them. However, it is important to recognize that various sociotechnical factors can significantly influence such projections and scenarios (as outlined in Table 10.1).

HRM professionals and employees have agency (Oliver, 1991). Thus, the diffusion of AI in HRM can be constrained by individual factors such as HRM professionals' attitudes and motivations toward AI and their AI-related knowledge, skills, and competencies (Tursunbayeva & Chaluz-Ben Gal, 2024), as well as employees' perspectives. Overall, employee experience has not improved in organizations for years. The Great Resignation has forced organizations to rethink their relationships with employees, without whom their businesses would not operate (McKinsey Themes, 2022). People, not "The Company," get stuff done. Thus, employees want to feel valued and appreciated. However, a recent Gartner survey revealed that only 13% of employees are fully satisfied with their experience (Baker, 2019). Thus, improving the employee experience is high on HRM leaders' agenda, and organizations are making significant investments to improve it through, for example, onboarding investments and workplace redesign. Many organizations are also turning to creating personalized experiences for workers, similar to how technology enables us to personalize consumer experiences (Chandra et al., 2022).

The individual responses to AI go beyond simply accepting or resisting it. According to Oliver (1991), there are at least five types of strategic responses individuals can employ to cope with institutional pressures, such as top-down AI implementation. These include acquiescence (conforming to expectations), compromise (balancing conflicting demands), avoidance (evading the need to conform), defiance (rejecting or opposing the expectations), and manipulation (attempting to alter the institutional expectations or influence the sources of these pressures).

The way AI can influence the future of work for HRM professionals also depends on advancements in AI technology itself. While numerous examples of AI's current and potential uses in various HRM practices are provided in this book, it is important to recognize that the current enthusiasm around AI may represent the "Peak of Inflated Expectations" in the Gartner (2023) hype cycle. This framework helps us understand the evolution of emerging technologies in terms of initial high expectations and their eventual roles within organizations. Typically, early developments lead to excessive excitement and unrealistic expectations, followed by a phase of disillusionment when those expectations are not met (Fenn & Raskino, 2008). For instance, e-books or Internet currency, among many others, are overpromoted technology products that failed to live up to their hype (Haskin, 2007). Given that generative AI is currently at the Peak of Inflated Expectations (Gartner, 2023), a disillusionment phase may also be approaching. Therefore, the progress, expectations, and realizations related to AI technologies can play a significant role in shaping the future of work for HRM professionals.

To conclude, it is evident that in future workplaces, HRM professionals will coexist with AI applications (Einola & Khoreva, 2023), incorporating various AI capabilities and functions (IBM, 2023). While some HRM activities will be fully automated, others will be supported by AI (Von Krogh, 2018; Raisch & Krakowski, 2021), as discussed in previous chapters. Thus, AI is unlikely to replace HRM professionals entirely, but HRM professionals who effectively integrate AI into their work will likely outpace those who do not.

# References

Abbott, A. (1988). *The system of professions: An essay on the division of expert labor*. University of Chicago Press. https://press.uchicago.edu/ucp/books/book/chicago/S/bo5965590.html

Autor, D. H. (2015). Why are there still so many jobs? The history and future of workplace automation. *Journal of Economic Perspectives, 29*(3), 3–30. https://doi.org/10.1257/jep.29.3.3

Baker, M. (2019). *Gartner says only 13% of employees are largely satisfied with their work experiences* [Gartner]. https://www.gartner.com/en/newsroom/press-releases/2019-10-29-gartner-says-only-13%2D%2Dof-employees-are-largely-satisf

Balasubramanian, S. (2024). Microsoft Partners to launch responsible AI initiative in Europe. *Forbes*. https://www.forbes.com/sites/saibala/2024/06/17/microsoft-partners-to-launch-responsible-ai-initiative-in-europe/

Balliester, T., & Elsheikhi, A. (2018). *The future of work: A literature review* (no. Research department working paper n°29). International Labour Organization. https://www.ilo.org/publications/future-work-literature-review

Berger-Böcker, S. (2022). 2022 HR budget and efficiency benchmarks. *Gartner*. https://www.gartner.com/en/documents/4013287

Bohr, A., & Memarzadeh, K. (2020). The rise of artificial intelligence in healthcare applications. *Artificial Intelligence in Healthcare*, 25–60. PMC. https://doi.org/10.1016/B978-0-12-818438-7.00002-2

Bolino, M. C., Kelemen, T. K., & Matthews, S. H. (2021). Working 9-to-5? A review of research on nonstandard work schedules. *Journal of Organizational Behavior, 42*(2), 188–211. https://doi.org/10.1002/job.2440

Chandra, S., Verma, S., Lim, W. M., Kumar, S., & Donthu, N. (2022). Personalization in personalized marketing: Trends and ways forward. *Psychology & Marketing, 39*(8), 1529–1562. https://doi.org/10.1002/mar.21670

Cherry, M. A. (2020). Back to the future: A continuity of dialogue on work and technology at the ILO. *International Labour Review, 159*(1), 1–23. https://doi.org/10.1111/ilr.12156

CIPD. (2021). *People Profession 2030: A collective view of future trends*. CIPD. https://www.cipd.org/uk/about/news/hr-shaping-new-future/.

Drucker, P. F. (1993). *Post-capitalist society*. HarperBusiness. http://archive.org/details/postcapitalistso00druc

Einola, K., & Khoreva, V. (2023). Best friend or broken tool? Exploring the co-existence of humans and artificial intelligence in the workplace ecosystem. *Human Resource Management, 62*(1), 117–135. https://doi.org/10.1002/hrm.22147

Fenn, J., & Raskino, M. (2008). *Mastering the hype cycle: How to choose the right innovation at the right time*. Harvard Business Press. https://www.semanticscholar.org/paper/Mastering-the-Hype-Cycle%3A-How-to-Choose-the-Right-Fenn-Raskino/33b509db0e07044ed22971f82ce705e8a612e10b

Fernandez,C.J.(2024).*HRisthefutureofAI:Whatwe'vedoneinMicrosoftHR*[LinkedIn].https://www.linkedin.com/pulse/hr-future-ai-what-weve-done-microsoft-christopher-j-fernandez-rlqgc

Fox, N. R. (1990). *Knowledge and organization*. https://www.semanticscholar.org/paper/Knowledge-and-Organization-Fox/46187ce1c27546d00e5126add44b993e30d103de

Gartner. (2023). *Gartner Says Generative AI is at the Peak of Inflated Expectations for Revenue and Sales Technology* [Gartner]. https://www.gartner.com/en/newsroom/press-releases/2023-08-17-gartner-says-generative-ai-is-at-the-peak-of-inflated-expectations-for-revenue-and-sales-technology

Graffin, S. D., & Ward, A. J. (2010). Certifications and reputation: Determining the standard of desirability amidst uncertainty. *Organization Science, 21*(2), 331–346. https://doi.org/10.1287/orsc.1080.0400

Harris, M., & Vining, G. W. (1987). The IE's future role in improving knowledge. *Industrial Engineering, 19*(7), 28–32.

Haskin, D. (2007). Don't believe the hype: The 21 biggest technology flops. *Computerworld.* https://www.computerworld.com/article/1647232/don-t-believe-the-hype-the-21-biggest-technology-flops.html

IBM. (2023). Types of artificial intelligence. *IBM.* https://www.ibm.com/think/topics/artificial-intelligence-types

Indeed Editorial Team. (2023). *HR to employee ratio: A definitive guide* [indeed]. https://www.indeed.com/career-advice/career-development/hr-to-employee-ratio

Janz, B. D., Colquitt, J. A., & Noe, R. A. (1997). Knowledge worker team effectiveness: The role of autonomy, interdependence, team development, and contextual support variables. *Personnel Psychology, 50*(4), 877–904. https://doi.org/10.1111/j.1744-6570.1997.tb01486.x

Johnson, R. D., Carlson, K. D., & Kavanagh, M. J. (2020). *Human resource information systems: Basics, applications, and future directions* (5th ed.). Sage. https://edge.sagepub.com/johnsonhris5e

Kelloway, E. K., & Barling, J. (2000). Knowledge work as organizational behavior. *International Journal of Management Reviews, 2*(3), 287–304. https://doi.org/10.1111/1468-2370.00042

Larson, B. Z., Moser, C., Caza, A., Muehlfeld, K., & Colombo, L. A. (2024). Critical thinking in the age of generative AI. *Academy of Management Learning & Education*, amle.2024.0338. https://doi.org/10.5465/amle.2024.0338

Løwendahl, B. R. (2005). *Strategic management of professional service firms* (3rd ed.). Copenhagen Business School Press.

McKinsey Themes. (2022). *How to improve the employee experience [McKinsey].* https://www.mckinsey.com/featured-insights/themes/how-to-improve-the-employee-experience.

McKinsey Insights. (2023). What is the future of work? *McKinsey.* https://www.mckinsey.com/featured-insights/mckinsey-explainers/what-is-the-future-of-work

Minbaeva, D. (2021). Disrupted HR? *Human Resource Management Review, 31*(4), 100820. https://doi.org/10.1016/j.hrmr.2020.100820

Nomikos, G. E. (1989). Managing knowledge workers for productivity. *National Productivity Review, 8*(2), 165–174. https://doi.org/10.1002/npr.4040080209

O'Hagan, C. (2024). AI ethics: 8 global tech companies commit to apply UNESCO's recommendation. *UNESCO.* https://www.unesco.org/en/articles/ai-ethics-8-global-tech-companies-commit-apply-unescos-recommendation

OECD. (n.d.). *Future of work.* OECD. Retrieved August 4, 2024, from https://www.oecd.org/en/topics/policy-issues/future-of-work.html

Oliver, C. (1991). Strategic responses to institutional processes. *The Academy of Management Review, 16*(1), 145–179.

PeopleCert. (n.d.). Looking into the future of certification. *PeopleCert.* Retrieved August 27, 2024, from https://www.peoplecert.org/news-and-announcements/peoplecert-future-of-certification

Raisch, S., & Krakowski, S. (2021). Artificial intelligence and management: The automation–augmentation paradox. *Academy of Management Review, 46*(1), 192–210. https://doi.org/10.5465/amr.2018.0072

Renkema, M., & Tursunbayeva, A. (2024). The future of work of academics in the age of artificial intelligence: State-of-the-art and a research roadmap. *Futures, 103453.* https://doi.org/10.1016/j.futures.2024.103453

Roper, I., & Higgins, P. (2020). Hidden in plain sight? The human resource management practitioner's role in dealing with workplace conflict as a source of organisational–professional power. *Human Resource Management Journal, 30*(4), 508–524. https://doi.org/10.1111/1748-8583.12311

Roth, G. (2019). *When we exceeded 1 billion knowledge workers* [Gartner]. https://blogs.gartner.com/craig-roth/2019/12/11/2019-exceeded-1-billion-knowledge-workers/

Rowley, M. (2020). *Human resources certification: What HR professionals should know*. Columbia Southern University. https://www.columbiasouthern.edu/blog/blog-articles/2020/october/human-resources-certification/

Ruël, H., Bondarouk, T., & Looise, J. K. (2004). E-HRM: Innovation or irritation. An explorative empirical study in five large companies on web-based HRM. *Management Revue, 15*(3), 364–380. https://www.jstor.org/stable/41783479

Schulte, P. A., Streit, J. M. K., Sheriff, F., Delclos, G., Felknor, S. A., Tamers, S. L., Fendinger, S., Grosch, J., & Sala, R. (2020). Potential scenarios and hazards in the work of the future: A systematic review of the peer-reviewed and gray literatures. *Annals of Work Exposures and Health, 64*(8), 786–816. https://doi.org/10.1093/annweh/wxaa051

Schwartz, J., Jones, R., & Anderson, S. (2019). What is the future of work? Redefining work, workforces, and workplaces. *Deloitte Insights*, 1–12. https://www2.deloitte.com/content/www/us/en/insights/focus/technology-and-the-future-of-work/redefining-work-workforces-workplaces.html

Snyder, K., Bottorff, C., & Sember, B. (2023). Key HR statistics and trends in 2024—Forbes advisor. *Forbes*. https://www.forbes.com/advisor/business/hr-statistics-trends/

Susskind, R., & Susskind, D. (2017). The future of the professions: How technology will transform the work of human experts. *Journal of Nursing Regulation, 8*(2), P52. https://doi.org/10.1016/S2155-8256(17)30099-6

Syrigou, A., & Williams, S. (2023). Professionalism and professionalization in human resources (HR): HR practitioners as professionals and the organizational professional project. *Journal of Professions and Organization, 10*(2), 151–164. https://doi.org/10.1093/jpo/joad008

Tubbs, M. (2022). Over half of HR managers say budgets are under threat, damaging business performance and economic recovery. *Personio GmbH*. https://www.personio.com/about-personio/press/hr-study-uki-2022/

Tursunbayeva, A., & Chaluz-Ben Gal, H. (2024). Adoption of artificial intelligence: A TOP framework-based checklist for digital leaders. *Business Horizons, 67*, 357. https://doi.org/10.1016/j.bushor.2024.04.006

van Vulpen, E. (2021, September 30). The current state of HR competencies: Only 2 in 10 HR professionals have future-proof skills. *AIHR*. https://www.aihr.com/blog/hr-competency-research-statistics/

Van't Noordende, S., & Scarpetta, S. (2022). Digital skills: How businesses and policymakers can respond to future demand in the labour market *World Economic Forum*. https://www.weforum.org/agenda/2022/11/digital-skills-labour-market-future/

Verlinden, N. (2023, July 27). 12 best HR training programs for 2024. *AIHR*. https://www.aihr.com/blog/human-resources-training/

Von Krogh, G. (2018). Artificial intelligence in organizations: New opportunities for phenomenon-based theorizing. *Academy of Management Discoveries, 4*(4), 404–409. https://doi.org/10.5465/amd.2018.0084

von Richthofen, G., Ogolla, S., & Send, H. (2022). Adopting AI in the context of knowledge work: Empirical Insights from German organizations. *Information (Switzerland), 13*(4), undefined-undefined. https://doi.org/10.3390/info13040199

Wells, R. (2024). 70% of employers say creative thinking is Most in-demand skill in 2024. *Forbes*. https://www.forbes.com/sites/rachelwells/2024/01/28/70-of-employers-say-creative-thinking-is-most-in-demand-skill-in-2024/

Wuthnow, R., & Shrum, W. (1983). Knowledge workers as a "new class": Structural and ideological convergence among professional-technical workers and managers. *Work and Occupations, 10*(4), 471–487. https://doi.org/10.1177/073088848301000400 5

Zielinski, D. (2023). *2023 HR technology trends: Talent marketplaces, expanding AI and optimizing existing systems* [SHRM]. https://www.shrm.org/topics-tools/news/technology/2023-hr-technology-trends-talent-marketplaces-expanding-ai-optimizing-existing-systems

# Chapter 11
# A Final Reflection

## 11.1 So What?

AI is already widely integrated into HRM and has the potential to be an "extraordinary force for good if contained appropriately" (Suleyman & Bhaskar, 2023). ChatGPT, for instance, is the "fastest-growing consumer application in human history" (Gordon, 2023). It reached 100 million users in just 2 months (Hu, 2023), while for comparison, TikTok reached the same user base in 9 months (Gordon, 2023). However, the concerns around AI and its implications for the Future of Work are also rapidly growing. For example, since the relevant to AI GDPR was enforced in 2018, 1701 fines have been issued for the total amount of €4,001,455,789 (Privacy Affairs, 2024).

Thus, this book was designed to provide a balanced exploration of AI's role within HRM, considering both the potential of AI for HRM and its pitfalls. The integration of AI in HRM is clearly complex, as it is reshaping HRM practices across all three configurations: operational, relational, and transformational. As the worldwide pace of innovation has been lowered, with potential consequences for productivity and growth (Mollick, 2024), AI might be the key that can help organizations and HRM functions to innovate, as they were called to do (Mallin, 2022). Moreover, AI's implications themselves are influenced by numerous sociotechnical factors, including human agency, organizational adoption strategies, regulatory frameworks, and technological development. It is thus important to keep in mind in reading this book that the AI we use today represents the least advanced version we will ever use (Suleyman & Bhaskar, 2023), meaning that many concepts and examples discussed in this book may become outdated by the time you are reading it. However, the book can still become an invaluable reference point because it merges the broader discussions on the Future of Work with the Future of HRM. It draws on established theoretical literature, empirical findings obtained with innovative research methodologies recommended for AI research (Orlikowski & Scott, 2023),



A. Tursunbayeva, *Augmenting Human Resource Management with Artificial Intelligence*, Contributions to Management Science,
https://doi.org/10.1007/978-3-031-75266-7_11

and real-life examples, thus providing the depth and breadth of the topic of AI in HRM that will continue to be relevant as AI evolves. Specific implications of the book are described below.

## 11.2 Theoretical Implications

Theoretically, this book proposes an approach for conceptualizing AI in HRM and its consequences by integrating two (so far) disconnected streams of literature on the Future of Work and HRM (Technologies). It thus addresses the gap in organizational theories that consider the complexity of AI (Trocin et al., 2021) and calls for building a more integrated body of research in this area (Tursunbayeva et al., 2017). This approach underscores the duality of AI's impact on HRM, encapsulated by the hype and fear perspectives previously discussed specifically for the broader Future of Work (Huysman, 2020) and not the future of people management. The positive hype perspective, emphasizing AI's transformative and augmentative potential in general (as discussed in Chap. 3), can be seen across all HRM practices, as well as across all configurations (see Chaps. 4–6), which illustrate AI's capacity to transform automation of operational tasks to algorithmic management, strengthen relational HRM practices, and augment HRM and organizations through previously unimaginable insights, types of analysis, and contributions to the top strategic goals such as sustainability. On the other hand, the fear perspective, which cautions against AI's potential to disrupt job markets and worsen inequalities, is addressed through discussions on ethical concerns and the challenges posed by algorithmic management and (ir)responsible AI-driven HRM solutions for employees, organizations, and society overall, including bias, transparency, and accountability (see Chap. 7).

The book also builds on the foundation of the configurational approach of e-HRM and HRIS research streams, which has been recommended for future AI for HRM research (Prikshat et al., 2021). This approach deepens the understanding of existing AI for HRM applications and offers a pathway to advance current knowledge, as well as opportunities for innovative developments and more effective application of these systems within organizations.

Moreover, the book brings to the HRM literature the discussion currently raised primarily in the information systems stream of research on RAI (Merhi, 2023). It is proposed in the Book as an approach (Klein & Potosky, 2019) to address the ethical challenges of AI for HRM research and practice at and across different levels of analysis (see Chap. 8).

By drawing on the approaches adopted by leading consulting companies (see Chap. 9) the book advocates for rethinking existing change management models for both adopting AI and change management with AI.

Finally, the book bridges the multi-topical, multidisciplinary, and multi-functional nature of existing research on AI and HRM (Strohmeier, 2022), bringing together these diverse research streams.

## 11.3 Practical Implications

From a practical standpoint, integrating AI in HRM offers significant benefits and improvements in efficiency, accuracy, and strategic alignment. As detailed in Chaps. 4–6, AI-driven tools for recruitment, training, performance management, and compensation are transforming traditional HRM practices. The book's real-life examples illustrate how AI for HRM vendor solutions can enhance decision-making processes, streamline operations, and support personalized employee development.

However, the practical implementation of AI in HRM has its challenges. Chapter 7 reveals that AI's ethical and legal risks, such as fairness, discrimination, and privacy, pose significant concerns at all levels. The practical implications call for a robust ethical framework, clear guidelines, and clarification on how these should be embedded in organizations (see Chap. 8) and converted to employee knowledge and skills to ensure that AI applications in HRM are aligned with organizational values and regulatory requirements.

Drawing on empirical research and the balanced insights, the book can increase knowledge about the best and worst cases of the application of AI for HRM. This will give the decision makers and managers a deeper understanding of the conditions under which AI for HRM adds value or becomes critical and what might be the intervention to improve their human-centered and responsible design and implementation across different sectors and industries. Specifically, unbiased and rigorous insights and recommendations of this book can facilitate synergy between technology and HRM practices and return on investments while safeguarding ethical and sustainable HRM, as the future of work depends on how technologies are embedded in organizations (Bondarouk et al., 2017).

The book also provides organizations with a foundation for assessing AI's impact, interactions, and potential complex consequences in HRM (Orlikowski & Scott, 2008). Additionally, it offers valuable insights for HR technology entrepreneurs to guide the human-centered design of AI in HRM, especially as related spinoffs and startups continue to emerge (As & Basu, 2022). The final chapters of the book (8–10) could be of particular interest to operational HR managers, as they provide a roadmap for responsible deployment of AI and their Future of HRM prospects.

## 11.4 Teaching Implications

The book is versatile and can be used for teaching across all academic levels and in executive education, as it offers practical insights and advanced knowledge that can be applied in professional settings. Whether used in a classroom environment or for specialized training programs, the book provides comprehensive and theoretically grounded content catering to various educational needs and learning objectives.

The research insights offered in the book could also highlight the areas where upskilling is needed to better engage with and grasp AI's potential and consequences (European Commission, 2020). For instance, for HRM professionals, this could include the RAI competencies discussed in Chap. 8 and the competencies needed for the Future of HRM work discussed in Chap. 10. This will enable them to better engage with and understand AI's potential benefits and consequences for their roles (EU Commission, 2020).

## 11.5 Methodological Implications

Empirically, it is one of the first integrated and theoretically informed inquiries that draws on multiple perspectives, data sources, and concrete examples of AI in HRM. The studies reported in this book also experiment with digital (e.g., netnography data collection on vendor AI for HRM solutions), mixed methodologies, and NLP (Kang et al., 2020) recommended for pioneering AI (Marda & Narayan, 2021) and management research.

The research insights offered in this book could serve as a benchmark for AI for HRM development, implementation use, and implications over time. For instance, the research findings could support the development or advancement of the HRM selection or training processes' guidelines in EU's public and private sectors.

The methodological contributions of this book are particularly relevant for (junior) researchers and practitioners interested in exploring AI's impact on HRM. The research approaches adopted by scientists in the age of AI are evolving. Unlike traditional studies conducted by an individual using a single dataset, analysis method, or location, modern research leverages multiple data sources, analysis techniques, and tools. It is often conducted by geographically dispersed international teams (National Academies Press, 2022). AI's rise has also enabled researchers to gather data from social media platforms such as LinkedIn (Di Lauro et al., 2023), Facebook (Franz et al., 2019), and Twitter (Takats et al., 2022) without directly interacting with research subjects, analyzing this data in ways that can be challenging even for other researchers to interpret (Schwartz, 2022). Recently, AI was even listed as one of 12 authors about using technology for medical education, generating debates among editors and publishers on whether it was appropriate, as AI cannot take responsibility for the content (Stokel-Walker, 2023). There are even suggestions that AI will be the only science in the future (Crawford, 2021).

As AI transitions from labs to real-world applications, scholars, especially junior ones, need to be aware of the ethical risks their research may pose. They must understand that scientific research is not conducted in isolation and can potentially cause harm to individuals, organizations, and society. However, implementing ethical practices in PA research is complex. Research in AI for HRM may originate from fields that typically did not address societal challenges in their research (Crawford, 2021), from contexts that "sparked debates and discussions" about research conduct (Parvatam, 2019), or with numerous ethical guidelines to be adhered to at different levels. Thus, whatever the methodological approach or the disciplinary lens, the complexity and diversity of research with AI mean that ethics must be considered across all research phases. Of course, it is impossible to anticipate every ethical dilemma that might arise. However, following ethical guidelines throughout the research phases can provide opportunities for reflection, help identify potential pitfalls, and enhance the quality of the research as a whole (Gilbert & Stoneman, 2016). If scholars fail to exhibit sufficient concern for the wider social consequences of their research, public confidence in the discipline could decrease. This may cause it to become an area that future researchers view as unattractive to work in, similar to the difficulties faced by studies on nuclear energy and the health consequences of smoking (Ada Lovelace Institute, 2022).

## 11.6 Policy Implications

The policy implications of this book are multifaceted, addressing both organizational and societal levels. For instance, as discussed in Chap. 6, AI has the potential to enhance organizational strategic objectives and support D&I efforts or sustainability, which highlights the need for policies promoting equitable and inclusive AI practices.

On a broader scale, the discussions in Chaps. 7 and 8 point to the necessity for regulatory frameworks that govern the ethical use of AI in HRM. Policymakers must work to create regulations that address ethical concerns, protect employee rights, and ensure that AI applications are used responsibly. This includes setting transparency, accountability, and fairness standards in AI systems and promoting collaboration between industry, academia, and government agencies. Here, the original research findings presented in this book could be invaluable as they identify the "grey areas" that require legislative attention (Guenole et al., 2018; Tursunbayeva et al., 2022), such as diversity attributes and neuroscience insights that previously were unavailable for collection or analysis in organizational settings.

## 11.7 Citizen Science Implications

The need for this book aligns with and responds to calls of the European Commission (2020) and other international initiatives to build a sustainable future for people at work and accountable, human-centered, and explainable AI. Thus, this book is written in a language accessible to non-specialist audiences, which can contribute to public awareness of AI's principal characteristics, opportunities, and risks (Kandlhofer et al., 2023).

## 11.8 Limitations and Future Research Directions

The book, as any publication, has some limitations. Although it extensively explores AI's potential positive and negative implications on HRM and organizations, it overlooks the context in which AI applications are adopted, a critical factor that could influence how AI objectives are translated into actual outcomes (Bondarouk et al., 2017). The book also provides numerous examples of how AI technologies can impact HRM and the potential implications of current AI applications. However, it is important to recognize that humans shape the outcomes of AI rather than AI exerting deterministic effects on its own. Additionally, what might seem like present-day AI applications to some could actually represent the near or even distant future for many of the examples and implications discussed in this book (Renkema & Tursunbayeva, 2024).

To identify future research directions, recognizing that a significant portion of upcoming studies will likely be conducted by or with the assistance of AI (Crawford, 2021), ChatGPT was consulted to suggest potential areas of focus (see Textbox* below).

*Employee Retention Prediction:* How can AI models predict employee turnover and identify key factors contributing to high attrition rates within an organization?

*Talent Acquisition Optimization:* How can AI improve the recruitment process by identifying the best candidates based on resume data, social media activity, and other digital footprints?

*Performance Evaluation Automation:* How can AI be used to develop unbiased and continuous performance evaluation systems that analyze employee performance using a combination of qualitative and quantitative data?

*Sentiment Analysis of Employee Feedback:* How can AI-driven sentiment analysis be used to interpret employee feedback from surveys, emails, and social media to gauge overall job satisfaction and organizational climate?

*Training and Development Personalization:* How can AI personalize learning and development programs based on individual employee needs, learning styles, and career aspirations?

*Predictive Workforce Planning:* How can AI be utilized to forecast future workforce needs and align them with business objectives, considering factors like market trends, technological advancements, and demographic changes?

*Diversity and Inclusion Analysis:* How can AI help in analyzing and promoting diversity and inclusion within the workplace by identifying patterns and biases in hiring, promotion, and retention practices?

*Health and Well-being Monitoring:* How can AI systems monitor and promote employee health and well-being by analyzing data from wearable devices, wellness programs, and workplace environment sensors?

*Remote Work Efficiency:* How can AI assess the productivity and well-being of remote workers by analyzing digital communication patterns, work habits, and project management data?

*Succession Planning and Career Pathing:* How can AI assist in succession planning by predicting potential leaders and creating optimal career paths based on employee performance data, skills assessment, and career aspirations?

*Prompt: "As a specialist in AI for HRM research, propose 10 HRM research questions that can be explored only with the help of AI"*

*Note: These research questions serve as an illustration of the potential of Generative AI, such as ChatGPT, for generating future HRM-related research inquiries that can be explored through AI. This process follows the prompting guidelines available on Prompting Guide (*https://www.promptingguide.ai*) and OpenAI's resources on prompt engineering (*https://platform.openai.com/docs/guides/prompt-engineering*). Key elements include crafting specific prompts (tasking the AI with proposing research questions), adopting a persona (positioning as a specialist in AI for HRM research), providing context (focusing on HRM-related research), and specifying a desired outcome (indicating the number of research questions to be generated)* (adopted from Renkema & Tursunbayeva, 2024).

* Created with ChatGPT, personal communication, September 01, 2024

The recommendations provided by ChatGPT are wide-ranging, covering topics across the entire employee life cycle. What emerges is that future research, at least as suggested by ChatGPT, will likely be highly empirical, drawing on novel Big Data sources and advanced analysis methods. However, it is crucial to remember that HRM research must also advance theories and contribute conceptually to the field, ensuring a balanced approach that combines empirical rigor with theoretical innovation. Such research should also be multi-level, multi-stakeholder, and longitudinal to assess the long-term impact of AI on HRM and to put forward new conceptual models to grasp the complex outcomes of AI for HRM. Finally, the research should also focus on employee outcomes, as this has been overlooked (Pereira et al., 2023), and on AI safety (Suleyman & Bhaskar, 2023). The latter currently comprises only 2% of all AI research, though it grew 315% between 2017 and 2022 (Emerging Technology Observatory, 2024).

## 11.9 Epilogue

The journey of integrating AI into HRM is ongoing. This represents a paradigm shift with far-reaching implications. We all want "a joy of the happy ending" (Tolkien, 1966) and bright technological future (O'Neill, 2021). As AI evolves, and there is no reset button in real life, organizations, researchers, and policymakers must remain vigilant and proactive in addressing its ethical, practical, and regulatory challenges. By adopting RAI practices and fostering a culture of ethical awareness and guardrails (Gasser & Mayer-Schönberger, 2024), stakeholders can harness AI's transformative power to enhance HRM practices, support employee well-being, and contribute to the broader goals of equity and inclusion. Our collective efforts will shape the bright future of people at work and can ensure that AI is used ethically, responsibly, and aligned with the organizational strategic optimism and objectives for sustainability (O'Neill, 2021). The insights and recommendations presented in this book aim to guide this journey, providing a roadmap for navigating the complexities of AI in HRM and paving the way for a more inclusive, responsible, and sustainable future of work and the HRM profession.

## References

Ada Lovelace Institute. (2022). *Looking before we leap. Expanding ethical review processes for AI and data science research.* Ada Lovelace Institute. https://www.adalovelaceinstitute.org/wp-content/uploads/2022/12/Ada-Lovelace-Institute-Looking-before-we-leap-Dec-2022.pdf

As, I., & Basu, P. (2022). *The Routledge companion to artificial intelligence in architecture.* Routledge. https://www.routledge.com/The-Routledge-Companion-to-Artificial-Intelligence-in-Architecture/As-Basu/p/book/9780367424589

Bondarouk, T., Parry, E., & Furtmueller, E. (2017). Electronic HRM: Four decades of research on adoption and consequences. *The International Journal of Human Resource Management, 28*(1), 98–131. https://doi.org/10.1080/09585192.2016.1245672

Crawford, K. (2021). *Atlas of AI: Power, politics, and the planetary costs of artificial intelligence.* Yale University Press.

Di Lauro, S., Tursunbayeva, A., Antonelli, G., & Moschera, L. (2023). Alignment of employees' competencies with espoused organizational values. *International Studies of Management & Organization, 53*(1), 1–18. https://doi.org/10.1080/00208825.2022.2148388

EC. (2020). *WHITE PAPER On Artificial Intelligence - A European approach to excellence and trust.* https://eur-lex.europa.eu/legal-content/EN/TXT/?qid=1603192201335&uri=CELEX:52020DC0065

Emerging Technology Observatory. (2024). *The state of global AI safety research* [emerging technology observatory]. https://eto.tech/blog/state-of-global-ai-safety-research/.

Franz, D., Marsh, H. E., Chen, J. I., & Teo, A. R. (2019). Using Facebook for qualitative research: A brief primer. *Journal of Medical Internet Research, 21*(8), e13544. https://doi.org/10.2196/13544

Gasser, U., & Mayer-Schönberger, V. (2024). *Guardrails: Guiding human decisions in the age of AI.* Princeton University Press.

Gilbert, N., & Stoneman, P. (2016). *Researching social life* (4th ed.). Sage. https://books.google.it/books?hl=it&lr=&id=Ff6ICwAAQBAJ&oi=fnd&pg=PA203&dq=%22unethical+research+questions%22&ots=fZOunmVgar&sig=qG4O8uUEpsU3xnMrCQPKksBUzf0#v=onepage&q=%22unethical%20research%20questions%22&f=false

Gordon, C. (2023). ChatGPT is the fastest growing app in the history of web applications. *Forbes.* https://www.forbes.com/sites/cindygordon/2023/02/02/chatgpt-is-the-fastest-growing-ap-in-the-history-of-web-applications/.

Guenole, N., Feinzig, S., & Green, D. (2018). The Grey area: Ethical dilemmas in HR analytics. *IBM.* https://www.ibm.com/downloads/cas/O3DLWXBQ

Hu, K. (2023, February 2). ChatGPT sets record for fastest-growing user base - analyst note. *Reuters.* https://www.reuters.com/technology/chatgpt-sets-record-fastest-growing-user-base-analyst-note-2023-02-01/

Huysman, M. (2020). Information systems research on artificial intelligence and work: A commentary on "Robo-Apocalypse cancelled? Reframing the automation and future of work debate." Journal of Information Technology, 35(4), 307–309. https://doi.org/10.1177/0268396220926511.

Kandlhofer, M., Weixelbraun, P., Menzinger, M., Steinbauer-Wagner, G., & Kemenesi, Á. (2023). Education and awareness for artificial intelligence. In J.-P. Pellet & G. Parriaux (Eds.), *Informatics in schools. Beyond bits and bytes: Nurturing informatics intelligence in education* (pp. 3–12). Springer Nature Switzerland. https://doi.org/10.1007/978-3-031-44900-0_1

Kang, Y., Cai, Z., Tan, C.-W., Huang, Q., & Liu, H. (2020). Natural language processing (NLP) in management research: A literature review. *Journal of Management Analytics, 7*(2), 139–172. https://doi.org/10.1080/23270012.2020.1756939

Klein, H. J., & Potosky, D. (2019). Making a conceptual contribution at human resource management review. *Human Resource Management Review, 29*(3), 299–304. https://doi.org/10.1016/j.hrmr.2019.04.003

Mallin, D. (2022). Council post: Why innovation is critical to the success of HR leaders in 2023 and beyond. *Forbes.* https://www.forbes.com/councils/forbesbusinesscouncil/2022/12/06/why-innovation-is-critical-to-the-success-of-hr-leaders-in-2023-and-beyond/

Marda, V., & Narayan, S. (2021). On the importance of ethnographic methods in AI research. *Nature Machine Intelligence, 3*(3), 187–189. https://doi.org/10.1038/s42256-021-00323-0

Merhi, M. I. (2023). An assessment of the barriers impacting responsible artificial intelligence. *Information Systems Frontiers, 25*(3), 1147–1160. https://doi.org/10.1007/s10796-022-10276-3

Mollick, E. (2024). Co-intelligence: Living and working with AI. *Portfolio.* https://www.amazon.com/Co-Intelligence-Living-Working-Ethan-Mollick/dp/059371671X

National Academies Press. (2022). *Fostering responsible computing research: Foundations and practices*. National Academies Press. https://nap.nationalacademies.org/resource/26507/public-briefing-slides.pdf

O'Neill, K. (2021). *A future so bright: How strategic optimism and meaningful innovation can restore our humanity and save the world.*

Orlikowski, W. J., & Scott, S. V. (2008). Sociomateriality: Challenging the separation of technology, work and organization. *Academy of Management Annals, 2*(1), 433–474. https://doi.org/10.5465/19416520802211644

Orlikowski, W. J., & Scott, S. V. (2023). The digital undertow and institutional displacement: A sociomaterial approach. *Organization Theory, 4*(2), 26317877231180896. https://doi.org/10.1177/26317877231180898

Parvatam, S. (2019). Cleaning up research conduct in India. *Nature India*. https://doi.org/10.1038/nindia.2019.100

Pereira, V., Hadjielias, E., Christofi, M., & Vrontis, D. (2023). A systematic literature review on the impact of artificial intelligence on workplace outcomes: A multi-process perspective. *Human Resource Management Review, 33*(1), 100857. https://doi.org/10.1016/j.hrmr.2021.100857

Prikshat, V., Malik, A., & Budhwar, P. (2021). AI-augmented HRM: Antecedents, assimilation and multilevel consequences. *Human Resource Management Review*, 100860. https://doi.org/10.1016/j.hrmr.2021.100860

Privacy Affairs. (2024). *GDPR Fines Tracker & Statistics* [privacy Affairs]. https://www.privacyaffairs.com/gdpr-fines/

Renkema, M., & Tursunbayeva, A. (2024). The future of work of academics in the age of artificial intelligence: State-of-the-art and a research roadmap. *Futures, 103453*. https://doi.org/10.1016/j.futures.2024.103453

Schwartz, M. D. (2022). Should artificial intelligence be interpretable to humans? *Nature Reviews Physics, 4*(12), 741–742. https://doi.org/10.1038/s42254-022-00538-z

Stokel-Walker, C. (2023). ChatGPT listed as author on research papers: Many scientists disapprove. *Nature, 613*(7945), 620–621. https://doi.org/10.1038/d41586-023-00107-z

Strohmeier, S. (2022). *Handbook of research on artificial intelligence in human resource management*. Edward Elgar Publishing. https://www.e-elgar.com/shop/gbp/handbook-of-research-on-artificial-intelligence-in-human-resource-management-9781839107528.html

Suleyman, M., & Bhaskar, M. (2023). *The coming wave: Technology, power, and the twenty-first Century's greatest dilemma*. Crown.

Takats, C., Kwan, A., Wormer, R., Goldman, D., Jones, H. E., & Romero, D. (2022). Ethical and methodological considerations of twitter data for public health research: Systematic review. *Journal of Medical Internet Research, 24*(11), e40380. https://doi.org/10.2196/40380

Tolkien, J. R. R. (1966). On fairy-stories. In *The Tolkien Reader*. Del Rey-Random House.

Trocin, C., Hovland, I. V., Mikalef, P., & Dremel, C. (2021). How artificial intelligence affords digital innovation: A cross-case analysis of Scandinavian companies. *Technological Forecasting and Social Change, 173*, 121081. https://doi.org/10.1016/j.techfore.2021.121081

Tursunbayeva, A., Bunduchi, R., Franco, M., & Pagliari, C. (2017). Human resource information systems in health care: A systematic evidence review. *Journal of the American Medical Informatics Association, 24*(3), 633–654. https://doi.org/10.1093/jamia/ocw141

Tursunbayeva, A., Pagliari, C., Di Lauro, S., & Antonelli, G. (2022). The ethics of people analytics: Risks, opportunities and recommendations. *Personnel Review, 51*(3), 900–921. https://doi.org/10.1108/PR-12-2019-0680

# Competing Interests

The author declares no competing interest.



A. Tursunbayeva, *Augmenting Human Resource Management with Artificial Intelligence*, Contributions to Management Science,
https://doi.org/10.1007/978-3-031-75266-7

# Statement

During the preparation of this work the author used ChatGPT to improve the quality of some of the text and to develop scenarios. After using this tool/service, the author reviewed and edited the content as needed and takes full responsibility for the content of the publication.


A. Tursunbayeva, *Augmenting Human Resource Management with Artificial Intelligence*, Contributions to Management Science,
https://doi.org/10.1007/978-3-031-75266-7

The manufacturer's authorised representative in the EU is Springer Nature Customer Service Centre GmbH, Europaplatz 3, 69115 Heidelberg, Germany. If you have any concerns regarding our products, please contact ProductSafety@springernature.com

Printed and bound by CPI Group (UK) Ltd, Croydon, CR0 4YY
01/10/2026
02225925-0020